CW00502039

Monty's Greatest Battles
1942–1945

*To the memory of General Sir Charles Richardson
and Major General 'Pip' Roberts.
Their advice has always been kept in mind.*

Monty's Greatest Battles
1942–1945

Adrian Stewart

Pen & Sword
MILITARY

First published in Great Britain in 2024 by
Pen & Sword Military
An imprint of Pen & Sword Books Limited
Yorkshire – Philadelphia

Copyright © Adrian Stewart 2024

ISBN 978 1 39904 601 5

Typeset by Mac Style
Printed in the UK by CPI Group (UK) Ltd, Croydon, CR0 4YY.

MIX
Paper | Supporting
responsible forestry
FSC® C013604
FSC
www.fsc.org

Pen & Sword Books Limited incorporates the imprints of After the
Battle, Atlas, Archaeology, Aviation, Discovery, Family History,
Fiction, History, Maritime, Military, Military Classics, Politics,
Select, Transport, True Crime, Air World, Frontline Publishing,
Leo Cooper, Remember When, Seaforth Publishing, The Praetorian
Press, Wharncliffe Local History, Wharncliffe Transport,
Wharncliffe True Crime and White Owl.

For a complete list of Pen & Sword titles please contact:

PEN & SWORD BOOKS LIMITED
47 Church Street, Barnsley, South Yorkshire, S70 2AS, England
E-mail: enquiries@pen-and-sword.co.uk
Website: www.pen-and-sword.co.uk
or
PEN AND SWORD BOOKS
1950 Lawrence Rd, Havertown, PA 19083, USA
E-mail: uspen-and-sword@casematepublishers.com
Website: www.penandswordbooks.com

Contents

Acknowledgements

For the narrative, my thanks to those kind people who shared experiences of service under Montgomery, their own or recently, sad to say, that of their father or uncle. Particular thanks to the officers and gentlemen mentioned in the Dedication.

For turning the narrative into a book, my thanks to my editor, Pamela Covey, my Agents, Johnson & Alcock Ltd, especially Ed Wilson, and the Birmingham & Midland Institute & Library and the Taylor Library for the photographs. Particular thanks to the staff of my Publisher, Pen & Sword Books Ltd, especially Brigadier Henry Wilson, to whom best wishes in his retirement, and Matt Jones, Production Manager and Liaison Officer Supreme.

My gratitude to you all.

Prologue

From the Dyle to the Desert

I t was the 13th day of August 1942 and the Second World War was at its height. For more than two years the Western Desert of Egypt and Libya had been the scene of savage clashes as the forces of Germany and Italy strove to reach the Nile Delta and the Suez Canal, while the soldiers of the British Empire and Commonwealth fought to prevent them. By this date, the Axis *Panzerarmee Afrika* of Field Marshal Erwin Rommel had pushed deeper into Egypt than ever before and, although held up in the Alamein 'gap' between the Mediterranean and a vast, trackless, chocolate-coloured quicksand called the Qattara Depression, was preparing to renew its advance. Against it was ranged the British Eighth Army and at 1830 on the 13th, its staff officers met at their headquarters on the Ruweisat Ridge to listen to an address by a newly-appointed Army Commander, Lieutenant General Bernard Law Montgomery.

Montgomery – small, wiry, sharp of face and sharp of nose – was not an impressive figure and, apart from Francis de Guingand, the Brigadier General Staff who had served with him before the war, few in Eighth Army knew anything about him. The officers naturally listened with outward respect but, as Major Edgar 'Bill' Williams, soon to become the army's Intelligence Chief, would later reflect: 'I think we had this rather arrogant view that we'd had rather a lot of generals through our hands in our day.' It came as quite a shock to them when this general told them bluntly and unequivocally: 'I do not like the general atmosphere I find here.'

Montgomery had had a great deal of experience in war. On leaving Sandhurst he had joined the Royal Warwickshires; a choice, he explains in his *Memoirs*, made because he liked its cap badge – an antelope – and knew it was not an expensive regiment. As a lieutenant in its 1st Battalion he first saw action on 26 August 1914 at the Battle of Le Cateau.

Montgomery's exploits in the First World War can be described briefly.[1] On 13 October 1914, he led his platoon in a bayonet charge that captured the village of Meteren, but was shot through a lung and so badly wounded that a grave was dug for him. Luckily he survived and was evacuated to England, where he learned that for 'conspicuous gallant leading' he had been promoted to captain and awarded the Distinguished Service Order, a decoration rarely given to a junior officer.

On recovery from his wounds, Montgomery was considered fit for staff duties in the field, so returned to France to hold a succession of important positions, being mentioned in despatches eight times. Throughout the inter-war years, he attracted the regard of his superiors, including the future Field Marshal Wavell who ensured that he assumed command of 9th Brigade in August 1937 and of 8th Division in Palestine in October 1938 and was promised that he would take over 3rd Division in England in August 1939.[2]

In May 1939, however, Montgomery fell gravely ill with an infection of the lung not wounded at Meteren. He demanded to be sent back to Britain, and on 3 July was carried aboard a passenger liner on a stretcher. The voyage across the Mediterranean and his own willpower brought about an amazing change. On 14 July he walked ashore, declaring that he was perfectly fit. After keeping him under observation for five days, the astonished doctors agreed. He took command of 3rd Division on 28 August.

Montgomery's recovery had come in the nick of time. On 1 September, German troops poured into Poland. On the 3rd, Britain and France declared war. On the 30th, Montgomery's 3rd Division arrived in Cherbourg as part of the British Expeditionary Force (BEF) sent to support the French army under Lieutenant General Lord Gort VC. By the greatest good fortune, the division formed part of II Corps, led by Lieutenant General Alan Brooke.

Brooke had got to know Montgomery well during the inter-war years, both having been instructors at the Staff College, Camberley. He was not an uncritical admirer since, according to General Sir David Fraser in *Alanbrooke*, he accused Montgomery of being 'prone to egotism, to misjudgement in personal matters' and to saying 'foolish and impetuous things'. However, he also believed Montgomery had no equal 'as a soldier of swift understanding, total calm in crises and iron will.'

Holding these views, Brooke inevitably came to replace Wavell as Montgomery's mentor. Hereafter, he would endeavour to support Montgomery, further his career when possible and, as he would ruefully reflect, 'guard him against his own foolishness'. In doing so he would issue stinging rebukes, but those who dismiss Montgomery as totally self-centred and self-satisfied should note that, as Brooke confirms, Montgomery accepted these strictures 'wonderfully well': he would admit he had been unwise, and express his gratitude for having his errors pointed out.

Brooke was soon to have abundant evidence that he was right to protect Montgomery. For the first months of the Second World War, the armies on the Western Front did little to harm or even hinder each other, but on 10 May 1940, the calm was shattered as German forces burst into the Low Countries. To the Allies, this seemed like a revised version of Germany's First World War Schlieffen Plan. They had always anticipated this move, so in accordance with previously agreed strategy, their own forces in the north of France, including the BEF, wheeled into Belgium to oppose it. Their intention was to secure the line of the River Dyle which runs northward from the neighbourhood of Namur to join the Scheldt just south of Antwerp. This would shorten their lines of defence, protect Brussels and incorporate the Belgian army into their Order of Battle.

Montgomery had spent the quiet months relentlessly training his division how to fight and how to move quickly and quietly by night as well as by day. He had even carried out a night exercise in which his men wheeled backwards into France as a mirror image of the advance to the Dyle. When the real advance was made, Montgomery brought his troops to the river near Louvain so rapidly that the Belgian defenders opened fire on them, believing they were German parachutists; fortunately, only one unlucky soldier was wounded. The 3rd Division quickly showed it could fight as well as manoeuvre. On 15 May, two German divisions broke into Louvain, but Montgomery's men drove them out again.

By then, however, it had become clear that the northern Allied armies had walked into a deliberate trap. The German plan, devised by General Erich von Manstein and eagerly supported by Adolf Hitler whose famous intuition was by no means always wrong, visualized the invasion of the Low Countries as a diversion. When Allied troops moved into Belgium to counter this, as the Germans were sure they would, other German forces, including the bulk of their armour, would strike over the Meuse at Sedan, head northwards to the sea and cut them off.[3] By nightfall on 15 May, the panzers had crossed the Meuse, reaching the Channel coast on the 21st. The retreat to Dunkirk began.

During this, Montgomery rose to greatness as a divisional commander. The strain on the BEF's leaders was immense. Lieutenant General Michael Barker in command of I Corps was so worn down by it that he could not sleep; he became exhausted, unable to issue clear orders or follow an agreed course of action. Even the immensely self-controlled Brooke broke down and burst into tears just before leaving for England. However, Brooke would record in Sir Arthur Bryant's *The Turn of the Tide 1939–1943* that in Montgomery's case, 'the very dangers and difficulties that faced us acted as a stimulus on him; they thrilled him and put the sharpest of edges on his military ability.'

Throughout the retreat, Montgomery kept a tight control over his division, his assessments of situations clear and confident and his orders simple and direct. He also did everything possible to ease his soldiers' burdens, for example by requisitioning cattle to provide 'rations on the hoof'. His actions and his attitude ensured that 3rd Division's morale remained high and it suffered fewer casualties than any other formation. Accordingly, on its return to England, it was given priority to be re-equipped in order to re-enter Europe as soon as possible. Luckily, the collapse of France prevented this.

For his part, Montgomery was well aware of and always acknowledged the debt he owed to his soldiers. The 3rd Division, he declares in his *Memoirs*, was 'like a piece of fine steel' and he was 'immensely proud' of it. The future Lieutenant General Sir Brian Horrocks, at this time one of 3rd Division's battalion commanders, states in his autobiography *A Full Life*: 'He [Montgomery] was convinced that he was the best divisional commander in the British Army and that we were the best division. By the time we had reached Dunkirk, I had come to the same conclusion.'

Montgomery and his 3rd Division had their finest hour on the night of 27/28 May. The Belgian army was disintegrating – it capitulated the next day – and a dangerous gap was opening to the north of the BEF. To block this, 3rd Division had to withdraw from an already exposed area, move at night behind a sector where fierce fighting was in progress and take up a new position on the British left flank. Montgomery, Brooke tells us, was 'exuberant in confidence', but Brooke was unable to conceal his own anxiety. Next morning he found that Montgomery 'had, as usual, accomplished almost the impossible'. 'I thanked heaven,' Brooke noted in his diary, 'to have a Commander of his calibre.'

On the morning of 30 May, Brooke, who had been instructed to return to Britain, appointed Montgomery temporary commander of II Corps. As such he attended a conference held that afternoon by Gort, who had also been ordered home. Since I Corps was scheduled to be evacuated last, Gort nominated Barker to succeed him and arrange terms of surrender if needed. This was not a decision that appealed to Montgomery, who rightly believed that Barker was in no fit state to be saddled with such responsibilities. He therefore requested a private word with Gort and bluntly said that Barker must be replaced by Major General the Hon. Harold Alexander, commander of I Corps' 1st Division, and then there would be no need for any surrender.

Much to his credit, Gort overlooked his subordinate's effrontery and accepted this demand thinly disguised as a recommendation. 'Alex got everyone away in his own calm and confident manner,' Montgomery rather smugly reports in his *Memoirs*. After seeing his own men embarked, Montgomery boarded HM destroyer *Codrington* on 1 June. Her voyage to England was harried by waves of enemy aircraft, but Montgomery, apparently 'in his seventh heaven', showed no alarm; rather an intense interest in the Luftwaffe's tactics, on which he kept up a running commentary. *Codrington*'s captain George Stevens-Guille considered him the 'coolest customer' he had ever met.

Back in England, Montgomery was promoted to lieutenant general on 28 July, and took command of V Corps guarding the coasts of Hampshire and Dorset. His immediate superior was the head of Southern Command, Lieutenant General Sir Claude Auchinleck, and they clashed almost immediately on a number of issues. Montgomery was not blameless, for he quite wrongly went 'over Auchinleck's head' to the War Office on matters he felt were of concern or to get officers he valued posted to V Corps.

The main cause of trouble, however, was a series of scathing reports from Montgomery to his superior about the poor state of V Corps' operational efficiency. Since Auchinleck had been its previous commander, he did not welcome these criticisms. He was further aggrieved when Montgomery cancelled his (Auchinleck's) former tactic of fixed beach defences and instead held the coastal area only lightly, using the main strength of the corps as a mobile reserve that could counter-attack any enemy penetration. Loyal staff officers would later declare that Montgomery's actions were a 'natural development' of Auchinleck's ideas, but that officer never accepted this interpretation and angrily – if vainly – commanded Montgomery to reverse his policy.

Montgomery also embarked on a programme of ferocious training exercises, demanding that: 'In rain, snow, ice, mud, fair weather or foul, at any hour of the day and night – we must be able to do our stuff better than the Germans.' One might have thought that this at least would earn Auchinleck's approval since he had earlier urged that training be made 'more realistic and less effeminate'. This, Montgomery's training certainly was. Unfortunately, Auchinleck retaliated for his subordinate's strictures by either dismissing Montgomery's methods as 'mostly rubbish' or damning them with faint sneer: 'All very inspiring and made me feel a bit inadequate. But I doubt if runs before breakfast really produce battle winners of necessity.'

Fortunately, Auchinleck left Britain in December to become Commander-in-Chief, India. Montgomery was frankly delighted. He had no more quarrels with superiors and his responsibilities and influence steadily increased. In April 1941, he was placed in charge of XII Corps defending Kent and Sussex. In November 1941, he took command of South-Eastern Command which included Surrey as well and controlled both XII and I Canadian Corps. He renamed it South-Eastern Army in the belief that it would one day see action on the Continent. In mid-1942, an opportunity for this suddenly arose.

At this time, both Prime Minister Winston Churchill and President Franklin Roosevelt were eager to find some way of assisting the Russians, then under terrible pressure from Hitler's armies. When it became clear that neither a full-scale invasion of France nor a limited assault on the Cherbourg Peninsula was yet possible, attention turned to a plan presented by Vice Admiral Lord Louis Mountbatten, Chief of Combined Operations, for a raid on the port of Dieppe. By May, the basic details of this had been approved by Churchill, by Brooke who had become Chief of the Imperial General Staff in the previous December, by Brooke's fellow chiefs of staff and by General Sir Bernard Paget, C-in-C of Britain's

Home Forces. It was decided that the troops for the assault would come from South-Eastern Army.

This meant notifying Montgomery of the plan. There were points in it with which his later record suggests he might be certain to disagree, in particular the cancellation of an intended preliminary attack by heavy bombers and the inadequacy of supporting naval firepower. Yet Montgomery raised no objection. It appears that after two years of waiting for an invasion of Britain that never took place, he was so eager for aggressive action that he was willing to accept any plan that promised this.

Still more surprisingly, Montgomery selected 2nd Canadian Division for the assault, although it was inexperienced and he was not entirely happy with its training. He had, however, been warned by Brooke that the Canadians, all tough, self-reliant volunteers, had come to resent his 'school-master' attitude and his unkind comments on the ability of their leaders. He therefore attempted to 'mend fences' by entrusting them with a role which both he and they regarded as an honour.[4]

It seems clear that, given time for consideration, Montgomery came to realize the plan's defects. After the raid, originally proposed for early July, was postponed by bad weather, he wrote to Paget, begging that it be abandoned altogether. The reason he gave was that security must have been compromised, but his urgent desire that the cancellation be 'for all time' suggests that this was merely a good excuse. His plea was ignored and the attack on Dieppe on 19 August proved a catastrophe, only redeemed by its providing vital lessons for the future. Montgomery had already decided that one lesson was that he must thoroughly examine and question any plan prepared by anyone else. This would have great significance after he arrived in Egypt in that same crucial August of 1942.

The tortuous paths by which Montgomery was appointed to command Eighth Army have been covered in numerous accounts, most notably in Field Marshal Lord Carver's *El Alamein* and General Fraser's *Alanbrooke*. Churchill and Brooke, concerned by a series of misfortunes in North Africa, arrived in Egypt to check for themselves on 3 August. On the 5th, they made a tour of Eighth Army positions, hearing many strong criticisms of General Auchinleck who then held the dual posts of Eighth Army Commander and Commander-in-Chief, Middle East. The leaders of the divisions from Australia, New Zealand and South Africa – the

Dominions as the self-governing parts of the British Commonwealth were then called – were particularly disapproving. By the end of the day, reports General Fraser, Brooke was willing to 'agree with any solution which took Auchinleck from Cairo'.

On 6 August, it was decided that Alexander should replace Auchinleck as C-in-C, Middle East. Brooke wanted Montgomery to take over Eighth Army, but Churchill insisted on Lieutenant General William 'Strafer' Gott, the army's senior corps commander. Then a tragic fate intervened. Gott was ordered to fly to Cairo for consultation, but the Bristol Bombay aerial transport in which he travelled was shot down by enemy fighters. Gott was killed. Brooke was not to be denied a second time. Montgomery arrived in Egypt on the morning of 12 August.

Churchill and Brooke had already set out, ultimately for Moscow, in the early hours of the 11th. Before leaving, the prime minister had expressed a wish that 'the transfer of responsibility' should take place forthwith, but Auchinleck had other ideas. His innate dignity had masked most of his understandable bitterness, but this had come out in a stormy interview with Brooke on 9 August. 'I had to bite him back as he was apt to snarl,' Brooke noted in his diary, 'that kept him quiet.'

Presumably, therefore, it was wounded vanity that led Auchinleck to decide not to give up his leadership of either the Middle East or Eighth Army until 15 August. Alexander, always good-natured, was persuaded to agree, and when Montgomery met Auchinleck soon after his arrival he was told, as Field Marshal Carver reports, 'to go down to the desert and look round but not to take over command until the 15th.'

This postponement irritated Montgomery and his irritation increased following meetings later that day with Major General John Harding, once his pupil at the Staff College, Camberley, now Deputy Chief of the Middle East General Staff, and early on the 13th with de Guingand. Both spoke bluntly of Eighth Army's lack of organization and loss of confidence. After talking to de Guingand, Montgomery proceeded to Eighth Army's dismal HQ on Ruweisat Ridge, where he cross-examined Lieutenant General Ramsden, the acting army commander. Montgomery then decided, says Field Marshal Carver, that 'he could not tolerate two days hanging about under these conditions.' Telling Ramsden to return to his corps, he assumed command of Eighth Army at 1400 and gave orders for an assembly of all staff officers that evening.

It was of course disobedience, and even some of Montgomery's admirers deplore what they describe as his cruel and offensive treatment of Auchinleck. It should be remembered, however, that Auchinleck would have been able 'to terminate his office in a proper and orderly fashion' as the critics demand had he only observed Churchill's wishes. Moreover, Eighth Army Intelligence had long warned that Rommel was receiving reinforcements and would launch a new offensive before the end of August; on the 26th it was now believed. Montgomery might therefore have only fourteen days in which to prepare for this. That Auchinleck should instruct him to waste one-seventh of this precious time 'looking round' is far more to be condemned and is frankly astounding.

Before Montgomery could meet the new German offensive, he had to create confidence in his own army and this would not be easy. Field Marshal Carver, who incidentally was then a staff officer in Eighth Army's XXX Corps, reports that: 'Few parts of the Army had lost faith in themselves or even in their commanders.' The trouble was that: 'The most general and the most dangerous tendency was that of different arms and formations to lay the blame on others.'

Thus Brigadier Howard Kippenberger, who commanded 2nd New Zealand Division's 5th Brigade, declares in his *Infantry Brigadier* that: 'At this time there was throughout Eighth Army, not only in the New Zealand Division, a most intense distrust, almost hatred, of our armour.' On their part, says Brigadier C.E. Lucas Phillips, then an artillery officer, in his *Alamein*, the infantry were accused of 'screaming for tank support' on every possible occasion. Neither armour nor infantry knew much about the other's problems and few of their commanders were used to working together.

Nor was there mistrust only between formations; there was also mistrust by those formations for the higher command. 'That there was such mistrust by this time,' states Carver, 'cannot be denied.' He particularly refers to the Dominion divisions and to 23rd Armoured Brigade that had been badly mishandled during July but, as Churchill has confirmed, the same view was held by leading airmen. It was even shared by Auchinleck's own staff officers. Thus Lieutenant Colonel Charles Richardson, then Eighth Army's Director of Plans, in his *Flashback: A Soldier's Story*, refers with admiration to Auchenleck's 'striking personality, which dominated almost without speech, his courage and his manifest integrity' but also declares 'I was unconvinced that General Auchinleck could turn the tide no matter what resources might come our way.'

For his part, Auchinleck blamed his men, complaining to Brooke: 'The 23rd Armoured Brigade, though gallant enough, lost control and missed direction. The infantry too seem to have made some avoidable mistakes. Perhaps I asked too much of them.' He seemed, however, unable to produce any positive directions or constructive ideas, as had become obvious to his staff, his field commanders and even knowledgeable onlookers.

Thus Richardson notes sadly that Auchinleck, instead of 'visiting his forward commanders', remained at his Headquarters 'day after day sitting in the sand spending long hours staring through binoculars at the distant void horizon.' 'For a long time,' complains Kippenberger, 'we had heard little from Army except querulous grumbles that the men should not go about without their shirts on, that staff officers must always wear appropriate arm bands, or things of that sort.' 'In itself,' reports the Australian War Correspondent Alan Moorehead in *The Desert War*, Eighth Army 'was ready for anything. But the things it lacked badly were a clearly defined purpose and a leader.'

It was now to get both. In his address to his assembled staff, Montgomery declared:

> I do not like the general atmosphere I find here. It is an atmosphere of doubt, of looking back to select the next place to which to withdraw, of loss of confidence in our ability to defeat Rommel, of desperate defence measures by reserves in preparing positions in Cairo and the Delta.
>
> All that must cease. Let us have a new atmosphere.
>
> The defence of Egypt lies here at Alamein and on the Ruweisat Ridge. What is the use of digging trenches in the Delta? It is quite useless; if we lose this position we lose Egypt; all the fighting troops now in the Delta must come here at once, and will. *Here* we will stand and fight; there will be no further withdrawal. I have ordered that all plans and instructions dealing with further withdrawal are to be burnt and at once. We will stand and fight *here*.
>
> If we can't stay here alive, then let us stay here dead.

In those few sentences, Montgomery showed his resolve, silenced the grumblers and united his staff behind him in relieved approval.

'We all felt,' reports de Guingand, 'that a cool and refreshing breeze had come to relieve the oppressive and stagnant atmosphere. The effect of the address was electric – it was terrific! And we all went to bed that night with a new hope in our hearts and a great confidence in the future of our Army.'

The reaction in the army's fighting formations was the same. Major General Leslie Morshead, commander of 9th Australian Division, summed it up in two simple words: 'Thank God!'

Notes

1. Full details of Montgomery's early life, including his service in the First World War, may be found in Nigel Hamilton's epic biography *Monty*, Volume I, *The Making of a General 1887–1942*.
2. Not all Montgomery's superiors shared Wavell's views and Wavell expressly comments that he personally 'was not afraid of' Montgomery's 'independent ideas and ways'.
3. In order to encourage the Allied move into Belgium, it was unhindered by the Luftwaffe; a circumstance that RAF officers rightly regarded as strange and rather sinister.
4. It may be mentioned that the chief staff officer of 2nd Canadian Division, Lieutenant Colonel Mann, attended the Dieppe raid conferences and had reservations about the plan. Yet he recommended its acceptance since he did not wish to deprive his men of their opportunity.

Chapter One

The Battle of Alam Halfa

Montgomery's description of the general atmosphere prevailing in Eighth Army and the reasons for this won the approval of its entire staff and the vast majority of its officers and men. However, it did not please Auchinleck who, in 1958, by which time he was a field marshal, protested in a letter to *The Sunday Times* that he had never contemplated any withdrawal 'since early in July 1942' and it was 'absurd and incorrect' to say otherwise.

In fact, a mass of evidence exists showing that in the last week of July and the first fortnight of August, neither Middle East nor Eighth Army headquarters gave much consideration to anything other than withdrawal. This included the possibility of retirement from Egypt altogether. Harding tells us that Auchinleck ordered him to plan a series of holding actions that would give time 'to extricate the bulk of his forces south of Cairo and then over the Suez Canal into Palestine.' Richardson was ordered to prepare plans 'for the possible withdrawal of Eighth Army to Khartoum'. Lieutenant Colonel Miles Graham, the army's Deputy Chief Administrative Officer, was instructed to make 'arrangements' in case it was necessary to 'evacuate Eighth Army' from Egypt.[1]

Much consideration was also given to a withdrawal from the Alamein 'gap' to positions guarding the cities of Egypt. The main ones were at Amiriya, south-west of Alexandria, at Khataba, north-west of Cairo and at Wadi Natrun between Alexandria and Cairo, blocking the 'Barrel Track', a rough desert road running from the southern part of the Alamein position to the Egyptian capital. This possibility was mentioned by Auchinleck personally in a letter to Brooke dated 25 July 1942.

Then on the 27th appeared an 'Appreciation of the situation in the Western Desert'. This was produced by Major General Eric Dorman-Smith, an Irishman of immense charm, ready tongue and consuming ambition, who Auchinleck had chosen to be his personal adviser. In it, Dorman-Smith declares flatly: 'To us the two vulnerable areas are Cairo

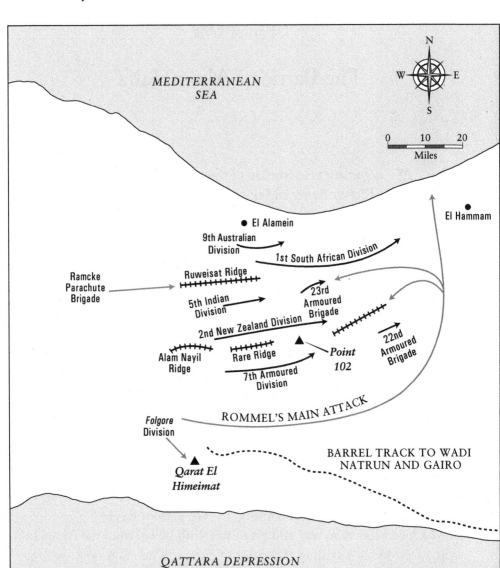

Map 1: Alam Halfa: The battle planned by Rommel and Auchinleck.

and Alexandria' and he holds forth at length on the importance of the 'preparation and manning of the Delta and Cairo defences'.

So great was this obsession that the last action taken by Auchinleck as C-in-C, Middle East was a request on 14 August that Eighth Army supply updated plans of the Wadi Natrun defences. He was probably not pleased

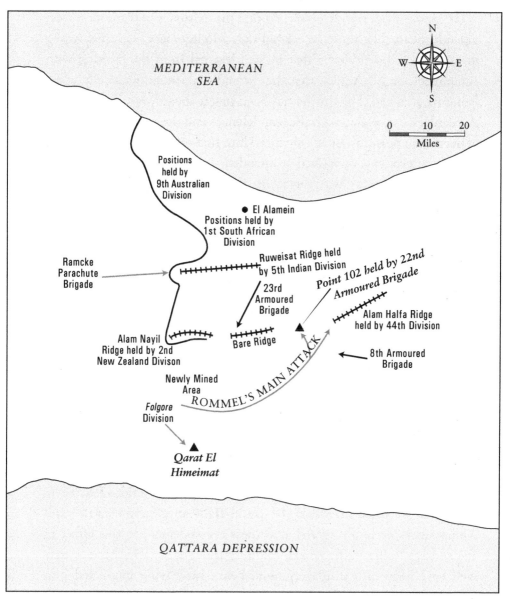

Map 2: Alam Halfa: The battle fought by Rommel and Montgomery.

when Lieutenant Colonel Hugh Mainwaring, Montgomery's Director of Operations, retorted that: 'In view of 8th Army Commander's new order for "no looking over your shoulder" and "fighting on present position" there is no need for a Wadi Natrun defensive position and therefore there is no action required.'

Of course it can rightly be argued that the existence of plans for retreat did not mean they must be carried out. Montgomery was thus wrong to indicate in his *Memoirs* that he had learned from his meeting with Auchinleck on 12 August that they would happen automatically when Rommel attacked. For this he has been much abused, but it seems that Auchinleck's obsession with the rear defences and the general atmosphere of pervading pessimism had convinced him that retreats would in practice occur whatever anyone wished or intended.

That Montgomery was correct in this belief seems almost certain. Within Dorman-Smith's Appreciation, says General Sir William Jackson in *The North African Campaign 1940–43*, there is 'a ring of defeatism or of realism, depending on the point of view of the reader.' Dorman-Smith reflects with relief that: 'The defences of Alexandria-Cairo-the Delta proper… and the Wadi Natrun area will be well forward by August 14', yet these would only be needed if Eighth Army could not hold its present positions. He explains delightedly that: 'The soft sand areas of the country east of El Alamein, notably the "Barrel Track" axis, the Wadi Natrun, the sand area to its north, are all added difficulties for the enemy's movement', yet the enemy would only reach these if Eighth Army could not hold its present positions. Clearly Dorman-Smith, and Auchinleck since he had approved the Appreciation 'without material alteration', doubted its ability to do so.[2]

Moreover, despite all the consideration paid to the reserve defences, Harding among others believed that if the Alamein positions fell, 'there was no other place in which you could fight an effective battle', and Montgomery certainly agreed as witness the statement to this effect in the address to his staff. Indeed, Harding thought that Auchinleck may well have been of a similar opinion, hence his having instructed him (Harding) to plan only holding actions.

Since the existence of the withdrawal plans was well known to all in Eighth Army, they were extremely dangerous. 'I don't say that it is not prudent to be prepared for the worst,' declares de Guingand, 'but on the other hand, if there is too much of this sort of thing it is most unlikely that the troops will fight their best in their existing positions.' 'The whole attitude of Eighth Army,' agrees Kippenberger, 'was that of having one foot in the stirrup.'

Fortunately, Montgomery's address on 13 August removed all chance of withdrawals of any kind under any circumstances. Thereafter he visited all the formations of his Eighth Army, first in a staff car and later in a specially modified Grant tank, frequently stopping to talk to individual soldiers who, according to his tank's driver, Sergeant James Frazer, 'were astonished that an officer of such exalted rank would take the trouble'. He also acquired an Australian slouch hat on which he stuck the badges of the units he had visited. This was later replaced by a more convenient black beret carrying his general's cap badge and that of the Royal Tank Regiment, to which he was not really entitled.

Montgomery's headgear delighted his troops and enraged the pompous, but what most concerned Eighth Army was Rommel's coming offensive and it had reasons for anxiety. Montgomery would later proclaim that Eighth Army was of 'truly magnificent material', but it had not been well used and he was knowledgeable enough to realize this. In *The Second World War 1939–1945*, Major General J.F.C. Fuller considers that Montgomery had been lucky to arrive in the desert when he did, because by that time the 'defects' in Eighth Army – he details these as 'lack of experienced officers and trained men, lack of equipment and inferiority of weapons' – had all been rectified. The reality, however, was very different.

Certainly the officers (and men) were experienced, but their experiences had made them cynical and distrustful: the fighting in the previous month was generally known as 'the nonsenses of July'. The men (and officers) had had much training, but not in vital matters like the combined use of infantry and armour, and sometimes in ways that were undesirable. For instance, while German tanks attacked infantry or supply units, British tanks delighted in making charges that resulted in frequent heavy losses to German anti-tank guns, particularly the fearsome 88mms, the deadliest killers on either side.

As for 'lack of equipment and inferiority of weapons', Eighth Army had always had a superiority in men, guns, tanks, motor vehicles and supporting aircraft, but this reached its maximum not in August but in July 1942 and had then been much reduced. The 2nd New Zealand Division, commanded by Major General Bernard Freyberg VC, had seen its 4th Brigade withdrawn from the battle area, while its 5th and 6th Brigades were well under strength. The 50th (British) Division, having lost one brigade already, lost another in July. The 1st Armoured

Division was also pulled out of the combat zone apart from its 22nd Armoured Brigade, led by Brigadier 'Pip' Roberts, which was transferred to 7th Armoured Division.

During August, Eighth Army's infantry losses had not been made good, though happily Montgomery's refusal to waste fighting men in rear defences would partially rectify this situation. The 10th Armoured Division did notionally replace 1st Armoured, but in practice it contained only Brigadier Neville Custance's 8th Armoured Brigade and two of its three armoured regiments had seen no previous action in the war or indeed since they had ceased to ride horses.

By contrast, in *Panzerarmee Afrika* reinforcements arrived that not only brought the existing divisions back to full strength but added to their number. To join the German *Afrika Korps* – 15th and 21st Panzer divisions plus 90th Light Division of mobile infantry – came 164th Light Division and the independent 288th Parachute Brigade, now used in an infantry role. The Italians' two armoured and four infantry divisions were joined by the *Folgore*, a very good 'dismounted' airborne division.

Panzerarmee Afrika improved in quality as well as quantity in early August. In his Official Despatch, Auchinleck states not as an opinion but as a fact that British armour was inferior to that of the Germans. In reality, tests made after the war showed that prior to August 1942, the opposite was the case.[3]

Of the original German tanks, the Panzer Mark IV fired high-explosive not armour-piercing shells, and the short-barrelled 50mm gun of the Mark III had less penetrative power than the 2-pounder in the British Valentines and Crusaders and the 37mm in the American Stuarts. All these also had thicker armour on their hull most of the time and on their turret all the time. Later the Mark III Special appeared with a long-barrelled 50mm gun, superior to those of the early Allied tanks. In the fighting in July, though, there were never more than 16 of these available, while Eighth Army had more than 160 American Grants with armour equal to that of the Mark III Special on the hull and stronger on the turret and both a 37mm in the turret and a 75mm in a sponson on the side, the latter being a much better anti-tank weapon than that on the Mark III Special.

When Montgomery took command of Eighth Army it still had about 160 Grants, but Rommel now had 73 Mark III Specials plus 27 Mark IV

Specials boasting a long-barrelled high-velocity 75mm gun. This fired armour-piercing shells and was far superior to that of the Grants and indeed that of the later Shermans, at last giving the Germans a better tank than any in Eighth Army. Add to this that their anti-tank guns, which always had been better, had doubled in number and their supporting warplanes had greatly increased in number and quality. Eighth Army was still larger, but it is not surprising that Captain B.H. Liddell Hart in his *History of the Second World War* reports that: 'The strength of the two sides was nearer to an even balance than it was either before or later.'

Rommel's only anxiety was his supply line, constantly harried by striking forces from Malta. This caused him to postpone his offensive until after dark on 30 August. By then, though, he had received almost 800 extra lorries, and while 3 Axis tankers had been sunk in August, 4 others had reached Tobruk safely. On the 30th, Field Marshal Albert Kesselring, Commander-in-Chief, South and also the Axis Air C-in-C, provided 1,500 tons of fuel from Luftwaffe stocks, giving Rommel sufficient for the seven days he estimated it would take to complete 'the final destruction of the enemy'.

Rommel's plan for what would be known as the Battle of Alam Halfa was a typically daring one. He knew that the northern British positions from the sea to the Alam Nayil Ridge were strongly defended, so here he intended to make assaults only on the Ruweisat Ridge and Alam Nayil and these chiefly to divert attention from his main thrust in the south. Here the *Folgore* Division would capture the 700ft-high Qarat el Himeimat (Mount Himeimat) and the rest of his striking force, 15th and 21st Panzer, 90th Light and the Italian *Ariete* (Armoured), *Littorio* (Armoured) and *Trieste* (Motorized) Divisions, would race eastwards between the Qattara Depression and the line of high ground that ran from Alam Nayil by way of Bare Ridge and Point 102 to the ridge of Alam el Halfa, or plain Alam Halfa as the soldiers called it.

Axis Intelligence had assured Rommel that this area was poorly defended and weakly mined, so he was confident that he could advance over 30 miles on the first night, outflanking all Eighth Army's defences. He would then head north-east to the sea, attacking Alam Halfa and Ruweisat Ridges from behind and savaging any supply units he encountered. Eighth Army would doubtless send its armour to rescue these, but Rommel was certain that his 88mms could master this as they had done so often in the past. Then Rommel would leave the bulk of his infantry to destroy the trapped remnants of Eighth Army and direct 21st Panzer on Alexandria and the rest of his striking force on Cairo and thence to the Suez Canal.

Dramatic as was Rommel's plan, British Intelligence had uncovered its whole outline long before this was finally confirmed by an Ultra intercept on 17 August. In his Official Despatch, Alexander would state that a plan to oppose it had therefore already been prepared and this was accepted in principle by Montgomery and himself. That was enough to enable Montgomery's detractors to declare that he had 'stolen' a marvellous visionary scheme, of which Dorman-Smith's Appreciation was the 'blueprint'.

In view of his other responsibilities as C-in-C, Middle East, however, it is not unreasonable to suggest that Alexander – who had no part in the preparations for Alam Halfa – might have been mistaken. De Guingand, who as chief of staff to first Auchinleck and then Montgomery was in the best possible position to judge, tells us that Montgomery never examined any previous plans but told him to 'burn the lot'. Indeed, after the lessons of Dieppe, Montgomery was unlikely to accept any existing plan, least of all one devised by Auchinleck who he had come to despise, or Dorman-Smith, who he had dismissed as clever but shallow when he had taught him at Camberley.

According to Alexander, Auchinleck's intentions were 'to hold as strongly as possible the area between the sea and the Ruweisat Ridge and to threaten from the flank any enemy advance south of the ridge from a strongly prepared position on the Alam el Halfa Ridge.' Certainly this was a good summary of the steps Eighth Army did take to oppose Rommel's advance, but that this reflected Auchinleck's intentions is contradicted by Auchinleck's own Despatch, Dorman-Smith's Appreciation and the War Diaries of Eighth Army's XIII and XXX Corps, all of which tell a totally different story.

For a start, Auchinleck's Despatch expressly states that the 'essence of the defensive plan' was 'fluidity and mobility'. Dorman-Smith's Appreciation confirms this. In the north it proclaims: 'We have to be prepared to fight a modern defensive battle in the area El Alamein-Hammam'; since El Hammam lay some 40 miles by road east of Alamein, this could only mean a battle of manoeuvre. It also refers to 'reserve positions' 10 miles or more from the front line. Known as Observation Posts (OPs), they were really defensive 'boxes', ten in number; it is suggested that the 'main front' might be withdrawn to these, leaving the existing fortifications as a mere 'outpost line'.

Both Field Marshal Carver and General Richardson confirm that Auchinleck agreed with this suggestion. Accordingly, orders were issued by XIII and XXX Corps to Eighth Army's divisions in the northern defences: 9th Australian, 1st South African, 5th Indian[4] and 2nd New Zealand reading from north to south. They can be found in the Public Records Office and make it very clear how mobile Eighth Army was to be.[5] The South Africans and incidentally 23rd Armoured Brigade were to retire east of the 'boxes', while the other divisions were to split up into 'battle groups', some to man the OPs and others, including most of the artillery, to manoeuvre between them, falling back into them if necessary.

These tactics were not highly regarded by the officers and men of Eighth Army. 'I never quite understood how it was to be done,' complains de Guingand, 'it was all too uncertain and fluid a plan for a sound defence. There was a great danger of the guns being driven hither and thither and confusion setting in.' A battle group, moreover, was cynically defined in Eighth Army as 'a brigade group which has been twice overrun by tanks.' How anyone could regard this as 'holding as strongly as possible the area between the sea and the Ruweisat Ridge' must remain an insoluble mystery.

It should be noted that Dorman-Smith's Appreciation makes no mention at all of the Alam Halfa Ridge, while the Corps' Operation Orders envisage it only as one of the many reserve positions. On 3 August, 21st Indian Brigade was sent to Alam Halfa, but it was very much under strength and had made hardly any progress in the construction of defences by mid-August. Bare Ridge and Point 102 had no troops manning them and no defences whatsoever. There was thus a gaping hole on the southern flank of 2nd New Zealand Division.

Not that this concerns Dorman-Smith. His Appreciation talks of organizing 'a strong mobile wing based on 7th Armoured Division', but this was clearly to be more mobile than strong for it would contain only light forces and not 22nd Armoured Brigade which was 7th Armoured's main tank strength. This was kept in reserve to cover the withdrawing infantry, counter-attacking if necessary. Since his tanks were somewhat battle-worn, Roberts was not eager for 'fluid and mobile' operations. He was further worried by being given a wide variety of potential duties of which the wrong one might easily be ordered in the confusion of combat or as the result of communications problems. To claim that an enemy advance would be threatened 'from a strongly prepared position on the Alam el Halfa Ridge' appears optimistic to say the least.

Few in Eighth Army were, in fact, optimistic and with good reason. Auchinleck's 'fluid and mobile' battle would have delighted Rommel as it was just the sort of engagement he wished for and at which his troops excelled. 'It would be difficult,' states Richardson, 'to conceive a tactical plan more unsuited to the units of Eighth Army at that time.' The 'suicidal notions' embodied in Dorman-Smith's Appreciation and set out in the Operation Orders to formations 'might almost' grumbles Lucas Phillips, 'have been written for Rommel's express benefit.'

It was just as well, therefore, that whatever anyone may have said, Montgomery did not accept, even in principle, his predecessor's plan but prepared a totally different one of his own that was quickly conveyed to his men by Operation Orders or word of mouth. Its 'essence' might unkindly be summarized as 'avoidance of fluidity and mobility'. On 14 August, the New Zealanders, who came under XIII Corps, were directed to hold their present front-line defences 'to last man and last round'. On the 16th, XXX Corps instructed the other three divisions in Eighth Army's northern positions to stand their ground 'at all costs'. There would be no withdrawals to the OPs or anywhere else.

To assist the defenders, labour units, previously working in the Delta, were brought forward to strengthen their positions, while additional food, water and ammunition was made available. The 23rd Armoured Brigade was ordered to transfer a squadron of tanks each to the Australians, the New Zealanders and 5th Indian Division, while its remaining Valentines came up just behind the Ruweisat Ridge in close support. The 50th Division – now really only 151st Brigade – previously guarding Alexandria became the army reserve and would also move into the battle-zone during the coming action.

These changes meant that Montgomery had no need for what Carver calls 'all this peculiar box business'. He further delighted Eighth Army by comprehensively rejecting the hated battle groups. Indeed, de Guingand tells us, he ordered that 'the expression ceased to exist. Divisions would fight as divisions and be allowed to develop their great strength.' His actions also ensured that each infantry division's artillery – normally three regiments of field guns and one regiment of anti-tank guns – were now concentrated, not scattered among battle groups and/or boxes, and they were strengthened by every possible gun that had previously been kept back from the combat zone.

At last the area from the coast to the Ruweisat Ridge really was defended 'as strongly as possible'. Not so, however, the area from the Alam Nayil Ridge, held by the New Zealanders, to the Qattara Depression. Yet this was just the place where, as British Intelligence had warned, Rommel had planned to make his major assault.

On 15 August, Horrocks, now a lieutenant general, reached Egypt, having been sent at Montgomery's request to take Gott's place as head of XIII Corps which defended Eighth Army's southern positions. He had control over 2nd New Zealand and 10th and 7th Armoured divisions but all were weak: 10th Armoured, as was mentioned earlier, consisted only of 8th Armoured Brigade. Horrocks had never previously commanded a corps in battle, but he soon found that Montgomery had already mapped out his course of action.

From the start, Montgomery had been determined that his armour, like his infantry, should not be 'fluid and mobile' but stand on the defensive. When Major General Renton, 7th Armoured's commander, had strongly argued against this, Montgomery on 14 August had removed 22nd Armoured Brigade from his control. This left only Brigadier Carr's 4th Light Armoured Brigade with a limited number of Crusaders and Stuarts and the mobile infantry and anti-tank guns of Brigadier Bosvile's 7th Motor Brigade to hold the southern part of the front line, but Montgomery had his ideas on how they could be assisted.

In Dorman-Smith's Appreciation, there is no mention of minefields: it is difficult, after all, to think of anything less 'fluid and mobile'. On 14 August, Montgomery ordered the 'enlarging and strengthening of minefields in 7th Armoured Div. front'. By the end of the month, two wide belts had been laid. In Dorman-Smith's Appreciation, Allied air power is casually dismissed as 'a very considerable if somewhat indefinable asset' and there had been no co-operation between the two services during July. By 16 August, Montgomery had moved Eighth Army's HQ from the

Ruweisat Ridge to the coast, side by side with that of the Desert Air Force, and the two staffs would plan all future moves together.

Just in case 7th Armoured could not halt Rommel's men, Montgomery also prepared a second line of defence. This again was only possible because he ignored Auchinleck's intentions. The 44th Division of Major General Ivor Hughes had been split up and entrusted with guarding the cities of Egypt, as Auchinleck considered it insufficiently well trained to fight his 'fluid and mobile' battle. Montgomery, though, believed it would fight well enough behind fixed defences. On 16 August, its 131st and 133rd Brigades moved to Alam Halfa Ridge, finally establishing there 'a strongly prepared position'.

Meanwhile, 44th Division's 132nd Brigade joined 2nd New Zealand Division. It did not operate on its own like Auchinleck's brigade groups or battle groups, so enjoyed the support of the division's other elements: field artillery, anti-tank guns, engineers, medical staff, signals staff and so on. Freyberg was now strong enough to guard both his front line and his flank on Alam Nayil. Montgomery also arranged for 23rd Armoured Brigade to be sent to Bare Ridge once it was certain that there was no breakthrough at Ruweisat, that 22nd Armoured Brigade should hold Point 102, and that 8th Armoured Brigade should take up station southeast of Alam Halfa. Both Roberts and Custance received extra anti-tank guns and all were told to stand strictly on the defensive.

Everything now depended on the soldiers and their comrades-in-arms of the Desert Air Force, and when the Battle of Alam Halfa began on the night of 30/31 August, they quickly showed their worth. In the north, the Axis forces had little success, as they might have done had the defenders been retiring to the OPs as Auchinleck had intended. Colonel Bernhard Ramcke's tough 288th Parachute Brigade did gain a foothold on Ruweisat Ridge and inflicted heavy casualties on 9th Indian Brigade, but at about 0700 on the 31st, 5th Indian Brigade recovered the ground lost. This enabled Montgomery, at about 1100, to send 23rd Armoured Brigade to Bare Ridge as planned.

It was in the south, where Rommel's main offensive was made, that Montgomery's new tactics proved most effective. The attackers, Rommel admits, 'came up against an extremely strong and hitherto unsuspected British mine-belt', behind which 4th Light Armoured and 7th Motor Brigades held their ground with 'extraordinary stubbornness'. They were supported by a pair of artillery regiments, Freyberg's guns on Alam Nayil and, after 0240 on the 31st, a whole series of air-raids.

Panzerarmee Afrika, though, was a formidable opponent. Many Axis formations remained entangled in the minefields well into 31 August. The tanks of the *Afrika Korps*, however, broke through the first minefield belt at about 0430 and by 0700 were past the second belt as well. Half an hour later, the *Folgore* Division captured Himeimet.

Nonetheless, Rommel had not outflanked Eighth Army's defences on the first night as intended and had lost some valuable senior officers. A bomb falling just in front of the command vehicle of General Walter Nehring, the *Afrika Korps'* leader, had gravely injured him and killed two of his staff, while Major General Georg von Bismarck, commander of 21st Panzer, had been killed, possibly by mortar fire but probably by a mine.

So discouraged was Rommel that he considered abandoning his offensive. Eventually he decided it should continue, but his own forces now seemed threatened by attacks from the flanks and he ordered only reconnaissance units to probe to the east. The *Afrika Korps*, under 15th Panzer's commander Major General Gustav von Vaerst, turned north-eastwards against Alam Halfa and Point 102, but even this move could make no real progress during the morning of 31 August.

With the coming of daylight, the air forces of both sides went into action, but while the Luftwaffe's raids were thwarted, those of the Allied airmen got through. The RAF Baltimore and South African Boston light bombers and the Hurricane and Kittyhawk fighter-bombers were particularly effective and, as was urged by Montgomery, concentrated their efforts against the hapless Axis supply vehicles struggling through the narrow gaps in the minefields. It was not until a severe dust storm in the late morning and early afternoon grounded all aircraft on both sides that von Vaerst was able to refuel and rearm, after which, at about 1400, the panzers resumed their advance.

Awaiting them on Point 102 was 22nd Armoured Brigade, its men tense with expectancy but delighted not to be advancing against enemy tanks or covering retiring infantry as Auchinleck had envisaged. Instead, as Roberts relates with satisfaction, they were standing defensively 'in good positions of our own choosing'. Roberts had stationed his three hardest-worked armoured regiments on the foothills south of Point 102. With a total strength of sixty-five Grants, thirty Crusaders and nineteen Stuarts, they formed a front of about 3 miles in an arc between Alam Halfa and Bare Ridge and were supported by the 6-pounder anti-tank guns of 1st Battalion, the Rifle Brigade, an artillery unit and an anti-tank battery.

Roberts had placed his fourth regiment, the Royal Scots Greys under Lieutenant Colonel Sir Ranulph Fiennes, on the north-eastern slopes of Point 102, some 2 miles behind the front line. Its troopers, not now mounted on the grey horses that had given their regiment its name, manned twenty-four Grants and nineteen Stuarts. Since all these were comparatively new and mechanically reliable, Roberts had chosen the Greys to be his 'mobile reserve'.

At 1730, the panzers appeared. They were heading for Alam Halfa but, on sighting the British armour, they turned towards Point 102. At 1800, 21st Panzer attacked the centre of the British position while 15th Panzer circled to engage its left flank. It was, Roberts tells us, 'fascinating to watch them, as one might watch a snake curl up ready to strike'. A deadly snake too, for in the van of 21st Panzer Roberts spotted several tanks with 'a very long gun on them, in fact it looks the devil of a gun. This must be the long-barrelled stepped-up 75mm the Intelligence people have been talking about.'

It was indeed, and the Mark IV Specials, here opposing Allied armour for the first time, opened fire from over 1,000 yards, destroying three Grants before they were able to hit back. As the range decreased, 21st Panzer began to suffer, but by the time it halted briefly to re-form it had knocked out nine more Grants and, says Roberts, torn 'a complete hole in our defence'. He hastily called the Greys forward, but before they could arrive 21st Panzer was on the move again, this time making for 1st Rifle Brigade. With admirable coolness, the gunners held their fire until the range was down to 300 yards. Then they opened up with considerable effect, being joined by every other British gun that could be brought to bear.

Again 21st Panzer halted briefly and as it resumed its advance, the Greys poured over the ridge in a cloud of dust, losing four of their Grants but blocking the gap in the defences. At 1900, 21st Panzer fell back, allowing Roberts to send reinforcements to his left flank where his men, aided by the guns of 44th Division on Alam Halfa, were still in action against 15th Panzer. At 1930, this also retired. The Germans had had twenty-two tanks destroyed, plus others disabled but later recovered, a task they always performed very skilfully. Despite its own tank losses, 22nd Armoured's casualties were just three men killed and some fifty wounded.

Though Montgomery sent his reserve formation 151st Brigade to Alam Halfa, the hour of greatest danger had in fact passed. On 1 September, 21st Panzer approached the right flank of 22nd Armoured, but was driven off by its tanks and the artillery of 23rd Armoured. The main German thrust, however, was made by von Vaerst's 15th Panzer on Alam Halfa, which Rommel apparently believed could only be lightly defended, as indeed it would have been had Montgomery not altered Auchinleck's plan. Custance's 8th Armoured Brigade appeared on von Vaerst's flank, only to be driven back by his anti-tanks guns, but 15th Panzer was itself thrown back by a succession of furious bombardments from 44th Division.

Rommel now decided to go on the defensive but, to his credit, had not yet lost all hope of victory. Later it would be said that Montgomery should have launched an immediate all-out assault, but was too cautious and unimaginative. These were accusations his critics often aimed at Montgomery, but thereby usually only demonstrate that he was better informed than they.

This was certainly the case at Alam Halfa. Had Montgomery allowed his tanks to go onto the attack, he would have given the panzers 'the opportunity for what must surely have been a certain revenge.' This at least was the opinion of Ronald Lewin, then an Eighth Army artillery officer stationed on the Alam Halfa Ridge, in *The Life and Death of the Afrika Korps*. He points out that

> Of the three [British] armoured brigades available, 8th was totally ignorant of desert warfare, 23rd consisted of the reinforced survivors from an almost total disaster, and only 22nd had maturity – but it was battle-weary and it is to be doubted whether it had grown out of all the bad old ways, though it had fought a most able defensive action on the 31st.

It was an assessment shared by Rommel who later reports that: 'Montgomery had attempted no large-scale attack to retake the southern part of his line, and would probably have failed if he had…. There is no doubt that the British commander's handling of this action had been absolutely right.' On 1 September, Rommel expressed the same opinion much less politely. 'The swine isn't attacking!' he complained angrily to Kesselring who was visiting the battle area. 'The swine', of course, was Montgomery.

Early on 2 September, Rommel received more bad news. Kesselring had, as promised, let him have a further 500 tons of fuel daily, though much of this was consumed on its journey to the front line. In addition, however, Marshal Ugo Cavallero, Chief of Staff of the Italian Armed Forces, had stated that five tankers would reach Tobruk in the first week of September. On the previous night, two of them had been sunk by aircraft from Malta and two more would be lost on the 4th, although the remaining one did reach Tobruk safely that same day. The sinking of the first pair, however, did give Rommel the chance of attributing his defeat to a shortage of petrol.

It was not a contention accepted even in most German accounts. Kesselring points out that the fuel carried in the tankers was not intended to supply Rommel for the seven-day battle he had envisaged, but to replenish the stocks the battle was likely to have consumed. He concludes that 'lack of petrol supplies could not be blamed' for the defeat. The German historian Paul Carell, after interviewing senior survivors of the *Afrika Korps*, declares in *The Foxes of the Desert* that Rommel's argument 'cannot be supported'. Von Vaest bluntly labels it 'a fallacy'.

Rommel would later claim that by the evening of 1 September, he 'had only one petrol issue left', but in a signal to Berlin the next day, he stated he could only continue 'at the full rate of expenditure' until 5 September, which gives a very different picture. Indeed, his complaint to Kesselring about Montgomery not attacking would have been pointless if he had not had the fuel to deal with the attacks when any came.

It seems clear therefore that Rommel's decision on 2 September to retire to his start line was caused by his inability to persuade Montgomery to fight a 'fluid and mobile' battle. His retirement appears to have been unhampered by any petrol shortage, even though, on Montgomery's instructions, Axis supply units were made the principal target for both army and air force. Montgomery's attempt to apply further pressure by having the New Zealanders push south from Alam Nayil proved a failure, however. Remembering past disasters, Freyberg allowed his two New Zealand brigades to attack only late on 3 September and then only if the very inexperienced 132nd (British) Brigade joined them. Montgomery and Horrocks, unwillingly and, as it transpired, unwisely, eventually agreed and the attackers suffered substantial casualties, 697 in 132nd Brigade alone, more than two-fifths of the Allied total for the entire battle.

Thereafter the Axis retirement was unhindered except from the air, and at 0700 on 7 September Montgomery called off the battle, leaving Himeimet and the two British minefields in the south in enemy hands. They scarcely justified Rommel's losses of almost 3,000 men, 55 guns, 49 tanks – 76 more were damaged but recovered – 41 warplanes and almost 400 'soft-skinned' vehicles. The battle cost the defenders 15 guns, 67 tanks – of which almost half were later repaired – 68 aircraft – not all of which were total 'write-offs' and half of whose airmen survived – and 1,750 casualties, dead, injured or prisoners.

It was Montgomery's first victory, revealing important aspects of his generalship, if also some myths. When the battle started, de Guingand awakened a sleeping Montgomery to give him the news. His leader muttered: 'Excellent, excellent!' and then went back to sleep. From this arose a legend that Montgomery would never allow his sleep to be disturbed and that his contribution to his battles was to make a brilliant plan and then leave it to his men to carry it out. Neither was correct. With the grim example of Barker in front of him, Montgomery did value his hours of rest, but we will see plenty of occasions when he would be awakened at a time of crisis. He also made sure that he was well informed of the progress of the battle and was quick to give any necessary orders to his soldiers.

Or any necessary requests to his supporting airmen. He was, says Horrocks, 'the most air-minded general I ever met.' His frequent arrogant references to 'his' 'magnificent air striking force' would come to infuriate certain senior air officers, but even in official RAF publications we find acknowledgements of his 'remarkably keen, clear and vigorous appreciation of the part that could and should be played by air forces in a land battle' and approval of the way 'air co-operation' was his 'gospel'. Indeed, Montgomery, in his own words a few months later, 'always maintained that the Eighth Army and the RAF in the Western Desert together constitute one fighting machine and therein lies our great strength.' His attitude and his actions would be followed very effectively by other commanders in North-West Europe, Italy and the Far East, but it was Montgomery who first set the example and for this he deserves immense gratitude.

Montgomery's calm poise, as demonstrated in his reaction to de Guingand's news, combined with his close supervision of his soldiers, enabled him to take his men into his confidence. He not only won a vital battle at Alam Halfa, but as Horrocks relates, won 'in exactly the manner he had said beforehand that he would win'. Moreover his experienced troops realized he had done so by his personal decisions and his personal alteration of previous intentions.

As a result, says Fuller rather austerely, 'this skilfully fought defensive battle raised the morale of his [Montgomery's] men.' 'From that tight-reined success at Alam Halfa,' declares Williams, 'sprang the morale needed for the victory at Alamein not too many weeks later.' Montgomery was always concerned about his men's morale, although one way he chose of raising confidence would cause him problems in the future.

This was Montgomery's insistence that events had gone entirely according to plan when some had clearly not done so. At Alam Halfa, for example, he would always imply that there was never any intention of doing more than delaying Rommel's offensive on the new minefields. In reality, the Operation Orders of his corps before the battle and his own orders and those of Horrocks during it clearly show a wish to halt Rommel here if possible. His attitude did increase confidence at the time, but unfortunately he persisted in maintaining it long afterwards. This was to his own detriment, for as well as providing ammunition for those jealous of him, it disguises instances of his own admirable flexibility.

Montgomery's closeness to his men, as Ronald Lewin points out, also caused him to be 'known affectionally throughout his army as a person'. After Alam Halfa, he was no longer the army commander; he was 'Monty', their leader and their mascot, 'unmistakable, unforgettable and unbeatable'.

That Alam Halfa was a personal triumph for Montgomery was always accepted by his enemies. Major General Friedrich Wilhelm von Mellenthin, Rommel's Intelligence Chief, states in *Panzer Battles* that: 'Montgomery is undoubtedly a great tactician – circumspect and thorough in making his plans, utterly ruthless in carrying them out. He brought a new spirit to Eighth Army and illustrated once again the vital importance of personal leadership in war.' Paul Carell in *The Foxes of the Desert* says simply that: 'From now on Bernard Montgomery dictated events.'

As to Alam Halfa's importance, it was, says von Mellenthin, 'the turning point of the desert war and the first of the long series of defeats on every front which foreshadowed the collapse of Germany.' 'Alam Halfa,' declares Paul Carell, 'has rightly been called the Stalingrad of the Desert.'

Notes

1. Graham was marking up a large map with details of the evacuation when he first met Montgomery. It says much for his ability that his career survived this unfortunate encounter.
2. Dorman-Smith's Appreciation is set out in all its depressing detail in an Appendix to *Auchinleck* by John Connell.
3. Details of the Allied and Axis tanks in the Desert campaigns are taken from the British Official History *The Mediterranean and Middle East* (Volume III) by Major General I.S.O. Playfair with Captain F.C. Flynn RN and Group Captain T.P. Gleave, *The Tanks* (Volume II) by Captain B.H. Liddell Hart, and *Tobruk* by Field Marshal Carver.
4. In every 'Indian' division, almost all the officers, the artillery units and one of the three battalions in every brigade were British; the other two battalions being Indian or Gurkha.
5. The relevant Operation Orders are No. 144 of 29 July for XIII Corps and Nos. 70 and 71 of 31 July and 10 August for XXX Corps. Those of XXX Corps were written by Field Marshal Carver.

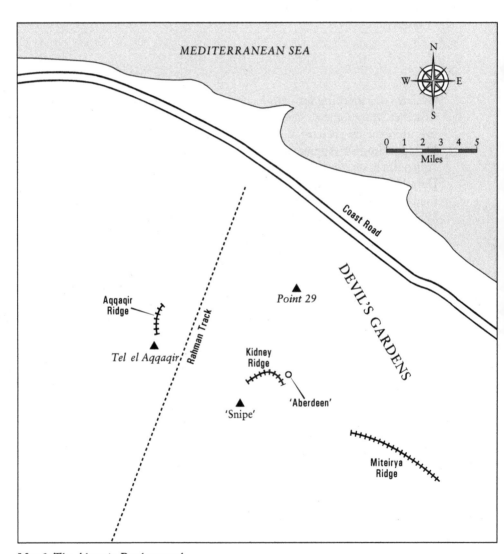

Map 3: The Alamein Battleground.

Chapter Two

The Battle of El Alamein

Victory at Alam Halfa had been vital for the Allied cause, because had it been lost, Rommel would have conquered Egypt. Yet ultimate triumph could still be his if only he could secure his supply lines.

It might seem astonishing that Eighth Army, the supply convoys for which had to travel some 14,000 miles round the Cape of Good Hope, never had shortages of men and matériel, whereas *Panzerarmee Afrika* frequently did, although the port of Messina in Sicily was only 350 miles from Tripoli. The reason was that 60 miles south of Sicily, right in the path of the Axis supply routes, lay the island-fortress of Malta, from which aircraft, submarines and for a time surface warships decimated Axis convoys. As Italian Naval Intelligence would sadly note: 'Malta was the rock upon which our hopes in the Mediterranean foundered.'

The need to suppress Malta was appreciated by the Axis leaders, who knew that Rommel could then be provided with limitless amounts of men and equipment with which to conquer the Middle East. Happily for the Allies, Rommel, intoxicated by his capture of Tobruk and the award of his field marshal's baton, decided to ignore previous arrangements and race at once for the Nile without waiting for Malta's suppression.

It was a catastrophic decision. Even after the fall of Tobruk, Eighth Army still had many more men, tanks, guns and supplies than Rommel. Every mile he advanced into Egypt saw his supply line less secure, his German troops more exhausted and his unmotorized Italian divisions and supporting warplanes further behind the *Afrika Korps*. Kesselring and Cavallero repeatedly warned of the dangers of this course of action, but Rommel won the support of Hitler and, more hesitatingly, that of the Italian dictator Benito Mussolini and he ignored them. He would later excuse his move as 'a plan with a chance of success – a try-on.'

It did not succeed. When Rommel reached the Alamein 'gap' on 1 July, his strength was down to about 1,500 infantrymen and 55 tanks, of which only 15 were Mark III Specials. The 1st South African Division, fighting from fixed positions and 'taking little account' says Field Marshal Carver, of Auchinleck's 'concept of moving columns of artillery around', repulsed his attack. On 3 July the Luftwaffe, which had now come up, attempted to blast a way through with dive-bombers, but it too was driven off by South Africans, this time the pilots of Hurricane fighters.

Thereafter, Rommel was unable to resume his offensive until he had been given reinforcements. During August, as we have seen, he received enough to bring *Panzerarmee Afrika* 'nearer to an even balance' with Eighth Army than at any other time. The Battle of Alam Halfa, however, ended his best chance of securing Egypt while Malta remained unsubdued, and during September and October it was Eighth Army that gained large reinforcements.

If Malta was overcome, though, and Rommel's supply lines secured, he had every chance of ultimate victory and Malta's position was extremely grave. It had been in a state of siege since February 1942, when Rommel had captured a great complex of airfields at Martuba near the town of Derna in Libya, then an Italian possession. This had previously provided a base from which RAF fighters could protect convoys to Malta from Alexandria. Now it provided a base from which Luftwaffe bombers could inflict such ruinous losses that no further convoys could reach the island from the east.

Convoys from Gibraltar had a better chance of success because aircraft carriers could give fighter cover part of the way. In August, four freighters, loaded with a mixture of flour, ammunition and aviation fuel in cans, and the American-built tanker *Ohio* got through. The loss of nine more merchantmen and four of the escorting warships warned, however, that this achievement was unlikely to be repeated before the end of November, when Malta's food and aviation fuel would run out.

To prevent Malta being starved into surrender therefore, Montgomery had to drive Rommel out of the Alamein 'gap', and then advance some 500 miles through Egypt into Cyrenaica, Libya's eastern province, and regain the Martuba airfields. Moreover, he must do this, as he reports in his *Memoirs*, in time to provide 'air cover to the last possible convoy to Malta' which 'was due to leave Alexandria about the middle of November'.[1]

Montgomery had always known that this would have to be done. Williams tells us that on his first meeting with Montgomery, he was questioned not only regarding Rommel's coming offensive, but 'about the enemy defences at Alamein. The new Commander of Eighth Army was one battle ahead of the rest of us.'

This policy of planning both the next battle and the next but one as well would be a characteristic of Montgomery's generalship. Thus in September while Alam Halfa was being fought, he had sent his Australians to make what was in practice an armed reconnaissance of the area where he would attack in due course. The most important example of this trait, though, would come at the end of Alam Halfa and will be examined later.

Once Alam Halfa was won, Montgomery ruthlessly replaced those officers in whom he lacked confidence. Sadly, he sometimes acted most unfairly, for he was far too quick in his judgements and if anyone incurred his displeasure he could rarely be persuaded to reconsider.

There was, for instance, the case of Brigadier Noel Martin, Eighth Army's senior artillery officer, who found himself blamed for its previous dispersals, against which he had in fact strongly protested. Any chance of his being retained was lost when Brigadier Maxwell, the senior gunner at GHQ, Cairo assured Montgomery that Martin was a delightful person and an amateur golfing champion. Montgomery's retort was obvious and immediate and poor Martin was duly replaced, as was the well-meaning but misguided Maxwell.

A more pleasant task was Montgomery's rearrangement of Eighth Army's formations to incorporate welcome if inexperienced reinforcements. XXX Corps was placed under the command of Lieutenant General Sir Oliver Leese who, like Horrocks, had been specially chosen by Montgomery. His corps lost 5th Indian Division, but in practice this meant 9th Indian Brigade. The division's other two brigades and its artillery were taken over by 4th Indian Division which had previously contained only 7th Indian Brigade. The 51st Highland Division also joined Leese, who thus had five divisions in the northern Alamein defences.

In the south, Horrocks retained command of XIII Corps. Under him were 44th Division which regained its 132nd Brigade but lost its 133rd, and 50th Division where 151st Brigade was joined by a re-formed 69th Brigade and a Greek brigade. Horrocks also controlled two Fighting French brigades and 7th Armoured Division, now under Harding, another of Montgomery's personal selections; this contained 22nd Armoured and 4th Light Armoured brigades.

Harding had also been responsible for arranging the creation of a new X Corps. It is said that Montgomery had originally intended to entrust this to Horrocks, but was persuaded that it would cause offence if none of Eighth Army's senior commanders were left in place. It was therefore led by Lieutenant General Herbert Lumsden and contained his former command 1st Armoured Division – 2nd Armoured and 7th Motor brigades – now under Major General Raymond Briggs, and Major General Alec Gatehouse's 10th Armoured Division: 8th Armoured Brigade, the newly-arrived 24th Armoured Brigade and the newly-motorized 133rd Brigade from 44th Division.

Finally, 9th Armoured Brigade under the red-haired, quick-tempered and utterly fearless Brigadier John Currie joined 2nd New Zealand Division, coming directly under Freyberg's control. This, like the provision of 133rd Brigade to Gatehouse, illustrated Montgomery's determination that infantry and armour should act together, as did a series of training exercises designed to give them experience of doing so.

The calibre of British armoured formations had also improved. Almost 80 Crusaders had replaced their 2-pounder gun with a 6-pounder, while more than 250 American Sherman tanks had arrived. With very strong armour and a 75mm gun in the turret instead of in a side-sponson like the Grant, the Sherman was the best tank in Eighth Army, although still inferior to Rommel's mercifully few Mark IV Specials and no match for his lethal 88mm anti-tank guns.

Later the Shermans would gain a deserved reputation for reliability, but in these early days many, as Lucas Phillips tactfully puts it, 'were found to be mechanically shaky'. Also some formations, in particular 8th, 9th and 24th Armoured brigades, received their new tanks too late to have any practice with them before Eighth Army's offensive opened.

For these reasons, Montgomery concluded it would not be possible to attack in September. He wished to do so on a night of clear moonlight followed by several similar ones, so it had to be the night of 23/24 October. Since this would leave Eighth Army little margin for error if it was to reach the Martuba airfields in time, Churchill was most unhappy about the delay and later writers have accused Montgomery of being over-cautious, considering that the Official History confirms the 'fighting strength' of

Eighth Army at 195,000 compared to 104,000 for *Panzerarmee Afrika*: 50,000 Germans and 54,000 Italians.

Yet Rommel had the priceless advantage of fighting in fixed positions that could not be outflanked. His front was guarded by half a million mines, set out in two main belts about 2 miles apart. Between these were other mines placed like the rungs of a ladder to box in attackers, together with every form of booby-trap that human ingenuity could devise. Well named the 'Devil's Gardens' by the Germans, this sinister barrier had a depth of between 2 and 4 miles. Behind it, any force, let alone *Panzerarmee Afrika*, could inflict fearful losses on any number of attackers.

After Montgomery had safely won his battle, later commentators would feel confident that he could not possibly have lost it. At the time, Churchill, Brooke and some of Montgomery's subordinates held other opinions, while Rommel hoped, almost to the end, that if he could hold on just a little longer, his opponent would give up in despair. He had good reason for this because in July General Auchinleck had attempted similar offensives and had failed miserably.

Accounts of July 1942 usually have headings that vary from the misleading 'The Stand on the Alamein Line' to the inaccurate 'The July Battles: Rommel's Advance is Halted'. In reality, Rommel's advance had been halted, temporarily at least, by 3 July. For the rest of that month, the stand on the Alamein line would be made not by Eighth Army but by *Panzerarmee Afrika* against five successive assaults.

Auchinleck had enjoyed a superiority in men and matériel greater than at any time before or since. He had received fresh infantry reinforcements, notably the three brigades of Morshead's highly experienced 9th Australian Division. His tank strength had reached more than 200 by 10 July and almost 400 by the 20th, while that of the *Afrika Korps* varied from less than 30 to about 50. Rommel had had no time to prepare fixed defences and although he had laid mines, they were only a fraction of those faced by Montgomery. His situation in fact was desperate, as an Ultra intercept revealed to Auchinleck on 5 July.

Unfortunately, Auchinleck, under the evil influence of Dorman-Smith, committed virtually every error possible. Infantry formations, already split up, were left unsupported by the armour which in turn was recklessly hurled against German 88mms. Artillery was not concentrated. Effective reconnaissance was not carried out. Co-ordination with the Desert Air Force was not achieved or apparently attempted.

These mistakes were costly. In one offensive on 21 and 22 July, 118 British tanks, mainly from 23rd Armoured Brigade, became total losses, while German tank losses were just 3. In this same offensive, the New Zealanders, unprotected by British armour, had some 900 casualties and lost 23 guns. In an earlier offensive on 14 and 15 July, the New Zealanders, again unprotected, had 1,405 casualties. In a later one on 26 and 27 July, the Australians and the British 69th Brigade were once more left 'naked before an armoured attack'. The 69th Brigade had to be removed from the front line after suffering 600 casualties. The Australians suffered 400, which brought their total in just over three weeks to 146 officers and 3,070 other ranks and Eighth Army's total for July to more than 13,000.

In October 1942, *Panzerarmee Afrika* was no longer exhausted or so heavily outnumbered and had better tanks and far better defensive positions. No wonder then that Montgomery should refuse to be hurried into neglecting any possible precautions. The wonder is that his attitude should have been so fiercely condemned in certain quarters.

One aspect of Montgomery's preparations was considered so important that it had its own code-name: Operation BERTRAM. This was a scheme co-ordinated by Richardson to disguise the time and place of the offensive. Montgomery had planned his main attack in the north of the 'gap', with only a subsidiary move in the south. Consequently, in the north tanks and guns were concealed by having the shapes of dummy lorries called 'sunshades' fitted over them, and supply dumps by being stacked in a way that resembled vehicles when seen from the air. By contrast, in the south dumps and artillery positions, often false ones, were deliberately badly camouflaged, while a bogus water pipeline made from petrol tins with pumping stations and water-towers was steadily laid towards the southern part of the front at a rate suggesting a completion date in early November.[2]

It was in this connection that the clearest example of Montgomery's foresight during the Battle of Alam Halfa was revealed: his refusal to attempt a recapture of Himeimat, despite the wishes of Horrocks and Roberts among others. He intended the peak to remain in Axis hands so that watchers on it could discover all the careful deception measures in the south. 'Leave them in possession of Himeimat,' he told Horrocks, 'that is where I want them to be.'

BERTRAM proved a complete success. It would later be learned from Ultra that Rommel believed Eighth Army would attack at several different points and develop the most promising. In consequence, he divided his armour, with 15th Panzer and *Littorio* divisions holding the northern defences while 21st Panzer and *Ariete* – the more experienced of the two Italian armoured divisions – were stationed in the south and 90th Light and *Trieste* Motorized divisions were kept well back in reserve. The date of the attack was also successfully hidden. When it took place Rommel was enjoying a well-deserved rest in Germany and his deputy, General Georg Stumme, had just sent a routine report to Hitler: 'Enemy situation unchanged.'

Montgomery intended that Leese's XXX Corps should make the main initial assault. When Churchill and Brooke had been in Egypt, they had concluded that 4th Indian Division was not of a high quality, having newly-trained units and inexperienced officers. Accordingly it was ordered to transfer its vehicles to the corps' other formations and restricted to making only diversionary moves.

Leese's remaining divisions – 9th Australian, 51st Highland, 2nd New Zealand and 1st South African, reading from north to south – were to break into the 'Devil's Gardens' on a front of some 6 miles under a very heavy bombardment. They could rely on the fact that a man walking normally was unlikely to set off an anti-tank mine, but would have to accept casualties from anti-personnel ones. Their objectives would be the Miteirya Ridge and the 'Kidney Ridge', really a depression of that shape with a ridge running north and east of it. In order to bring up their vehicles, anti-tank guns and supporting 9th and 23rd Armoured brigades, their Royal Engineers would have to clear gaps through the minefields; an immense undertaking, both difficult and dangerous.

This part of Montgomery's plan would be criticized by Major General Francis Tuker, the able but acerbic commander of 4th Indian Division. His complaints were that a narrower concentrated attack would have been more effective, and that all the artillery should have supported XXX Corps without any assisting XIII Corps' diversion in the south. Neither can be justified. Throughout the battle, Eighth Army suffered from a lack of 'elbow room' causing congestion and traffic problems, and a narrower thrust would have made this infinitely worse. The southern attack had to be supported by artillery: if not, this would have 'given the game away' that it was not a major effort and Axis armour and mobile infantry would not have been kept away from the main area of conflict.

Tuker would also assert that Montgomery contributed nothing new to Eighth Army except firm leadership. In reality, Montgomery's new contributions had already been shown at Alam Halfa and would continue to be shown thereafter. As one small example of this, at Alamein a number of aged Matilda tanks had been fitted with heavy chains that revolved to strike the ground, destroying any mines encountered. Sadly these – known as 'Scorpions' – soon broke down as a result of overheating. They do, however, indicate Montgomery's readiness to use new weapons. It was a trait that would reappear several times and reach its culmination on the beaches of Normandy.

A more important example of Montgomery's new approach at Alamein can be seen in his intentions for Lumsden's X Corps. Once the infantry had secured their initial objectives, X Corps' sappers would clear two wide 'corridors' through which the British tanks would pass: 1st Armoured Division through the northern corridor and 10th Armoured Division through the southern. They would then take up positions from which to resist the enemy armour when it tried to regain the important ground lost, fighting on the defensive with the aid of anti-tank guns. This was a different tactic for an Eighth Army offensive since previously British tanks had always tried to seek out the enemy armour and invariably come to grief from the 88mms.

Montgomery did originally follow the traditional principle adopted by both sides in the Desert campaigns that the enemy armour should be destroyed first and the infantry 'mopped up' at leisure. By 6 October, however, Montgomery had begun to doubt whether his own armour was sufficiently well trained for this task. He therefore decided to destroy the enemy infantry first. This would be done by XXX Corps in a protracted battle of attrition: a procedure Montgomery called 'crumbling'. He was convinced that the impulsive Rommel would send his panzers to the rescue; they would be opposed by British tanks once more standing on the defensive.

With his plans in place, Montgomery explained his intentions in detail to senior officers, made it clear to different formations what was expected of them, encouraged officers and men by his confidence and generally raised the morale of his entire army. Lieutenant Colonel Victor Buller Turner, CO of 2nd Battalion, the Rifle Brigade, summed up the usual reaction to this approach: 'Absolutely thrilling.'

At the same time, Montgomery never promised too much. Fuller describes him as 'audacious in his utterances and cautious in his actions.' Before the Battle of El Alamein it was his actions in reversing all previously approved tactics that might be described as audacious, while his utterances, if not cautious, were certainly cautionary. He warned that results would not come quickly and the fighting would last twelve days. Privately he advised his staff to expect 13,000 casualties. Even the code-name chosen for the offensive had grim implications for a battle fought among minefields: Operation LIGHTFOOT.

It began at 2140 on 23 October, when a tremendous barrage from 474 artillery pieces fell on the Axis gun batteries. At 2155, there was a five-minute pause; then the shellfire switched onto the Axis infantry positions, moving slowly forward ahead of the advancing Eighth Army infantry.

These enjoyed mixed fortunes. In the south, the diversionary attack broke through the first minefield belt but not the second one. Despite the energetic efforts of commanders of the calibre of Horrocks, Harding and Roberts, XIII Corps could make no further progress before 26 October when Montgomery called off operations in this area. Nonetheless, it had successfully performed its main task of keeping 21st Panzer and *Ariete* divisions away from the major assault in the north.

Here by early on 24 October, XXX Corps had captured 80 per cent of its objectives, including most of the Miteirya Ridge. It subsequently secured the remaining ones; the last of them, a stronghold code-named 'Aberdeen' on the eastern end of Kidney Ridge, at dawn on 27 October. In addition, the corps had taken about 1,000 prisoners and killed General Stumme, the acting enemy commander.[3]

As usual in a battle fought by Montgomery, his supporting aircraft played a major role. On the first night, Wellingtons dropped 125 tons of bombs. Next morning, Royal Air Force and South African Air Force squadrons of anti-tank Hurricanes, each aircraft carrying a pair of 40mm cannons, put out of action 'Battlegroup Kiel', a German armoured formation using captured British tanks. Thereafter, throughout the conflict, Allied aircraft constantly attacked Axis targets on or behind the front line and safely intercepted Luftwaffe attempts to retaliate.

With one important exception. The tanks of Lumsden's X Corps had not been able to pass through the infantry as planned. On Kidney Ridge, 1st Armoured Division's 2nd Armoured Brigade under Brigadier Frank Fisher beat off an attack by 15th Panzer and *Littorio*, destroying twenty-six Axis tanks. Fisher lost thirty-one of his own, but Eighth Army could afford this rate of exchange and *Panzerarmee Afrika* could not. Montgomery, though, had hoped that Gatehouse's 10th Armoured Division containing both 8th and 24th Armoured brigades would push on from Miteirya Ridge. Unfortunately, when it attempted to do so on the night of 24/25 October, 8th Armoured Brigade was illuminated by enemy aircraft dropping parachute flares and a bombing attack that followed hit its supporting vehicles, setting twenty-two petrol or ammunition lorries ablaze.

Brigadier Custance was naturally disheartened by this and suggested to Gatehouse that the armoured advance should be discontinued. Gatehouse strongly recommended as much to Lumsden, who in turn notified de Guingand, adding that he was inclined to agree. De Guingand consulted Leese, who seems to have reached the same conclusion. This has been disputed, but Leese would have had every reason for such an opinion. Freyberg had already told him that he doubted X Corps' ability to make further progress and Leese could scarcely expect his infantrymen to win the battle on their own.

De Guingand decided that Montgomery must be informed. He woke his chief and arranged for a conference with Leese and Lumsden at 0330 on 25 October. At this, to quote General Jackson, both corps commanders 'believed that the battle had gone so wrong that it should be broken off to avoid further profitless expenditure of life and resources.'

Montgomery, de Guingand tells us, remained cool and calm but very firm. He made it clear that his basic instructions were unchanged. He warned Lumsden that if necessary he would appoint new leaders for the armour who would ensure his commands were carried out. He contacted Gatehouse on the field telephone, learned he was at his Main Headquarters almost 10 miles behind his armoured brigades and angrily ordered him to 'lead his division from in front and not from behind'. This was in fact most unfair to (and never forgiven by) Gatehouse who had been at his

Main HQ at Lumsden's request so that he could be contacted easily. It was, however, further evidence of Montgomery's insistence that the needs of the armour must be subsidiary to those of the army as a whole.

Montgomery's firmness had no immediate effect, for next morning neither Custance nor Fisher was able to move forward and both lost ten tanks in the attempt. As a result, many commentators including Montgomery's biographer Nigel Hamilton have tended to deny the importance of this conference. De Guingand, by contrast, considers it the first of the 'stepping stones to victory'. There can be no doubt that he is correct. Montgomery's resolution did not win the battle, but it did prevent it from being prematurely abandoned.

As well as firmness, Montgomery showed remarkable flexibility; an unusual combination masked by his stupid insistence that everything always went exactly according to plan. By midday on 25 October, he had decided to abandon his intended moves south-west of Miteirya Ridge and have his armour stand on the defensive, but continue 'crumbling' assaults on the enemy infantry. That night, 26th Australian Brigade captured Point 29, the most prominent feature on a dominating spur north of the Australian positions. This brilliant attack was another example of Montgomery's co-ordination of all arms, for the Australian infantry were supported by 30 Valentines from 40th Royal Tanks, 7 regiments of field or medium artillery and 115 tons of bombs dropped by Wellingtons.

Late on 25 October, Rommel resumed his command of *Panzerarmee Afrika*, but at first merely continued the counter-attacks that had previously cost his armour dear. By the evening of the 26th, 15th Panzer's tank losses had risen to seventy-seven and those of *Littorio* to about fifty, so Rommel ordered 21st Panzer, part of *Ariete* and supporting artillery up from the south and 90th Light and *Trieste* forward from their reserve locations. This led to some ferocious clashes on 27 October, the most remarkable of which was fought out on an unnamed ridge to the south-west of the Kidney Depression that was known by the undramatic code-name of 'Snipe'.

The 'Snipe' position had been captured on the previous night by 2nd Battalion, the Rifle Brigade, commanded by an officer mentioned earlier, Lieutenant Colonel Victor Buller Turner. Under him were fewer than 300 men, the most important being Major Thomas Bird's anti-tank company equipped with 13 6-pounder guns plus 6 others from 76th Anti-

Tank Regiment. As dawn broke, 15th Panzer and *Littorio* were sighted, moving towards the Kidney Ridge. The defenders of 'Snipe' promptly opened fire on them, destroying eleven tanks or self-propelled guns and temporarily knocking out five more. Then a single unarmed German soldier, who had been lying concealed in the heart of the defences, sprang to his feet and made a dash towards his fellow countrymen. Not a shot was fired at him and he made it to safety.

Plenty of shots would be fired by both sides later in the day. Throughout the morning and early afternoon, the Axis tanks assaulted 'Snipe'. They were always beaten off, but the defenders steadily lost guns destroyed or put out of action and men were killed or wounded, among the latter being Turner as he was carrying ammunition to one of his guns, and Bird, both hit in the head. In late afternoon, a new foe appeared: 21st Panzer on its way to assist attacks on Kidney Ridge. The 'Snipe' defenders took full advantage of the targets presented as the new arrivals passed their position and were in turn subjected to repeated attacks, all of which they repulsed. By now Turner's men had suffered seventy-two casualties and only one 6-pounder, commanded by Sergeant Ronald Wood, was not disabled. At 2315 the survivors fell back to Kidney Ridge, bringing their last gun with them.[4]

So great was the fame of this action that a Committee of Investigation examined the site a month later. It concluded that a minimum of thirty-two tanks – twenty-one German including five of Rommel's precious Mark IV Specials and eleven Italian – plus five self-propelled guns had been totally destroyed and another twenty tanks knocked out but recovered, few of which could have been repaired before the battle ended. Among the twenty-four decorations awarded to the defenders were three Distinguished Conduct medals, a Distinguished Service Order for Bird and a Victoria Cross for Turner; he insisted that he received it as the representative of his men.

Montgomery, meanwhile, was again demonstrating his flexibility by varying the direction of his main thrust. The Australians were to advance northward from Point 29 on the night of 28/29 October, and on the night of the 30th/31st, the New Zealanders would attack down the coast road from the Australian position: a move code-named Operation SUPERCHARGE. To prepare for it, 2nd New Zealand Division and 9th Armoured Brigade were pulled back from the front line into reserve. When this news reached Churchill he was most alarmed, angrily telling Brooke that Montgomery was 'allowing the battle to peter out'. Brooke had his own anxieties, but he reassured the prime minister and Montgomery was spared interference from London.

However, on the morning of 29 October, Alexander, for the only time during the battle, did interfere. He arrived at Eighth Army Headquarters, followed later by Air Chief Marshal Sir Arthur Tedder, the Middle East Air C-in-C, to learn Montgomery's intentions. Alexander had reason for concern because not only was it necessary that the Martuba airfields be captured quickly so as to preserve Malta, but an Anglo-American invasion of Vichy French North Africa – Operation TORCH – was planned for 8 November. Alexander had suggested this date which he considered would give enough time for Eighth Army 'to destroy the greater part of the Axis army facing us' but not enough for the enemy to send out substantial reinforcements. 'Both these facts,' Alexander believed, 'would have a strong effect on the French attitude.'

Alexander was thus anxious that Montgomery should not just win his battle but win it soon. Intelligence reports had indicated that Rommel was massing his German troops in the north but – unfortunately quite wrongly – that an attack just north of Kidney Ridge would meet only Italian opposition. Alexander therefore felt that this should be the area in which SUPERCHARGE should take place. Montgomery had already received similar advice from de Guingand and Williams, but rejected it because a successful attack down the coast road would effectively cut off Rommel's entire force, whereas one further south would leave this road as an enemy escape route.

Nonetheless, Montgomery could appreciate that an early success at Alamein must benefit Malta and TORCH, and Alexander had brought with him a telegram to this effect from Churchill. After Alexander had left, de Guingand approached his chief again and Montgomery agreed to execute SUPERCHARGE further south where, he accepted, he could win his battle more quickly if, as he thought probable and as turned out to be the case, less completely.

Montgomery's strategic knowledge had triumphed over his tactical skill and in fact SUPERCHARGE was not delivered as soon as had been hoped because Freyberg required a postponement until the early hours of 2 November. Meanwhile Montgomery ordered the Australians to continue the attacks begun on the night of 28/29 October in order to persuade Rommel that the break-out was still planned in the north, thereby tying down as many of the enemy as possible.

Montgomery's choice of the Australians for this rather thankless role reveals another facet of his generalship. As he declares in his *Memoirs*: 'All men are different.... Therefore all *divisions* are different.' When a particular task had to be performed, he tried to find the division where its men were best suited to carry it out. For the savage combats in the north of the Alamein 'gap' he rightly thought the Australians were ideal, possessing unquestioned courage, stubborn determination and quite remarkable stamina.

So from 26 October to 2 November, the Australians, supported by the Rhodesian 289th Anti-Tank Battery, pushed forward, fighting off counter-attacks by enemy infantry and enemy armour. On 26 October Private Percival Gratwick and on 30 October Sergeant William Kibby earned Victoria Crosses, both sadly posthumous ones. In an article for *The Sunday Times Magazine* twenty-five years later, Montgomery concluded an account of Alamein with the declaration: 'We could not have won the battle in 12 days without that magnificent 9th Australian Division.' Immediately after it was over, Horrocks hastened to congratulate the divisional commander. 'Thank you, General,' replied Morshead, 'the boys were interested.'

At 0105 on 2 November, another moonlit night, SUPERCHARGE began. Like LIGHTFOOT it was accompanied by a 'creeping barrage' and air attacks, but it was carried out by only two brigades, 151st from 50th Division and 152nd from 51st Highland, both of which, it should be noted, were not acting independently but as part of and fully supported by 2nd New Zealand Division. That night they advanced 4,000 yards, bringing them just east of the Rahman Track which ran south-westwards from the coast road, beyond which was the Aqqaqir Ridge and Rommel's last line of defence.

It had been intended that 9th Armoured Brigade – also, it will be remembered, part of 2nd New Zealand Division – would cross both the track and the ridge under cover of darkness, thereby opening a path for the bulk of the British armour. Montgomery considered this so important that he told Brigadier Currie he would accept 100 per cent casualties if 9th Armoured was successful. Unfortunately, delays in assembling prevented 9th Armoured from crossing the Rahman Track at night and when daylight came, it was confronted by the familiar threat of 88mms. It desperately charged these, destroying 35 of them, but of its 94 tanks, 70 were knocked out – though many were later recovered – 230 of its men were killed and no gap had been opened for the British armour.

Luckily, Rommel now engaged the New Zealand salient, with calamitous results. The 1st Armoured Division, containing both 2nd and 8th Armoured brigades, fighting strictly on the defensive, destroyed seventy German and thirty-seven Italian tanks for the loss of only fourteen of its own. The Desert Air Force's light bombers joined in, making seven attacks on the enemy, while two dive-bomber raids by the Luftwaffe were so disrupted by Hurricanes that they dropped their bombs on their own troops.

That evening, Montgomery again varied the direction of his main thrust, ordering 152nd Brigade to attack southward from the New Zealand salient. This finally proved decisive. On the morning of 3 November, Rommel ordered his Italian infantry divisions to retreat while his mobile forces held firm as long as possible to cover them.

At 1530, Rommel received a signal from Hitler ordering him to 'stand fast' and show his troops 'no other road than that to victory or death'. Rommel would later pretend that this order prevented him from making an orderly retirement, but his claim cannot be accepted since he did not obey it. Instead, as night fell on 3 November, he withdrew his mobile troops from the Aqqaqir Ridge, thus surrendering the defensive line that had hitherto defied Eighth Army. At the same time, Montgomery renewed his push southward with fresh formations. That night 154th Brigade from 51st Highland captured Tel el Aqqaqir, the ridge's highest point, and 5th Indian Brigade from 4th Indian Division reached the Rahman Track 4 miles to the south.

Through the gap torn in the Axis defences poured the British armour. In the early afternoon of 4 November, 22nd Armoured Brigade fell upon *Ariete* which Rommel had belatedly brought into the battle-zone: it was all but wiped out, losing 450 men as prisoners at a cost to Roberts of 1 Stuart tank and 3 men wounded. At about the same time, Brigadier Fisher's 2nd Armoured Brigade threw back a final counter-attack by the panzer divisions and 90th Light. The *Afrika Korps'* leader, Lieutenant General Wilhelm Ritter von Thoma, was captured. That evening he dined with Montgomery, rather touchingly inviting his conqueror to visit him in Germany when the war was over.

By 1730 on 4 November, *Panzerarmee Afrika* was in full flight. As at Alam Halfa, there was enough petrol to enable the mobile units to escape, but the four Italian infantry divisions, whose problem was not a shortage of petrol but an absence of any vehicles in which to put it, had no option except to surrender; eight Italian generals followed von Thoma into captivity.

The Battle of El Alamein, as Montgomery had foretold, had lasted twelve days and Eighth Army had suffered 13,500 casualties, little more than those in the 'nonsenses of July'. It had also lost 100 guns and 97 of its supporting aircraft. It has been widely stated that 500 tanks had been destroyed, but in fact total losses were 150 and the remainder, mostly suffering damage to tracks or suspension in the minefields, were quickly back in action. The Axis powers had lost more than 1,000 guns and 450 tanks plus 75 more abandoned by the Italians in the pursuit and 84 warplanes. Their manpower casualties are variously estimated, but probably between 20,000 and 25,000 were killed and wounded. There is no doubt that well over 30,000 were taken prisoner, 10,700 of them Germans.

On 6 November, Churchill received a signal from General Alexander: 'Ring out the bells!'

Notes

1. Montgomery was a far better strategist than Auchinleck who, as late as August 1942, could state that Malta's retention was not absolutely necessary to his plans.
2. Richardson's *Flashback* gives full details of the deception plan which would set a precedent for similar operations in the future. He was rewarded with the grant of a rare OBE (Military).
3. Soon after dawn, Stumme had set out for the front line to check the situation. He was just getting out of his staff car when it came under fire from Australian troops. The driver made off at high speed, unaware that his general was outside the car, clinging on to it. Stumme suffered from high blood pressure and had a fatal heart attack. His body was found the next day.
4. A brilliant, detailed description of 'The Great Stand at "Snipe"' is given by Lucas Phillips in his *Alamein*.

Chapter Three

'On to Tripoli!'

Victory at El Alamein had immensely valuable consequences for the Allied cause and not only with regard to the campaigns in the desert. On 8 November, British and American troops under the overall command of Lieutenant General Dwight David Eisenhower landed at Algiers and Oran in the Mediterranean and Casablanca on the Atlantic coast. This was Operation TORCH. It suffered from considerable delay, confusion and losses but, as Alexander had anticipated, was saved by the achievements of Eighth Army.

It so happened that Admiral Jean Darlan, heir apparent to the aged Marshal Pétain as Vichy's Head of State, was in Algiers visiting a son dangerously ill with polio. His dislike of the British was notorious and

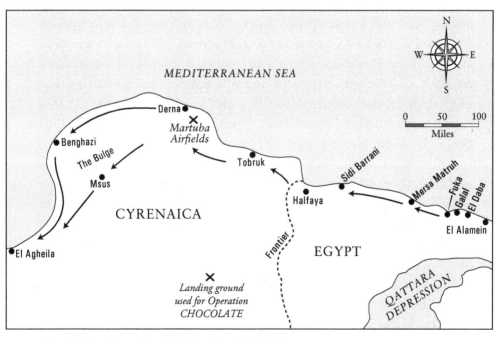

Map 4: The advance from El Alamein to El Agheila.

his first act on learning of the landings was to arrest Mr Robert Murphy, the US Consul General. He was, though, a realist and, accepting the inevitable, at 1120 on 10 November, he ordered all French troops in North Africa to end their resistance.

Darlan's abrupt conversion to the Allied cause did him little good, for on Christmas Eve he was shot dead by a youthful anti-Vichy fanatic named Bonnier de la Chapelle – himself hastily court-martialled and shot two days later – but it did bring Morocco and Algeria under Allied control. It also greatly alarmed Hitler and so led to further dramatic developments.

Hitler had two main anxieties: that Vichy France would now join the ranks of his enemies and that Allied forces would move eastward through Tunisia into Libya and engage Rommel from the rear. This latter prospect delighted Montgomery. Eighth Army had no railway beyond Tobruk and only a single satisfactory coast road to the main Axis base of Tripoli. In Tunisia, by contrast, good roads and railways stretched almost to the Libyan frontier. It should therefore be much easier to capture Tripoli by a thrust through Tunisia than by a long haul from Egypt. Montgomery saw this very clearly and said as much to Alexander in a letter of 18 November.

It was not to be. Hitler acted with admirable speed and complete ruthlessness. On 11 November, ten German and six Italian divisions poured into and overran the unoccupied part of France. Earlier still on 9 November, the first German contingent arrived in Tunisia in transport aircraft. It was pathetically small, consisting of just one parachute regiment and the personal guard unit of Field Marshal Kesselring, but reinforcements were soon to follow. By early December, there were 15,000 German and 9,000 Italian soldiers in Tunisia, including the men of 10th Panzer Division. Formed into Fifth Panzer Army under General Jurgen von Arnim, a harsh, grim man who had previously commanded a corps in Russia, they quickly checked the advancing Allies.

By his prompt action, Hitler had temporarily saved the situation in North Africa but, it quickly became clear, only at the cost of a catastrophe elsewhere. The troops transferred to Vichy France and Tunisia had been destined for Russia and their absence greatly aided the Russian counter-offensive at Stalingrad which, on 22 November, cut off the German Sixth Army. This could undoubtedly have fought its way out during the next week, but Hitler refused to allow this because he could not tolerate another major German retreat so soon after the one from El Alamein. Moreover, some 400 operational warplanes and numerous aerial transports were sent from the Russian front to the Mediterranean, thus preventing the Sixth Army being supplied by air as Göring had promised.

Indeed, when it is considered how widespread the benefits of El Alamein were, it is extraordinary that most later commentators view its results in North Africa with at best lukewarm approval and at worst fierce hostility. Denis Richards and Hilary St George Saunders, authors of the Official History *Royal Air Force 1939–1945*, admirably if unintentionally sum up the irony in two successive sentences: 'The subsequent pursuit, however, did not quite satisfy our most ardent desires. It swept across the breadth of Africa.' In the three previous years of war the soldiers, politicians and general public of the Allied countries would have been more than grateful for such an 'unsatisfying' occurrence.

The trouble was that *Panzerarmee Afrika* had been defeated but not destroyed, and it is suggested that all that was needed to achieve this was a swift relentless pursuit. It is forgotten that Eighth Army and the Desert Air Force alike were worn out by the physical and mental demands of twelve days of action, and this moreover had been continuous since Montgomery had deliberately avoided giving his opponents any intervals of rest as had happened in Auchinleck's July offensives.

For a swift relentless pursuit, in fact, fresh troops were desirable. During the battle de Guingand and Richardson had tried to create a reserve force for this purpose but, inevitably perhaps, its units had been thrown into the fighting. Montgomery can be criticized for this, but it is difficult to do so severely when previous events are recalled. In July, Auchinleck had laid much stress on pursuing a defeated foe, but unfortunately had been unable to achieve his defeat in the first place.

Major General Tuker was particularly indignant that his 4th Indian Division, of which only 5th Indian Brigade had seen major action in the battle, was not used for the pursuit. Yet his other two brigades were still back behind the minefields and all of them were short of transport vehicles, as Tuker had often complained. Accordingly, Montgomery decided to use formations that were already well forward and at least not too tired. These were X Corps' 1st, 7th and 10th Armoured divisions and Freyberg's 2nd New Zealand Division, reinforced by 4th Light Armoured Brigade. These were surely better choices for the pursuit force, even if far from perfect for a number of different reasons.

For a start, the armoured divisions' supply echelons were still making their way – with difficulty – through the minefields. Their absence was the more serious because the Shermans now revealed another defect: they consumed 'fantastic quantities of fuel', a problem previously concealed by the static nature of the fighting at Alamein. In addition, all the British tanks were handicapped by the poor 'going' they were compelled to cross in order to outflank Rommel who could move down a good coast road. Nor were matters helped by poor communications between Lumsden as head of X Corps and his divisional commanders Briggs, Harding and Gatehouse, and between Lumsden and Freyberg.

These problems were increased by an error on the part of Montgomery. During both Alam Halfa and Alamein, he had maintained a tight control over his army which, although unpopular in some quarters, proved very effective. He believed, however, that in a fluid situation such as a pursuit centralized control was unsuitable. He therefore laid down a proposed course of action and left it to Lumsden and Freyberg to carry this out. After 7 December, Montgomery implicitly admitted his mistake by resuming firm control, but by then much had already happened.

Yet the main reason why the Germans made good their escape was that Eighth Army was badly misled by Ultra. The exaggerated praise bestowed on this form of Intelligence has tended to mask its sometimes serious flaws. There was, for instance, an inevitable delay before the intercepts were communicated to the combat zone. The signal had to be detected: not easy as the Germans regularly changed their radio frequencies. Then it had to be deciphered, translated, errors corrected and gaps caused by poor reception filled. Finally it had to be re-encoded and radioed to the appropriate British Intelligence Officer in the field. By that time several hours, sometimes as much as three days, would have passed and the situation revealed might well have altered completely, especially in the fast-moving desert campaigns.

Worse still, the signal could only reveal the intention of its originator at one particular moment. It would be grossly misleading if he had changed his mind or been overruled or, in Rommel's case particularly, had received orders that he did not propose to obey or had stated plans that he did not propose to carry out.

This is what now happened. On 3 November, Ultra reported that on the previous day Rommel had warned Hitler that his men were exhausted, his non-motorized units would probably 'fall into the hands of the enemy' – as they did – and his mobile troops were also threatened because 'the shortage of fuel will not allow of a withdrawal to any great distance.' A second signal issued on the same day and again reported to Eighth Army on 3 November stated that Rommel therefore proposed to retire fighting 'step by step'.

Thus when on 4 November another Ultra intercept revealed that Rommel intended 'to gain some time at the next intermediate position El Daba' 20 miles west of El Alamein before retiring a further 30 miles to Fuka, this seemed in accordance with, or indeed confirmation of, the previous signals. It therefore appeared to Montgomery that he had a marvellous chance of trapping Rommel at El Daba. Some of his tank commanders would later say that he should have sent one of his armoured divisions on a wide sweep to the Egyptian frontier. So he might have done had he been the cautious unimaginative commander described by his critics. Instead he committed all his advanced forces in a daring attempt to crush Rommel's mobile units once and for all.

Montgomery sent 2nd New Zealand Division to Fuka, 1st and 7th Armoured divisions directly to El Daba and 10th Armoured to Galal midway between Fuka and El Daba, urging them to move all night if necessary. In fact, the night of 4/5 November was an exceptionally dark one and little progress was made before daylight. Next morning, 1st Armoured Division secured El Daba but took only 150 prisoners; 10th Armoured at Galal intercepted the remnants of the Italian armour, destroying 33 tanks and 100 lorries and taking 1,000 prisoners. There was, however, no sign of the main prize: Rommel's *Afrika Korps*. There had been one fatal flaw in Montgomery's seemingly admirable plan: Ultra had given him inaccurate information because Rommel had changed his mind and was not attempting to stand at El Daba after all.[1]

On 6 November, Montgomery ordered a further attempt by 1st and 7th Armoured to cut off the *Afrika Korps* between Fuka and Mersa Matruh, but they were handicapped by 'bad going' and, at about 1500, by a rainstorm described as 'torrential' by a grateful Rommel. This continued throughout the night, reducing the desert to a quagmire in which vehicles sank to their axles and ending all chance of outflanking movements for the rest of 6 November and the whole of the 7th. Montgomery did later send Harding on a wide sweep to the frontier, but he made little progress even before he was bogged down by more heavy rain on the 10th.

Just Gatehouse's 10th Armoured Division, which could move down the coast road, was unaffected. At midday on 6 November it entered Fuka, adding another 300 Italians to Eighth Army's growing haul of prisoners. On the 7th, though, its rather weak efforts to reach Mersa Matruh were checked by determined resistance from Rommel's rearguard, the battered but undaunted 90th Light Division. Only the urging of Montgomery, who arrived at the front in person later that afternoon, led to a further assault and another Axis withdrawal: to Sidi Barrani.

Montgomery was certainly leading his army from the front on 7 November; in fact he was unwise to be so far forward. The dangers of this were demonstrated on this same day when an advance party of his staff officers looking for a site for their headquarters in the Matruh area collided with the enemy. Among those captured were Lieutenant Colonel Mainwaring, Head of Operations, and Montgomery's stepson Major Richard Carver.[2] However, the whole episode does indicate Montgomery's determination that the pursuit should be kept up relentlessly.

For this Montgomery has received little credit. Later critics delight in describing the Eighth Army's advance as cautious, ponderous, sluggish, lumbering and, worst of all, dull. This was not how it appeared to the Germans. Paul Carell, who, as was mentioned earlier, gained his information from Rommel's chief subordinates, declares that: 'Montgomery was pressing on with unusual speed' and that 'the boldness of the British pursuit was conspicuous.'

Carell also emphasizes that Montgomery gave the Germans 'no time to reorganize or dig in for a defence.' Rommel confirms that he planned to defend Fuka 'long enough for the Italian and German infantry to catch up', but he was driven out so quickly that his unmotorized units had no choice but to surrender. He hoped the rainstorm would enable him to 'hold on to Mersa Matruh for a few more days' while defences in the frontier area were constructed, but Eighth Army's pressure soon changed his mind. He intended to keep Sidi Barrani at least until the evening of 10 November, but was forced to retire a day earlier. Finally on the night of 10/11 November, a brilliant attack by Kippenberger's 5th New Zealand Brigade captured Halfaya Pass and 600 Italians and compelled Rommel to abandon his frontier defences, once more 'earlier than anticipated'.

Thereafter Rommel was not prepared to risk defending any Cyrenaican towns, not even Tobruk which he hastily decided possessed only 'symbolic value'. He continued to retreat, still closely followed by Eighth Army, or at least part of Eighth Army for, despite later claims, Montgomery's strength was not only not overwhelming but was steadily diminishing. His splendid Australian and South African divisions were recalled to their home countries and the problem of supplies that bedevilled every advance in the desert resulted in other formations having to halt in the frontier area. The pursuit through Cyrenaica, therefore, was carried out only by Harding's 7th Armoured Division: 22nd Armoured and 4th Light Armoured brigades.

Harding kept up continual pressure, aided by Montgomery, typically, having insisted that the Desert Air Force must advance with Eighth Army. Indeed he gave it priority, although this placed a further strain on his supply system because 11,500 RAF and AA personnel were brought forward, together with their food and equipment and fuel for their aircraft.

The Desert Air Force responded with an operation with the innocuous code-name of CHOCOLATE. On 13 November, two squadrons of Hurricane fighter-bombers flew to a landing-ground deep in the desert about 140 miles behind the enemy lines. From then until the 16th when their base was discovered and they had to retire, these aircraft, for the loss of two of their number to AA fire, flew continuous sorties against Axis targets. In the course of these, they totally destroyed about 130 vehicles together with their wretched occupants and crippled some 170 more, almost all of which had to be abandoned; a brilliant little achievement.

A less welcome air force interference was provided by Air Chief Marshal Tedder, who urged that Eighth Army abandon the coast road and cut across the base of the Cyrenaican 'Bulge', trapping Rommel at Benghazi. Montgomery did send armoured cars in this direction, but declined to divert his main forces. De Guingand was in complete agreement, pointing out that Montgomery's resources were already stretched, and bad weather and enemy aircraft would have made the action suggested by Tedder unlikely to succeed in any case. Post-war critics, however, have decided that Montgomery was over-cautious and missed a great opportunity.

In reality, it seems that both de Guingand and the later critics missed a point clearly seen by Montgomery. Wisely and rightly, he again chose a strategic necessity over a tactical opportunity. The greatest strategic prize in North Africa at this date was the Martuba airfields, the time limit for their capture was desperately close and Montgomery was not prepared to weaken the forces making for them under any circumstances.

His decision was soon justified. On 15 November, 4th Light Armoured Brigade captured the airfields. On the 17th, a convoy of four merchantmen, code-named STONEAGE, left Alexandria for Malta. Enemy air attacks were broken up by fighters from Martuba and early on the 20th the convoy reached the island, raised the long siege and ended the last chance of the Axis being able to dominate the Mediterranean. In his diary, Brooke recorded a simple 'Thank God!'

With Martuba safely secured, Montgomery was prepared to consider an advance across the base of the 'Bulge'. He therefore sent 22nd Armoured Brigade to follow up the armoured cars – which had captured Msus on the 17th – and hurried forward Sherman tanks on transporters as reinforcements. As de Guingand had forecast, however, rain and enemy air-raids held up this move, while 4th Light Armoured, having taken Benghazi without resistance on the 20th, was checked on the coast road

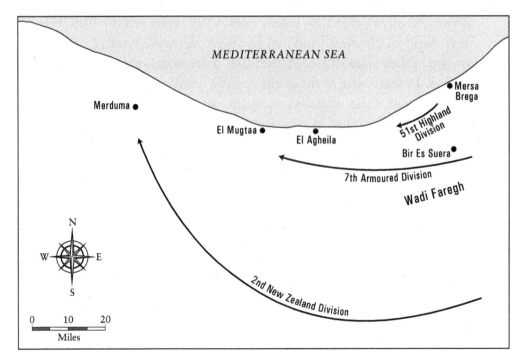

Map 5: The Battle of El Agheila.

by the skilful delaying tactics of the redoubtable 90th Light. By the 23rd, all Rommel's men were safely behind the fixed defences of El Agheila.

It had been the longest, most rapid retreat in Germany's proud military history and when considering the criticisms levelled at Eighth Army in general and Montgomery in particular, it is worth recalling an earlier victorious advance that had begun on 7 December 1941. From the then front line running roughly southward from Tobruk, it took Eighth Army until 5 January 1942 to reach El Agheila: thirty days to cover 470 miles by the coast road. No criticisms ever seem to have been made of this achievement. Instead they are reserved for the advance from El Alamein to El Agheila that took nineteen days from 5 to 23 November to cover 840 miles by the coast road; almost twice the distance in less than two-thirds of the time.

For those who feel this is singularly unfair, there is the consolation that the Allied leaders at the time had a different appreciation of what Eighth Army had accomplished in October and November 1942. On the 11th of the latter month, its leader became a full general and a Knight Commander of the Bath.

In January 1942, Eighth Army had been unable to progress beyond El Agheila. Nor had an earlier Allied advance through Cyrenaica at the expense of the Italians in February 1941. Inevitably, there were many who feared that history might repeat itself; their anxiety did not escape Montgomery, always very conscious of and susceptible to the moods of his army.

Nor was this concern unreasonable. Alexander in his Official Despatch would call the El Agheila position the strongest in Libya. El Agheila itself lay at the centre of the defences, but they began at the little port of Mersa Brega some 40 miles to the east. They could only be approached between the sea and the Wadi Faregh, a deep, narrow gorge running parallel to it. The fixed defences blocked the gap, then swung south-westwards to south of El Agheila. Soft sand, salt marshes and broken ground restricted freedom of movement and the natural difficulties, as at El Alamein, had been increased by vast quantities of both anti-tank and anti-personnel mines that spread all over the front and stretched back as far as El Mugtaa some 17 miles west of El Agheila. The position could be outflanked, but only by a very wide sweep of 200 miles through exceptionally difficult country.

These strong defences helped to restore Axis morale, as did the arrival of Italian reinforcements: the re-formed *Ariete* (Armoured), the fresh *Centauro* (Armoured) and two infantry divisions. The defenders' only weakness was their leader. Rommel had lost his will to resist. Field Marshal Kesselring, an invincible optimist and, like Montgomery and indeed Alexander, at his very best when matters were going badly, reports that: 'He [Rommel] wanted to get back to Tunis; if possible still further away, to Italy and the Alps – wishful thinking that clouded his strategic judgement.'

So low was Rommel's personal morale that it is possible that Montgomery really was over-cautious when he paused and prepared for a set-piece attack in mid-December instead of assaulting at once. It is difficult, though, to blame him, because Ultra had made clear the Axis leaders' determination to hold El Agheila, but not Rommel's reluctance to do so. Not until 6 December, when Rommel persuaded Mussolini and Cavallero to allow his unmotorized infantry to be sent back to Buerat some 250 miles further west, did Montgomery get an indication of his opponent's real state of mind.

By this time, Montgomery had already done much to reorganize his army, ready for the assault. XIII Corps virtually ceased to exist for a time and Horrocks took over X Corps which was pulled back between Benghazi and Tobruk to guard against any Axis counterstrike into Cyrenaica. The luckless Lumsden returned to England, Montgomery reporting to Brooke: 'He [Lumsden] is a good trainer. He is young and may come along later. At present he is quite unfit for a Corps Command.'[3]

Only the three divisions of Leese's XXX Corps took part in the Battle of El Agheila. On the night of 13/14 December, 51st Highland Division attacked down the coast road, apart from its 153rd Brigade. This, together with 8th Armoured and 131st Motorized Infantry brigades, was included in Harding's 7th Armoured Division; another indication of Montgomery's integration of the different branches of his army. Harding attacked at Bir es Suera, about 15 miles south of the Highlanders' offensive. On the previous night, Freyberg's New Zealanders, accompanied by the forty-five tanks of 4th Light Armoured Brigade, set out on a lengthy outflanking move aimed for the coast road at Merduma, well to the west of El Mugtaa.

Naturally Montgomery's plans have not been allowed to escape criticism. According to Rommel, he was at fault for not postponing his main offensive until Freyberg was in a position to cut the coast road. However, since Montgomery's alleged error did not prevent Freyberg from doing this, Rommel's complaint seems irrelevant at best. At worst it seems stupid. The distance that Freyberg's force had to travel made it almost inevitable that it would be detected by air reconnaissance and then be dangerously exposed. Indeed, when it really was detected at 1700 on 14 December, Rommel's officers urged him to make an armoured attack on it, but he dared not take the risk while he was under pressure from Eighth Army's main assault. Had Montgomery delayed this, Freyberg, whose tank strength had been reduced to seventeen by bad going and the Shermans' unreliability, might have endured a very unpleasant experience.

Lieutenant General Leese, by contrast, was very conscious of the dangers faced by Freyberg, who he thought should have been given every tank and gun available. However, as de Guingand has pointed out, any larger force could not have progressed rapidly over the very difficult terrain. In any case, if the main attacking force was deprived of its accompanying bombardment and powerful armoured support, it might not be able to break through El Agheila's strong defences, in which case Freyberg would be isolated and Eighth Army's advance halted in its tracks.

It would seem that Montgomery had again been wiser than his critics and the course of the battle confirms this. The defences and minefields proved considerable obstacles and although Rommel might have lost heart, the re-formed *Ariete* and ever-reliable 90th Light certainly had not. They resisted so strenuously that it was not until 15 December that 7th Armoured, supported as always by the Desert Air Force, broke through to sweep south of El Agheila, whereupon Rommel decided he would have to withdraw.

Meanwhile, the New Zealanders were pressing on with the outflanking movement, their progress aided by Montgomery having earlier arranged a reconnaissance of their route by the armoured cars of 1st King's Dragoon Guards under Captain Chrystal. By late afternoon of 15 December, Freyberg had reached the coast road near Merduma, although sadly was not strong enough to trap the enemy completely. That night the Axis soldiers, splitting up into small groups, burst past the New Zealanders, leaving behind as prisoners only some 450 men, and although Freyberg continued to harry them, they made good their retirement, ultimately to Buerat.

So ended the Battle of El Agheila. It was neither large nor memorable, but it was immensely important: Eighth Army had finally overcome a barrier that to many had seemed impassable and was advancing ever further into the Libyan province of Tripolitania. It was slowed by a seemingly never-ending sequence of minefields, but the Royal Engineers, not without casualties, steadily cleared a way through these and by 29 December, 4th Light Armoured Brigade at the head of Eighth Army had reached Rommel's defensive position at Buerat.

By this time Montgomery, and everyone else for that matter, had accepted that there was not the remotest possibility of Allied forces pushing through Tunisia to attack Tripoli from the west. This therefore was up to Eighth Army, but it was at the end of an exceptionally long and increasingly uncertain supply line and Tripoli was still 230 miles away. Moreover the offensive could be made only by XXX Corps' three divisions: 2nd New Zealand; 51st Highland which included 23rd

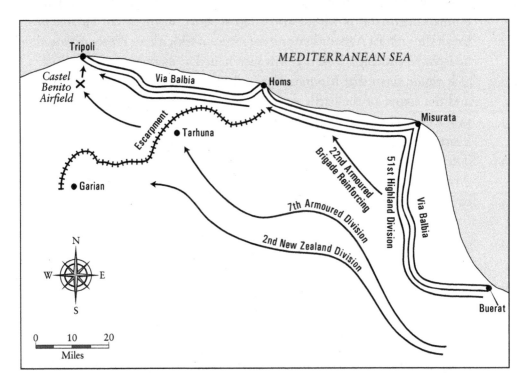

Map 6: The capture of Tripoli.

Armoured Brigade; and 7th Armoured, still with 8th Armoured and 131st Infantry brigades and now joined by armoured cars from 4th Light Armoured Brigade; plus 22nd Armoured Brigade in 'Army Reserve'.

It was not a large force with which to master the many difficulties facing it. Buerat admittedly was not such a good position as El Agheila. It was less strong naturally, had fewer artificial defences apart from another mass of minefields, and was much more easily outflanked. After Buerat had been passed, however, Eighth Army's problems became really serious.

There were two possible lines of advance after Buerat. Eighth Army could follow the coast road – the Via Balbia, as it was called in Libya – as far as the little town of Misurata, where it turned due west to run directly to Tripoli. Or Eighth Army could strike due west immediately from Buerat over open country, then turn north-westwards and finally due north to attack Tripoli from the south. Neither was particularly attractive. The latter presented every possible natural obstacle: miles of soft sand, steep wadis, high cliffs and appallingly broken ground covered with great boulders. The former met not only natural obstacles – before Misurata it was hemmed in by salt marshes – but man-made ones as well such as mines, booby-traps, 10 destroyed bridges, 6 anti-tank ditches and 177 craters blown in the road.

Whichever route was followed, before it could reach Tripoli it would be blocked by a formidable natural obstacle that aroused the apprehension of Montgomery and de Guingand and, interestingly, was well-known to Mussolini. This was a massive escarpment that, beginning at Homs on the coast, curved in a great arc through Tarhuna and Garian to protect Tripoli from the east, south-east and south. Montgomery's biographer, Nigel Hamilton, considers it 'the best natural defensive line between Alamein and Tunisia.'

For the defence of Tripoli, *Panzerarmee Afrika* had lost the services of 21st Panzer Division which had been sent to Tunisia, but since it had previously transferred its tanks and artillery to 15th Panzer, this was not as significant as it appears at first glance. In addition to 15th Panzer, Rommel had at Buerat 90th Light, 164th Light, the Ramcke Parachute Brigade and other German and Italian units including the *Centauro* (Armoured) Division. The revived *Trieste* (Motorized) and three Italian infantry divisions held the Homs-Tarhuna escarpment. The Axis troops are reported as resolute and showing no signs of being disheartened.

Montgomery now demonstrated conclusively that the portrait of him as a cautious unimaginative general is arrant nonsense. His plan – code-named Operation FIRE-EATER – called for Eighth Army to gain Buerat, capture the Homs-Tarhuna escarpment 'on the run' and reach Tripoli all in one swift movement. To do this, he would launch two widely separated thrusts: one along the coast road and the other due west over the desert. This should have the benefit of splitting the enemy forces, with the added advantage that if either thrust was held up, its opponents would be threatened with being outflanked by the other one.

Montgomery entrusted the advance over open country to Leese, to whom was given both 2nd New Zealand and 7th Armoured divisions. That down the Via Balbia would be the responsibility of 51st Highland Division and since Montgomery considered it would be difficult for a single corps commander to control both moves, he took personal charge of this one. His decision was perhaps not entirely to the satisfaction of Major General Douglas Wimberley, the Highlanders' CO, who found himself being constantly harried by Montgomery, sometimes with scant regard for the difficulties he faced. There was, however, a very good reason for the army commander's urgency.

On 4 January 1943, as Montgomery relates in his *Memoirs*, strong gales caused havoc at Benghazi, Eighth Army's nearest supply port: 'Ships broke loose and charged about the harbour; heavy seas broke up the breakwater and smashed into the inner harbour; much damage was done to tugs, lighters and landing places.' A vessel carrying 2,000 tons of ammunition and three other large freighters were sunk, and supplies received at Benghazi fell from 3,000 tons a day to just 400 tons.

Montgomery refused to be daunted. Horrocks and his X Corps became a transport service, delivering supplies to the front from the more distant port of Tobruk. Their best efforts, though, could not provide the forces advancing on Tripoli with more than ten days' supplies if FIRE-EATER should proceed as planned on 15 January. Yet Montgomery insisted that this date be met. This again was scarcely the action of a cautious commander and indeed was one of considerable moral courage, for if Rommel could hold Tripoli for say fourteen days, Eighth Army would have been forced into a humiliating retreat for lack of the necessary provisions.

Rommel was still in no mood for holding on. Kesselring, who was frankly disgusted, declares that the Axis soldiers were given no leadership because their leader was only interested in retreating. 'Fighting,' Kesselring snarls, 'went by the board.' How different was the attitude of Montgomery, who in a message to his army on 12 January declared that nothing could stop them, and concluded: 'ON TO TRIPOLI!'

Operation FIRE-EATER began at 0715 on 15 January, when Leese's two divisions struck westward into Axis-held territory south of the Buerat defences. That evening, 51st Highland Division attacked those defences directly. Both moves were hindered, the former by 15th Panzer and the latter by Axis minefields. Rommel, however, intended to do no more than impose delay and by dawn on the 16th, the entire Buerat position was in Eighth Army's hands.

Thereafter, Leese and Montgomery pressed forward rapidly, both being aided, as usual, by the fighters and fighter-bombers of the Desert Air Force. Leese had to contend chiefly with the terrible terrain, but Montgomery, opposed by 15th Panzer, 90th Light, 164th Light and the Ramcke Brigade, had a more difficult task. Nonetheless, 51st Highland captured Misurata on 18 January and Montgomery then called on 22nd Armoured Brigade to further support his push down the coast road. On the 19th this reached Homs, but here it was brought to a halt by increasing Axis resistance.

It was now, though, that Montgomery's decision to advance on two separate lines proved its worth. By 19 January, away to the south, 7th Armoured Division had reached the narrow pass between high ridges that led to Tarhuna, while 2nd New Zealand Division, backed by 4th Light Armoured Brigade, was moving south of Tarhuna towards Garian. Fearing that he might be outflanked from the south and trapped, Rommel sent almost all his German troops to the Tarhuna front, leaving only 90th Light to defend Homs.

At this point, 7th Armoured's progress was halted by an unhappy incident. Harding was standing on top of a Grant tank directing operations when a shell burst in front of this, killing one of its crew and knocking Harding to the ground severely wounded in the chest, legs and particularly his left arm and hand, from which he lost three fingers. Fortunately, his senior staff officer Lieutenant Colonel Michael Carver – the future field marshal – was able to arrange his removal to hospital in a light aeroplane, but it was 20 January before Roberts could arrive to take command and the 21st before the pressure against Tarhuna could be resumed.

Again, however, Montgomery's dual thrusts proved invaluable. The Highlanders, encouraged by Rommel's transfer southward of most of its defenders, renewed their assault on Homs which fell on the afternoon of 20 January. The news once more made Rommel fearful of being outflanked and trapped, this time from the north. On the 21st, he fell back from the Tarhuna Pass. The 7th Armoured Division followed up, heading for the main Axis air-base of Castel Benito south of Tripoli. It was checked on the 22nd by a double anti-tank ditch, but that night the 1/6th Queen's Royal Regiment from 131st Brigade under Lieutenant Colonel Roy Kaulback attacked this and took it by storm.

Rommel could resist no longer. Despite Italian protests, his army began a hasty retreat to Tunisia. At 0530 on 23 January 1943, three months from the start of the offensive at El Alamein, the 11th Hussars from 7th Armoured Division entered the capital of Libya from the south. They were just ahead of the 50th Battalion of the Royal Tank Regiment from 23rd Armoured Brigade coming down the coast road with men of the 1st Gordon Highlanders riding on their Valentines. Montgomery and Leese met and shook hands, while their desert veterans crowded into the main square to gaze with delight at the plumes of white water from the fountains of Tripoli.

Notes

1. The Ultra signals can be found in *British Intelligence in the Second World War* by Professor F.H. Hinsley. Montgomery was not the only commander badly served by Ultra. In February 1943, for instance, II US Corps in Tunisia was warned by Ultra of a planned attack through the Fondouk Pass. When it in fact came through the Faid Pass, not only did it achieve complete surprise, but reinforcements were held back in the belief that it must be only a preliminary diversion.

2. Both Mainwaring, disguised as an Italian peasant, and Carver escaped from prisoner of war camps in Italy and made their way back to Eighth Army.

3. Lumsden, a dashing cavalryman, was of a type very appealing to Churchill and he was knighted on his return to England. Churchill later sent him to the Far East as a liaison officer to General MacArthur. He was killed by a Kamikaze suicide attacker while watching the American landings at Lingayan Gulf in the Philippines on 6 January 1945.

Chapter Four

The Battle of the Mareth Line

The fountains of Tripoli. For almost two and a half years they had been for the British and Commonwealth soldiers a beautiful mirage, tempting and taunting them, sometimes appearing tantalizingly close, sometimes impossibly distant. Now that the goal had been reached, it was only fitting that the victors should enjoy a moment of relaxation and celebration that culminated on 4 February 1943, when Churchill, Brooke and Alexander, the first two openly shedding tears of relief and joy, visited them to watch a triumphant parade and march-past. It is only a pity that the moment should have been of such brief duration.

For Montgomery was determined to keep Rommel 'on the run' and on this same 4 February, 7th Armoured Division was following the coastal road across the border of Tunisia. More bad weather and supply problems caused by the enemy having effectively blocked Tripoli's harbour and destroyed its port facilities dictated a pause, but when large quantities of stores at last began to arrive on 14 February, Montgomery took full advantage of the situation.

On 16 February, 7th Armoured, reinforced by 22nd Armoured Brigade, captured the coastal stronghold of Ben Gardane. Next day, 51st Highland Division also joined 7th Armoured and they combined to capture Medenine together with the four landing-grounds in its vicinity. The day after, Foum Tatahouine also fell. It should be recorded that Rommel considered that all this happened 'rather earlier than we had bargained for'.

Rommel, incidentally, had recovered much of his old aggressive spirit, having found the situation in Tunisia most encouraging. The Allied force there, First (British) Army under Lieutenant General Sir Kenneth Anderson, part of which was the II US Corps, was bogged down on a front running southward from the Mediterranean along a line of hills called the Eastern Dorsale that could not be outflanked because it rested

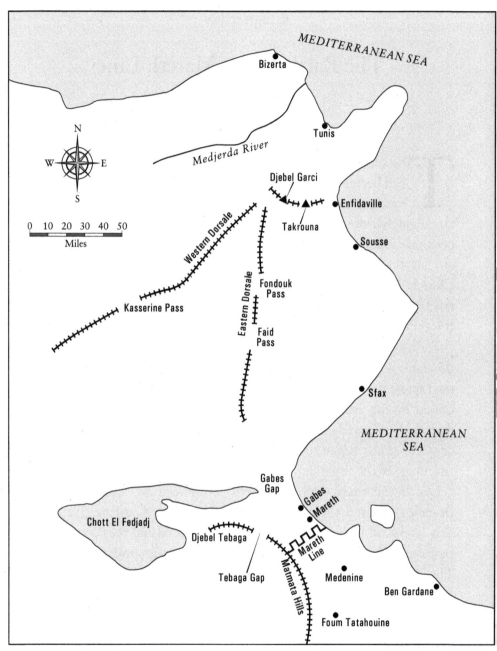

Map 7: The Tunisia battleground.

on a vast trackless salt marsh, the Chott el Fedjadj, beyond which was an almost equally impassable sea of sand, the Grand Erg.

Equally encouraging for Rommel was the inexperience of the Allied troops. Even the commander-in-chief, Eisenhower, though promoted on

11 February to a full 'four star' general, was a staff officer who had never seen action previously. It had therefore been decided that on 20 February, Alexander would become deputy C-in-C and commander of a new Eighteenth Army Group controlling both First and Eighth Armies.

When Alexander arrived in Algiers on 15 February, he was appalled by the absence of any firm direction or centralized control. He therefore took up his command two days early on the 18th and, having little confidence in Anderson, in effect also took over the tactical leadership of First Army, much as Montgomery had done in Egypt, although whereas Montgomery has been roundly condemned, Alexander has escaped all criticism. Alexander, though, had little time to rectify the situation. On the 19th, Rommel struck at the south of the Allied line, making for another line of hills known as the Western Dorsale. By the 21st, he had broken through the Kasserine Pass and taken about 4,000 prisoners.

Early on the 22nd, Montgomery received an urgent signal asking that Eighth Army assist by putting immediate pressure on Rommel. His reaction was prompt and generous. Declaring: 'Alex is in trouble; we must do everything we can to help him', he ordered Eighth Army's advanced formations to push forward, assisted by the Desert Air Force's fighter-bombers. He also sent a cheerful signal to Alexander – which did not reflect his true feelings – saying that they might get Rommel 'running about between us like a wet hen'.

These actions had the desired effect, strengthening Rommel's concerns about Eighth Army's recent captures, especially that of Medenine. He abandoned his offensive at Kasserine and though he later offered many excuses for this, his real reason emerged in a signal to Hitler – intercepted by Ultra – on the evening of 22 February: it was 'necessary to collect my mobile forces for a swift blow against Eighth Army before it had completed its preparations.'

Rommel gave the same reason to Kesselring, who approved his withdrawal and promoted him to command a newly-created Army Group *Afrika*. This gave Rommel control over both von Arnim's Fifth Panzer Army and his own *Panzerarmee Afrika*, now renamed First Italian Army and entrusted to General Giovanni Messe, who had commanded an Italian corps in Russia with sufficient ability to earn him the award of a Knight's Cross from Hitler. Rommel used his authority to halt an offensive by von Arnim in northern Tunisia and set about preparing for his own 'blow against Eighth Army'.

To deliver this, Rommel collected 10th, 15th and 21st Panzer divisions with a total of 141 tanks, 90th Light, 164th Light and two Italian infantry divisions. These would be supported by all available artillery including new weapons, superior to any Allied equivalents, that the Germans had just introduced. These were the six-barrelled *Nebelwerfers*, literally 'smoke projectors' but really mortars that could discharge their six 150mm missiles in only ten seconds. Soon to be joined by a five-barrelled 210mm version, the 'Moaning Minnies' as the British called them would be used extensively hereafter and with deadly effect.

Had this force been able to strike immediately, Eighth Army's forward units would have been in great danger, as Montgomery was well aware. His actions had once more not been over-cautious since his X Corps was

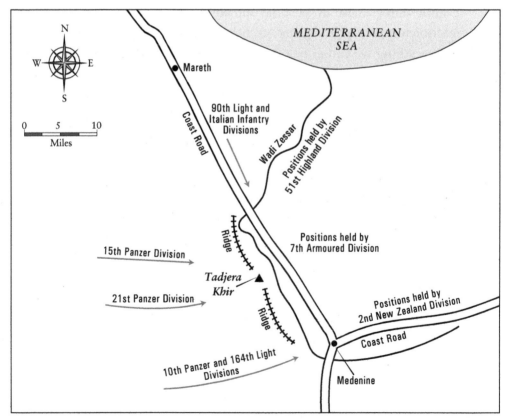

Map 8: The Battle of Medenine.

still at Benghazi and 2nd New Zealand Division was still at Tripoli. He later admitted to de Guingand that he 'had sweated a bit at times'.

Though the Ultra intercept reporting Rommel's intentions did not reach Montgomery until 25 February – a not uncommon delay – and revealed neither the date nor the direction of the coming assault, it did confirm Montgomery's anxieties and he increased his aerial reconnaissance missions. On 4 February, he had personally persuaded Churchill to supply the Desert Air Force with a pair of Mosquitos that were ideal for this task and their work indicated that Rommel's attack would be made on a date between 3 and 7 March.

This gave Montgomery just enough time to provide his forward units with substantial reinforcements. Eighth Army's administrative staff managed magnificently and by the evening of 4 March, 2nd New Zealand Division, 201st Guards Brigade and 23rd Armoured Brigade had all reached the front and were assisting to prepare what Kippenberger calls 'our masterpiece in the art of laying out a defensive position under desert conditions.'

Beginning on the Mediterranean coast some 20 miles due north of Medenine, the position moved south-westward following the line of the Wadi Zessar, then crossed the coastal road to a convenient ridge. This northern section of the line was very strong, being protected by extensive minefields since Montgomery believed that it would be here that Rommel would deliver his main assault. This was a correct interpretation of Rommel's intentions, but in practice he was overruled by his panzer commanders who felt they would have insufficient room for manoeuvre and he had withdrawn into a sulky indifference, being content to demand 'the utmost commitment' from his men.[1]

Fortunately, Montgomery's error had no ill effects because with his usual thoroughness – his critics may call it caution if they wish – he had guarded Medenine and its landing-grounds against attacks from the west and south-west as well. His defences extended southward for 16 miles down the ridge, the most important feature of which was a small but steep hill called Tadjera Khir. The northern defences and the angle between these and the western ones were held by 51st Highland Division supported by 8th and 23rd Armoured brigades. The Tadjera Khir area was held by 131st and 201st Guards brigades backed by 22nd Armoured

Brigade. The New Zealanders and 4th Light Armoured Brigade protected the direct approaches to Medenine.

Although the defenders included more than 300 tanks and some 350 artillery pieces held under XXX Corps' control to ensure concentrated fire, their main weapons were their 460 or so anti-tank guns. This was nothing new in itself, but Montgomery had again introduced a new tactic and a new weapon. The anti-tank guns were not there to support their own armour or protect their infantry; instead they were carefully sited where they would be best able to destroy Rommel's panzers. In addition, their usual 6-pounders and 2-pounders had been joined by some brand-new 17-pounders: formidable weapons bearing the innocuous name of 'Pheasants'.

At 0900 on 6 March, the Axis forces appeared out of the morning mists and the Battle of Medenine had begun. A thrust down the coastal road was made by 90th Light and the Italian infantry; 15th and 21st Panzer assaulted the Tadjera Khir ridge; 10th Panzer and 164th Light made a wide sweep to strike directly at Medenine itself.

It all looked very threatening, but the Axis opportunity had already passed. Every attack met with resolute resistance. The two flanking moves were thrown back with heavy losses. In the centre, XXX Corps' concentrated artillery fire forced the panzer divisions' infantry regiments to seek shelter, but their tanks closed right up to Eighth Army's defences, 15th Panzer engaging 131st Brigade and 21st Panzer the Guards Brigade.

What the minefields had achieved at Alam Halfa, however, the anti-tank guns achieved still more effectively at Medenine. This time the panzer divisions could not even penetrate the front-line defences and both lost tank after tank. The assaults of 15th Panzer were so continuous that 22nd Armoured Brigade sent a squadron of Shermans to provide close support, but this was the only time the British armour took part in the fighting. The Shermans put seven panzers out of action and did not suffer a single loss.

By midday, the panzers had had enough and retired to reorganize. At 1530, attacks from all sides were renewed but with a noticeable reduction in determination; all had been repulsed by 2030. That night the Germans attempted to recover some of their knocked-out tanks. They were driven off by artillery fire, but their actions convinced the defenders that morning would bring further enemy assaults. In fact, none materialized.

Eighth Army had suffered only 130 men killed or wounded against an Axis loss of 635 dead, injured or taken prisoner, more than two-thirds of them Germans. The victors counted fifty-two German tanks wrecked and abandoned on the battlefield.

This latest defeat reduced Rommel to a sick, disillusioned man, his condition plainly revealed by unsightly boils that disfigured his face. On 9 March he handed over his Army Group to von Arnim and left Africa forever.

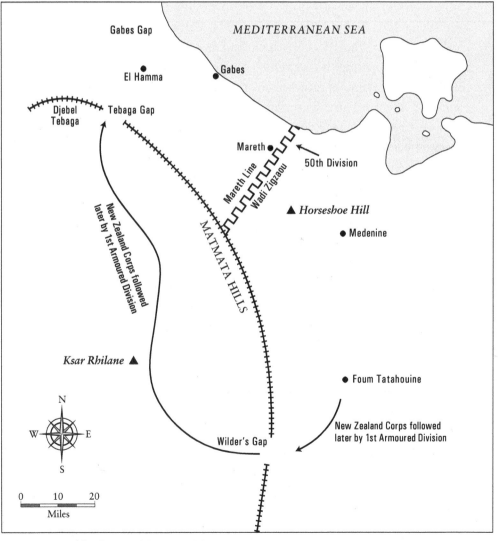

Map 9: The Battle of the Mareth Line.

Alexander, by contrast, delighted by a triumph achieved with 'about half the equipment which the Americans possessed in Tunisia' as General Jackson rather unkindly reminds us,[2] wished Eighth Army to advance as soon as possible to the central Tunisian plain and form a continuous front with the rest of his Army Group. This, though, would not be easy, for between Eighth Army and the plain lay a whole series of impressive obstacles, both natural and man-made.

The huge salt-marsh known as the Chott el Fedjadj has already been mentioned. A long tongue of this reached out to within 15 miles of the Mediterranean just north of the little town of Gabes to produce a 'bottleneck' called the Gabes Gap. The eastern section of this was blocked by the Wadi Akarit which had been deepened, widened and mined. The remainder was covered by a line of ridges, as much as 1 or 2 miles in width, rising in places to steep hills of 500 or even 1,000ft. They contained plentiful artillery and machine-gun posts, passes through them were closed by wide anti-tank ditches and approaches to them were guarded by some 4,000 mines.

Furthermore before Eighth Army could reach the gap it would have to pass through another bottleneck, this one 22 miles wide between the sea and the rugged Matmata Hills that ran parallel to it. The barrier across this was the Mareth Line: a series of fixed fortifications designed by the French to guard against an Italian advance from Libya but now ironically manned by, among others, Italians. They consisted of mutually supporting artillery posts connected by trenches, behind which were strongholds as much as 1,200 yards long by 400 yards deep that could accommodate a full battalion. In front of and around the defences were the usual mines – 100,000 anti-tank and 70,000 anti-personnel – not to mention booby-traps.

Like the ancient castles, the Mareth Line had a 'moat', in its case a double one: the inner man-made, an anti-tank ditch; its outer natural, the Wadi Zigzaou. This was 20 to 30ft deep, from 60 to 200ft wide, its sides artificially steepened and its bed covered with up to 8ft of water. In de Guingand's words, it alone presented a 'horrible obstacle'.

It was admittedly possible to move west of the Matmata Hills. As far back as December 1942, Montgomery, as usual looking 'one battle ahead' – in this case more than one – had asked the Long Range Desert Group to check this area. South-west of Foum Tatahouine, a New Zealand officer, Lieutenant Nicholas Wilder, had discovered a pass – henceforth called Wilder's Gap in his honour – that would enable troops to head northward along the western edge of the hills. Unfortunately progress would be blocked eventually by salt marshes and the Grand Erg sand-sea, so they would have to turn eastward towards the coastal area through the Tebaga Gap – 'Plum Pass' as it was called in Eighth Army – guarded by an anti-tank ditch, strongpoints and minefields and at only 4 miles wide the narrowest bottleneck of all.

Montgomery, however, was sure he could overcome all obstacles. His plan for doing so was not a cautious one and, incidentally, answers post-war criticisms of his conduct of the Battle of Medenine. These are that he should have followed up his retiring enemies immediately. In fact he did not know they were retiring: they did so after dark and, as described earlier, events during the night served to conceal their intentions. Nor would a pursuit have been very safe when the Axis troops could retire into the fortifications and minefields of the Mareth Line. Yet in any case Montgomery wanted all Eighth Army and not just XXX Corps available to participate in his next move.

In essence, Operation PUGILIST, as this was called, would be a repeat of Operation FIRE-EATER. In that action, Montgomery had taken the Buerat position, seized the Homs-Tarhuna escarpment 'on the run' before its defenders could organize resistance and captured Tripoli, all in one continuous series of encounters. In PUGILIST he intended to take the Mareth Line, seize the Gabes Gap 'on the run' before its defenders could organize resistance and capture the Tunisian ports of Sfax and Sousse and perhaps even the capital itself all in one continuous series of encounters.

This could only be difficult and Montgomery was given fair warning of just how difficult by two very different preliminary clashes. First, Eighth Army's 'Force L' got into trouble. The initial stood for General Philippe Leclerc, who on 1 February had joined Montgomery at Tripoli at the head of more than 3,200 French and colonial volunteers after a march of about 1,000 miles from French Equatorial Africa. Montgomery sent the Fighting Frenchmen to secure Wilder's Gap. Then on receiving Alexander's plea to put pressure on the enemy, Leclerc had been ordered to advance further and reached Ksar Rhilane, a craggy massif about a third of the way towards Tebaga. Here on 10 March, he was attacked by a powerful German reconnaissance unit reinforced by tanks.

Eighth Army was too distant to help 'Force L', but the Desert Air Force was not. The anti-tank Hurricanes of South African Squadron Leader Weston-Burt's No. 6 Squadron proved particularly effective and the Germans retired, having lost six tanks, five half-tracks, thirteen armoured cars, ten lorries, a mobile gun and a wireless van. The squadron had set a most important precedent and thoroughly deserved the congratulations it received from Montgomery, Tedder and, presumably with special fervour, Leclerc. At the same time, this incident did surely indicate that the Axis powers were very ready to offer resistance.

A still stronger warning was given when 201st Guards Brigade attacked a German outpost at Sidi el Guelaa – 'Horseshoe Hill' to the British for obvious reasons – on the night of 16/17 March. The defenders, a detachment from 90th Light, expected this, having captured a British artillery officer who carried a map giving full details of the supporting fire plan. The Guards lost 38 officers and 484 men killed, wounded or taken prisoner. Leese, himself a Coldstream Guardsman, was distraught.

Montgomery realized he had underestimated the strength of the defenders and of the position's considerable minefields. To his credit, he wrote to Brigadier Gascoyne, apologizing for his error and accepting full responsibility. He was, though, much more blameworthy for not heeding the warning the action had given. He remained dangerously overconfident and his plans for PUGILIST are open to a good deal of criticism; although not, please, by those who label his usual very thorough planning as over-cautious.

On the evening of 19 March, a sizeable force left the coast, passed through Wilder's Gap and headed for Tebaga. It was based on 2nd New Zealand Division, its 5th and 6th Infantry brigades being joined by 8th Armoured Brigade with about 100 Shermans and 50 Crusaders. Freyberg also commanded an armoured car formation, Field, Medium, Anti-Tank and AA regiments and at Ksar Rhilane added Leclerc's Force L to his strength. Officially his command was the 'New Zealand Corps', though he appointed no subordinate divisional commander and remained in direct control.

With his usual foolish insistence that everything had gone exactly according to plan, Montgomery would later emphasize this flanking manoeuvre and 'play down' his coastal advance. Yet the testimony of New Zealand officers like Kippenberger and his own expressed hope that

Freyberg might distract attention from the coastal attack make it clear that this was the main one. Freyberg, incidentally, certainly did provide distraction, for by 22 March the Tebaga Gap was guarded by 21st Panzer, 164th Light and seven battalions of Italian infantrymen.

At 2230 on 20 March, a typical Eighth Army artillery barrage heralded the start of PUGILIST's coastal thrust. At 2345 50th Division, its 151st Brigade in the van and elements of its 69th Brigade in support, burst over the Wadi Zigzaou. By the morning of 21 March, battling with a determination symbolized by the award of a Victoria Cross to Lieutenant Colonel Derek Seagrim, CO of 7th Green Howards, the attackers had secured a bridgehead 1 mile wide and 800 yards deep.

It had been intended that the advance should be backed by fifty-one Valentines of 50th Royal Tanks, but the first one to enter the wadi got stuck and the Royal Engineers, working under heavy fire, had to construct another crossing for them. Over this four tanks passed carrying 'fascines', large bundles of wood bound firmly together, which they dropped into the anti-tank ditch beyond the wadi and so got across this also. The fifth tank to arrive, however, broke through the wadi's floor, sank up to its turret and completely blocked the crossing. Despite the heroic efforts of the sappers, a new one could not be prepared during 21 March.

Infantry reinforcements did get over the wadi and that evening, aided by attacks from the Desert Air Force's light bombers, 50th Division resumed its advance, capturing five major strongholds and large numbers of prisoners. In the early hours of the 22nd, forty-two Valentines at last were able to use the new crossing, although they damaged it so badly that no other vehicle could do so, but then Operation PUGILIST began to go wrong.

For this there was one major cause. Montgomery and, under Montgomery's influence, Leese were directing their attention not towards winning the Battle of the Mareth Line but towards the dramatic operations that would follow after it had been won. This had disastrous results. Even without the New Zealand Corps, Montgomery had more than enough strength to smash through the defences as X Corps had come up to the front line. Yet just one division and one tank formation carried out the coastal assault, while XXX Corps' 51st Highland and 4th Indian Divisions and X Corps, now with both 1st and 7th Armoured divisions under its command, were, Horrocks tells us, held back 'ready to exploit success towards Gabes'.

This lack of attention also meant that no guidance was given to 50th Division's CO, Major General Nichols. Worse still, Nichols, who was not nicknamed 'Crasher' for nothing, personally crossed the wadi to hearten and encourage his men, leaving his headquarters without direction. Command thus in practice fell on 151st Brigade's CO Brigadier Beak VC who had never before led it into action.

In short, Montgomery had made exactly the same mistake that Auchinleck had done in July 1942; an error he had always avoided hitherto. It can only be explained by Montgomery again having been misled by Ultra. This had reported that both Rommel and von Arnim favoured withdrawing to the Gabes Gap or even further north, thereby suggesting that only a token resistance would be offered at the Mareth Line. It was just unfortunate that Ultra had not reported that Hitler, Kesselring and Messe all insisted that the Mareth Line be held at any cost.

It seems that Montgomery realized his mistake – though he would never admit it – because he belatedly turned his attention to the battle in hand. He was certain the enemy would launch an armoured counter-attack and had learned that his own inexperienced commanders had concentrated on bringing up tanks, not the anti-tank guns that had proved so effective at Alam Halfa, Alamein and Medenine. In the afternoon of 21 March he made repeated enquiries whether these were being brought across the wadi and on the 22nd, he gave specific orders that this must be done 'at once', but he was too late.

For at 1340, 15th Panzer, 90th Light and the Germans' own anti-tank guns launched the expected counter-attack. There were no British 6-pounders to oppose them and no aircraft either; more heavy rain had grounded the Desert Air Force's light bombers. The Germans regained three of their captured strongholds, 151st Brigade was badly mauled and 50th Royal Tanks lost thirty Valentines. At 0200 on the 23rd, Montgomery was aroused from sleep to learn that the Eighth Army bridgehead had been all but eliminated.

On hearing this news, Montgomery temporarily lost the cool self-confidence that was one of his greatest assets; the first of only two occasions according to his staff officers that this happened in the whole of the war.[3] Paradoxically, this was a supreme tribute to his generalship.

He must surely have recalled how at Alamein he had been similarly awakened with pleas to call off his attack but had curtly refused. It would not have been surprising if he had now felt that resolution was all that was needed to save the situation and persisted in his coastal thrust. Instinct and experience, however, warned him that this time the situation was different and demanded a radically new approach.

Montgomery summoned de Guingand to confer with him and by 0900 when Horrocks and Leese had joined them, he had regained his self-control. He ordered that the coastal thrust be abandoned and its troops fall back over the Wadi Zigzaou, which they did that night. Instead he hoped, as he had already suggested to Alexander, that II US Corps under Major General George Patton might strike at Messe from behind. Patton made several attempts, but although his 38,000 troops were opposed by only 8,000 Axis soldiers of whom only 1,000 were German, he had no success apart from ensuring that 10th Panzer Division's forty tanks were unable to join the forces opposing Eighth Army.

Patton's move also revived von Arnim's belief that Messe should fall back from the Mareth Line, but any chance of this happening was quelled when the unquenchable Kesselring visited Messe on the afternoon of 24 March and forbade any withdrawal. His firmness convinced Messe and even von Arnim, and Patton's final efforts were broken on the 25th, though this did not prevent him from boasting later that he had won the Mareth Line battle for Eighth Army.

What really won the battle was a new move by Montgomery, officially for morale reasons entitled Operation SUPERCHARGE after the decisive attack at El Alamein, but known throughout Eighth Army as 'The Left Hook'. This was a planned assault through the Tebaga Gap, and it had to be done quickly before Messe, who on 25 March had added 15th Panzer Division to Tebaga's defenders, strengthened them still further. Moreover, it could not possibly be achieved by the New Zealand Corps alone.

Montgomery therefore sent X Corps' troops, chiefly 1st Armoured Division under Major General Raymond Briggs, through Wilder's Gap to Freyberg's assistance. To speed up their arrival, the armour was loaded onto tank-transporters manned by former long-distance lorry drivers, who somehow coped with the difficult country. By the afternoon of 26 March, the artillery of two field regiments and one medium regiment had joined the New Zealand Corps and its 8th Armoured Brigade had been strengthened by Brigadier Fisher's 2nd Armoured Brigade containing 67 Shermans, 13 Grants and 60 Crusaders, 22 of them carrying 6-pounder guns.

Montgomery, now back in tight control of the battle, had ordered an afternoon attack when the sun would be behind the attackers and in the eyes of the defenders; it was the first time Eighth Army had attacked from west to east and could enjoy this advantage. He had also firmly rejected Freyberg's suggestions that attempts be made to outflank the Tebaga Gap or that this be taken by a series of 'set-piece' operations and demanded one single all-out assault. Since he knew that Freyberg had not forgotten past occasions when his New Zealanders had been left unsupported, on 24 March Montgomery sent Horrocks and his staff to Tebaga, confident that the enthusiastic and thrusting X Corps' commander would override any doubts or hesitancy.

It was hardly likely that Freyberg would welcome the arrival of Horrocks, but for once Montgomery was tactful. He explained that the number of troops employed needed an experienced Corps HQ to handle them and de Guingand sent all messages to both Horrocks and Freyberg as equal joint commanders.[4] Tuker was also critical of this appointment; he would declare that neither Horrocks nor Leese had the character or initiative to act outside Montgomery's direct control. However, Leese had already proved him wrong during the final advance on Tripoli and, happily, Horrocks now proved him wrong again. 'If we punch the hole,' queried Freyberg, 'will the tanks really go through?' 'Yes they will,' retorted Horrocks, 'and I am going with them.'

Freyberg was also worried because despite the additional artillery given to him, he rightly considered that more was necessary. Fortunately an alternative could be found. On 1 February 1943, Harry Broadhurst, the youngest air vice marshal in the RAF, had taken command of the Desert Air Force. Its senior air staff officer since the previous November, he had enjoyed a happy relationship with Richardson, Eighth Army's Director of Operations after the loss of Mainwaring, and Lieutenant Colonel Jock McNeill, the officer directly responsible for army/air force liaison. Recalling the Desert Air Force's role at Ksar Rhilane, Richardson and McNeill urged de Guingand to request Broadhurst for similar direct support at Tebaga, and this at very low level where the aircrafts' cannons could do more damage than bombs dropped from a higher altitude.

This was quite a favour to ask. Only the anti-tank Hurricanes had previously practised this technique and the AA guns with which the sides of the Tebaga Gap were liberally supplied threatened severe losses. Some of Broadhurst's superiors were so concerned that they warned him that in the event of failure, his entire future career would be at risk. To his credit, though, he took no notice. 'I will do it,' he promised de Guingand, 'you will have the whole boiling match – bombs and cannon. It will be a real low-flying blitz.'

To carry this out, Broadhurst committed two squadrons each of Boston, Baltimore and Mitchell light bombers, five of Spitfires, sixteen of fighter-bomber Kittyhawks or Warhawks, one of fighter-bomber Hurricanes – sent south by the ever-helpful Alexander – and of course No. 6 Squadron's Hurricane 'tank-busters'. Arrangements were quickly made for giving all the locations of friend and foe by smoke or shell-bursts and Wing Commander Darwen, the brilliant organizer of Operation CHOCOLATE, went up to the front in an armoured car to control the aerial assaults; a practice later employed with outstanding success in North-Western Europe, Italy and Burma.

At 1530 on 26 March, the new Operation SUPERCHARGE began with the Desert Air Force 'screaming in at zero feet' as Horrocks recalls. In just over two hours, 412 sorties were flown. Despite previous fears, only one Baltimore and thirteen single-engine aircraft were lost, six of their pilots getting back safely to their units. The 'brilliant and brave work' of the airmen, reports Montgomery in his *Memoirs*, 'completely stunned the enemy'.

At 1600, Eighth Army's artillery joined in and at 1623 the soldiers moved forward, the barrage advancing ahead of them. First, 2nd New Zealand Division with 8th Armoured Brigade in the van advanced 4,500 yards, capturing the high ground on either flank in the process. Then at 1800, as Horrocks had promised, 1st Armoured Division headed by 2nd Armoured Brigade raced through the hole that had been 'punched'. Eighth Army suffered about 600 casualties but 2,500 prisoners, all Germans, were taken, 15th and 21st Panzer divisions were terribly mauled and 164th Light lost almost all its vehicles and heavy weapons.

By 0210 on 27 March, the remaining defenders of the Tebaga Gap were in full retreat north-eastward to the little town of El Hamma.

A few strongholds that had been cut off continued to resist, the last of them only falling that evening after a final assault led by a Maori officer, 2nd Lieutenant Ngarimu, who won a Victoria Cross – posthumously, as he was shot dead at the moment of victory – but the Battle of the Mareth Line had been won. On the line itself, the Axis troops fell back in desperate haste to avoid being trapped; only a rearguard, the valiant 90th Light, retired in good order. About 7,000 Axis soldiers were killed or wounded, with the same number taken prisoner. On 29 March, 1st Armoured Division captured El Hamma and soldiers from both X and XXX Corps moved into Gabes.

Ahead lay the Gabes Gap that Montgomery had hoped to take 'on the run'. Sadly, this hope had disappeared with the repulse of his coastal thrust at the Mareth Line and he therefore paused while he completed his preparations to attack it. This has, of course, been declared overcautious but not by anyone in Eighth Army, not even the eager, aggressive Horrocks.

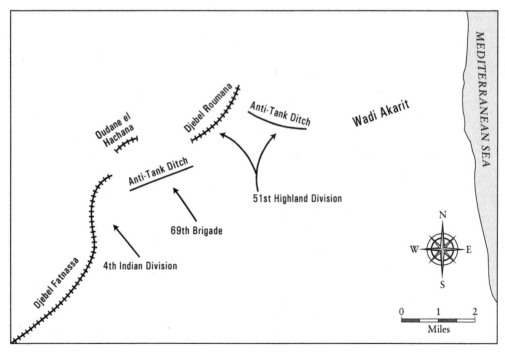

Map 10: The Battle of Wadi Akarit.

The Battle of Wadi Akarit, as it would rather oddly be called, began with two typical facets of Montgomery's generalship. One was a new tactic. 'As time was important,' de Guingand explains, 'the Army Commander decided to attack on a dark night – with no moon. We had not attempted this before and so he hoped to obtain a measure of surprise.' The night in question was that of 5/6 March and it did indeed find the enemy largely unprepared. Moreover, von Arnim, not anticipating so early an encounter, had withdrawn 10th and 21st Panzer divisions for rest and replenishment and though he at once ordered them back, they were too late to participate in the fighting.

Montgomery also displayed his trait of choosing divisions for tasks that best suited them. He had not regarded 4th Indian Division as very skilled in desert combat, but since it had been specially trained for mountain warfare, he did consider it ideal to assault the ridges blocking the Gabes Gap. In a conference on 2 April, he declared its objective should be the Djebel Roumana, 500ft high, too steep to be crossed by vehicles and protected on each side by anti-tank ditches. At the same time, 51st Highland Division would strike over the eastern anti-tank ditch between the Djebel Roumana and the Wadi Akarit. The initial breakthrough would be followed up by X Corps' New Zealanders – now back to the status of a division – and 1st Armoured Division, with 7th Armoured in reserve.

Meanwhile 1st Battalion, Royal Sussex Regiment, one of 4th Indian's British battalions, had been carrying out night patrols in the ridges west of the Djebel Roumana. They discovered that the defenders of the 1,000ft-high Djebel Fatnassa, overestimating the difficulties of its forward slopes, had sited their heavy weapons to fire only east and west. Moreover, while the Djebel Roumana/Wadi Akarit area was guarded by 15th Panzer, 90th Light and three Italian infantry divisions, the whole western ridge was held only by the *Pistoia* Division plus what was left of the shattered 164th Light. Major General Tuker was thus convinced that 4th Indian could take the Fatnassa position in a surprise night attack.

Curiously enough, Tuker did not express his belief at the 2 April conference, but later he raised the matter privately with his corps commander Leese, who in turn persuaded Montgomery to adopt the suggestion. This demonstrated Montgomery's flexibility, but it did cause difficulties for other Eighth Army formations. The Highlanders now had to take the Djebel Roumana as well as the anti-tank ditch to its east. Montgomery had to order 50th Division up to the front line to fill the space between 4th Indian and 51st Highland divisions by taking the anti-tank ditch west of the Djebel Roumana. The losses suffered by 151st Brigade at the Mareth Line meant that in practice only 69th Brigade could do so and there was no time to arrange support by the divisional artillery.

As darkness fell on 5 April, British and Gurkha soldiers made a stealthy advance onto the Fatnassa position. There was no artillery bombardment so as not to warn the defenders, but at 0330 on the 6th, 450 guns covered the attacks of 51st Highland Division and 69th Brigade. The Djebel Roumana and both its anti-tank ditches were captured along with 2,600 Italian prisoners, but 69th Brigade in particular suffered heavily, among those killed being Lieutenant Colonel Seagrim, the Mareth Line VC, and Private Eric Anderson of 5th East Yorkshires, a stretcher-bearer who won a posthumous VC for three times rescuing wounded comrades under intense fire before being killed in an attempt to rescue a fourth.

On the Djebel Fatnassa another Victoria Cross was earned by Subedar Lalbadur Thapa of 2nd Gurkha Rifles,[5] who captured three machine-gun posts, the last single-handed after all his men had been mown down. By morning, 4th Indian Division had gained all its objectives and was moving round behind the western anti-tank ditch. At 0845, Tuker jubilantly assured Horrocks that the way was clear for X Corps' breakthrough. Horrocks notified Montgomery, who gave permission for X Corps to advance at once and sent off a triumphant signal to Alexander.

Unfortunately, X Corps did not break through and Tuker would later be scathingly dismissive of Horrocks and 1st Armoured Division's CO, Major General Briggs. Yet the fault was not theirs but Tuker's own: he had simply got his facts wrong. For a start, another line of hills, the Oudane el Hachana, had still to be taken by 4th Indian Division. This was only attacked at 0935, when another 1,000 Italian prisoners were taken and Briggs then found his way blocked by part of 15th Panzer, a line of 88mms and field guns in protected positions which, incidentally, were still killing some of Tuker's men as late as 1600. Tuker would argue that Briggs should have charged the anti-tank guns, but this was not a practice recommended by the lessons of the past.

In any case, by late morning the British commanders had become reluctant to commit the armour until they were certain where this would be most needed. On both the Djebel Roumana and the eastern anti-tank ditch, 51st Highland was subjected to desperate counter-attacks by 90th Light. The Highlanders were forced off the crest of the Djebel Roumana, captured it again, were driven off it again, and once more regained it. At the anti-tank ditch where elements of 15th Panzer were assisting 90th Light, the fighting was fiercer still but all afternoon and into the evening, 51st Division held firm, its efforts crowned and symbolized by yet another VC, this one awarded to Lieutenant Colonel Lorne Campbell, CO of 7th Battalion, Argyll and Sutherland Highlanders.

That night Messe ordered a general retirement, cleverly covering it by a number of thrusts at 69th Brigade. However, Eighth Army quickly followed up on 7 March, mauling the enemy rearguard, the luckless *Pistoia* Division. As Messe retreated, the Axis garrisons in the Eastern Dorsale fell back with him and Eighth Army at last made contact with II US Corps. Thereafter Montgomery's men were handicapped mainly by the number of prisoners they were taking: about 1,000 every day. The port of Sfax fell on 10 April, the port of Sousse fell on the 12th, and by the evening of the 13th Eighth Army had covered 150 miles and reached Enfidaville at the north of the central Tunisian plain.

Meanwhile on 10 April, General Eisenhower had received a personal message from Montgomery: 'Captured Sfax early this morning. Please send Fortress.' In February, Montgomery had assured Eisenhower's Chief of Staff Lieutenant General Walter Bedell Smith that his men would be in Sfax by 15 April. Bedell Smith, knowing the difficulties involved, thought this was quite impossible and very unwisely said that if it could really be done, Eisenhower would give Montgomery 'anything I liked to ask for'. Montgomery immediately said he would like a Flying Fortress with its crew who would remain on the US payroll. Sfax duly fell and Montgomery demanded that Eisenhower 'pay up'.

This was an appalling example of bad manners, bad taste and lack of consideration for others, but Montgomery treated it as a good joke, even when Brooke showed his anger. Yet, much to their credit, Eisenhower and Bedell Smith swallowed their indignation in recognition of the magnitude of Montgomery's achievement. He duly got his Fortress[6] but the long-suffering Bedell Smith is reported to have said that to serve under Montgomery would be a great privilege for anyone, but to serve over him was hell!

Also on 10 April, Montgomery signalled to Alexander that either First or Eighth Army should assault the remaining Axis positions in Tunisia while the other merely exerted pressure: 'on no account must we split our effort.' He was probably not pleased when his superior decided that the main effort would be by First Army and it would be reinforced by the transfer of 1st Armoured Division from Eighth Army.

Alexander's decision was undoubtedly correct. First Army had an easier line of attack and for political reasons it was essential that II US Corps should participate in the final assault. By contrast, Montgomery at Enfidaville faced a line of ridges similar to that blocking the Gabes Gap, except that behind the Enfidaville ones were not open plains but more hills running almost all the way to Tunis. Montgomery was ordered to put 'maximum pressure' against these defences to draw in enemy reserves, but it seems clear that he secretly hoped he might break through them and give his Eighth Army the honour of taking Tunis.

His attack was launched on the night of 19/20 April. The 4th Indian Division captured some, though not all, of the 1,000ft-high Djebel Garci, Halvidar-Major (Sergeant Major) Chhelu Ram of 4/6th Rajputana Rifles winning a Victoria Cross, and the steep-sided crag of Takrouna was taken equally gallantly by 2nd New Zealand Division. Yet the Indians suffered 550 casualties, the New Zealanders 500, and it seemed obvious that further progress would prove difficult and costly.

At this point, Montgomery's vision appears to have failed him. He showed none of his usual flexibility, but ordered the attempt to break through to be continued by fresh troops. Those chosen were the men of 56th (British) Division who had just come all the way from Iraq and were completely inexperienced. They delivered their attack on the night of 28/29 April and were thrown back in disorder the next day.

In fairness, Montgomery was far from well at this time and in fact had retired to bed on the 27th, suffering from influenza and tonsilitis. By the 29th, if still too ill to travel, he had recovered sufficiently to cancel all Eighth Army attacks and request Alexander to visit him. Alexander did so promptly, intending to order a further transfer of Eighth Army formations to the First Army front. It was an order never to be given.

Montgomery had regained his vision and his flexibility. Air Vice Marshal Broadhurst who was present at the meeting reports that Montgomery 'got in first', offering Alexander the use of 7th Armoured

Division, 4th Indian Division and 201st Guards Brigade and advising him to use them to assist a single concentrated thrust. 'You'll be through in 48 hours,' he promised. Alexander added the Eighth Army units to the British 6th Armoured and 4th Infantry divisions in his IX Corps and prepared for an attack in the Medjerda River Valley. To command it, Montgomery also supplied Horrocks, bearing in mind his experience at Tebaga.

The end came quickly. At 0600 on 6 May, Horrocks began his assault, following the pattern used at Tebaga: first air-raids and an artillery bombardment, then an infantry attack and finally the breakthrough by the two armoured divisions. By noon, both of these were on their way to Tunis. Their armoured cars entered the city in the afternoon of 7 May, while II US Corps took the port of Bizerta at almost the same moment. There remained only 'mopping-up' operations during which, General Fraser reports, 'over 100,000 German soldiers passed into Allied captivity – a greater number than taken at Stalingrad a few months before – and nearly 90,000 Italian.'

There would later be rather pointless arguments over whether the armoured cars of the 11th Hussars from 7th Armoured or those of the Derbyshire Yeomanry from 6th Armoured got to Tunis first. Horrocks tactfully calls it a draw, but de Guingand (probably) and Montgomery (certainly) vote for the 11th Hussars. In any case, Eighth Army formations had their fair share of the final triumphs. By midday on 9 May, 7th Armoured Division had accepted the surrender of the German panzer units, while on the 12th, 4th Indian Division accepted that of von Arnim.

Even when Fifth Panzer Army had given up, First Italian Army's matchless 90th Light Division continued to defy Eighth Army at Enfidaville. However, at midday on 13 May, Field Marshal Messe – his promotion well-earned if inappropriate in its timing – ordered it to cease its resistance. Ronald Lewin watched the white flags go up: 'White everywhere as if butterflies were dancing over the hill.' Finally Messe made his personal surrender to the renowned Eighth Army. That evening, he dined with Montgomery and 'we discussed various aspects of the battles we had fought against each other.'

Notes

1. Montgomery would study a photograph of Rommel when deciding what action his enemy would take. This has been the subject of mockery, but the fact remains that Montgomery was absolutely correct in his reading of Rommel's mind, not just on this occasion but also at Alam Halfa, Alamein and later at Normandy.
2. Jackson served as an officer in First Army, so was hardly prejudiced in Eighth Army's favour.
3. The other one came in December 1944, when Montgomery was warned that Eisenhower would no longer tolerate his insubordination.
4. De Guingand told them that he felt he was writing 'to the old combination – Hindenburg and Ludendorff!' This was perhaps rather less tactful.
5. A subedar was a senior 'Viceroy's Commissioned Officer'. These were Indians or Gurkhas of similar rank to British warrant officers, but having the privilege of being saluted by their own soldiers although not by British troops.
6. It was 'written off' on 28 July in a crash-landing in Sicily, whereupon Eisenhower generously replaced it with a less impressive but more manageable Dakota.

Chapter Five

The Struggle for Sicily

All Axis forces in North Africa had been eliminated and Allied attention turned to *Festung Europa* ('Fortress Europe') as Hitler was beginning to call it. Hitler rudely described Italy as the 'groin' of his fortress and his view was shared by Churchill who considered Italy the 'soft under-belly of the Axis'. Long before the final triumph in Tunisia, at the Casablanca Conference in January 1943 in fact, Churchill, Roosevelt and their chiefs of staff were pondering the action to be taken once that triumph had been achieved and inevitably it was to Italy that their interest was mainly directed.

There was a good deal of discussion and honest differences of opinion at Casablanca, but it was eventually accepted by everyone that the first

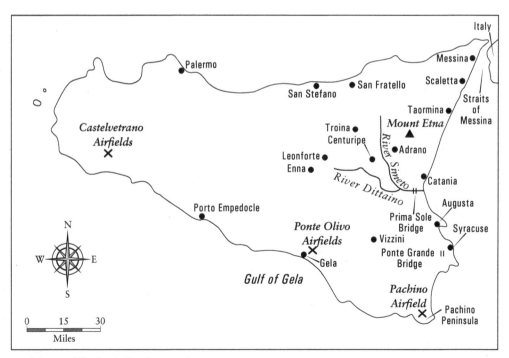

Map 11: The Sicily Battleground.

move after Tunisia should be an invasion of Sicily. Enemy aircraft stationed there were still making effective attacks on Allied shipping and an occupation of the island would end this threat, secure total Allied control of the Mediterranean and avoid the need to send convoys all the way round the Cape of Good Hope. It would also, it was hoped, reduce Axis pressure on Russia where the Germans were again on the offensive – they would recapture Kharkov on 15 March – and deal a final blow to an already tottering Italy.

It was at Casablanca that Alexander was appointed Eisenhower's deputy and head of the new Eighteenth Army Group controlling both First and Eighth Armies. As if those duties were not enough, he was made responsible for planning the subsequent invasion of Sicily code-named Operation HUSKY, a task he wisely delegated to a special planning unit under Major General Charles Gairdner. This originally met in the Hotel St George, Algiers and was designated 'Force 141' after the number of the room in which its first meetings were held.

By the end of February 1943, Gairdner had produced an initial draft plan that anticipated a number of widely dispersed landings in western and south-eastern Sicily. This did not appeal to Alexander, who suggested it would be better to make one concentrated attack on the south-east of the island, but Gairdner assured him that the ports in the area would not be able to handle the volume of shipping this unified assault would require.

On 13 March, the plan was approved in principle by Eisenhower and his air and naval commanders, Tedder and Admiral of the Fleet Sir Andrew Cunningham. Montgomery was also advised. He of all people favoured looking ahead, but at this moment was far too concerned with the need to break through first the Mareth Line and then the Gabes Gap to give the plan more than cursory attention. Even this, though, was enough to show him that the three Eighth Army divisions that were to land in the south-east of Sicily would not be strong enough to attain their objectives. His argument was accepted and he was promised a fourth division.

There was good reason for Montgomery's concern. While a successful attack on Sicily promised rich benefits, a failed assault on Fortress Europe, 'striking for the first time at the enemy in his own land', as Admiral Cunningham put it, would have dire consequences. Moreover many felt that failure was not at all unlikely, notably Mountbatten who had not forgotten the disastrous Dieppe raid.

Sicily, after all, was ideal defensive country. An island of 10,000 square miles, it had few main roads and away from them advances had to be made over narrow winding lanes with high stone walls on either side. Apart from its small coastal plain, it was rugged and mountainous, particularly in the north-east where the approaches to the vital port of Messina were guarded by the massive volcano Mount Etna, surrounded by great fields of solidified lava that could cut like a razor and injuries from which had an unpleasant tendency to turn septic.

Defending Sicily was the Sixth Italian Army, controlled officially by the 66-year-old General Alfredo Guzzoni but in practice by Kesselring. It consisted of four Italian mobile infantry divisions and six Italian static coast defence divisions, backed by the Hermann Göring Panzer Division and 15th Panzer Grenadier Division, a motorized infantry formation containing one tank battalion. It could also be reinforced easily since the Straits of Messina separating Sicily from the Italian mainland are only 2 miles wide at one point and 5 miles wide on average.

Kesselring was genuinely eager to assist, encourage and establish good relationships with the Italians and his efforts had been rewarded by a high level of co-operation between German and Italian soldiers, at least as far as the mobile Axis formations were concerned. The Sicilians, however, were a proudly independent people who had not wanted the war and had little liking for Mussolini. The coast defence divisions shared these views and were frankly reluctant to fight. This, though, was not known to either Montgomery or Alexander, both of whom therefore judged the resistance the Italians were likely to give on their fine performance in Tunisia. This, however, was perhaps no bad attitude, for resistance by the Axis mobile units alone was not to be taken lightly.

Nor were the defenders unprepared for the Allied invasion. A brilliant if macabre deception was put into effect on 30 April, when the body of 'Major William Martin of the Royal Marines' was washed ashore on the Spanish coast. Among the papers carried by this fictitious officer was a letter to Alexander from Lieutenant General Sir Archibald Nye, Vice Chief of the Imperial General Staff, indicating that the real Allied objectives were Greece and Sardinia. Axis agents in Spain provided copies to Hitler and the German high command who swallowed the bait and sent reinforcements to those areas. Sadly, however, Kesselring was not deceived. A fine airman, he was certain the Allies would invade only where they could be protected by their shore-based Spitfire and Mustang fighters. That could only be Sicily, and Kesselring in fact received reinforcements during June. He also correctly estimated that the invasion would come in July.

That it would take place as early as July seemed unlikely to some, but with the Mareth Line and the Gabes Gap safely behind Eighth Army and the final destruction of the Axis forces in Tunisia clearly only a matter of time, Montgomery turned his full attention to HUSKY. On 15 April, de Guingand, promoted to major general, was sent to Cairo to co-ordinate its planning. Montgomery personally flew to Cairo on the 23rd. Next day, he had lengthy conferences with de Guingand and Admiral Sir Bertram Ramsay, once the organizer of the Dunkirk evacuation but now responsible for landing Eighth Army in Sicily, after which he acted promptly and vigorously.

It had been intended that the invasion would be conducted, under Eisenhower's overall control, by a new Fifteenth Army Group replacing Eighteenth Army Group but again led by Alexander. Under this would be Montgomery's Eighth Army and a new Seventh US Army led by Patton. This last would contain three infantry divisions, the 1st and 45th which together formed Major General Omar Bradley's II US Corps, and the 3rd under Patton's direct control. These units would make two separate attacks: one against the port of Palermo in north-west Sicily and the other against the south-west of the island to take the airfields at Castelvetrano.

Eighth Army would employ two corps, each containing two infantry divisions. In Leese's XXX Corps would be the veteran 51st Highland Division and 1st Canadian Division which was sent out from the United Kingdom. In XIII Corps, thus resuming its active role, would be an existing Eighth Army division, the 50th, and the 5th Division which had come from the Middle East. The corps commander was Lieutenant General Miles Dempsey, another personal choice of Montgomery who rightly considered him loyal, hard-working, efficient, capable of explaining plans clearly and simply and possessing an uncanny ability to visualize the ground over which a battle was to be fought after studying it on a map. Eighth Army was to make a number of dispersed landings on both sides of the Pachino Peninsula in the south-east of Sicily and in the Gulf of Gela on its south coast.

It was the first time that Montgomery had been presented with someone else's plan since that of Auchinleck for Alam Halfa. He surely remembered that he had altered this and won his battle precisely because of his alterations whereas he had accepted the Dieppe plan with disastrous results, and his reaction was predictable. On 24 April, he sent a signal to Alexander declaring that the multiple landings risked being overwhelmed separately one after the other. He therefore insisted that all Eighth Army's divisions land together on one single front stretching from the Pachino Peninsula to just south of Syracuse and the landing in the Gulf of Gela be abandoned.

Since Alexander had always favoured a concentration of his forces, he was naturally sympathetic, but others were frankly hostile and for this it is difficult to blame them. Montgomery's signal and indeed his entire attitude was tactless, arrogant, dictatorial and dogmatic. Inevitably it aroused justifiable resentment and instinctive resistance, particularly on the part of Cunningham and Tedder who were concerned that the abandonment of a landing on the south coast would mean that the Ponte Olivo airfields would not be attacked and so left free to strike at the assault shipping.

On his return to Tunisia, Montgomery fell ill, as was described earlier. He was thus unable to attend a conference held in Algiers on 29 April. De Guingand was intended to go instead but his aircraft crashed on take-off, putting him in hospital with concussion. Leese, who replaced him, was treated disgracefully. No-one met him at the aerodrome, he had to get into the city by hitching a lift in a lorry and then, apart from Alexander who Leese tells us 'was splendid and stood up for me from the start', the senior officers refused to discuss the matter unless Montgomery was present in person.

As we know, Alexander visited Montgomery to arrange the final moves in Tunisia and it seems that Montgomery then informed him of his latest ideas about Sicily. These were to cancel the proposed operations in the west of the island and land the Americans in the Gulf of Gela, thus enabling the Ponte Olivo airfields to be captured quickly, securing Eighth Army's left flank and simplifying the fighter protection for the landing. On 2 May, Montgomery flew to Algiers, found Bedell Smith and 'sold' the plan to him. He in turn convinced Eisenhower, but in view of continuing objections from Cunningham and Tedder, it was agreed to leave the final decision to Alexander who had been prevented by bad weather from attending the conference. Next day, Alexander was consulted and he fully supported Montgomery.

Naturally some post-war critics would be less supportive. Captain Liddell Hart, for instance, regrets the abandonment of the Palermo landing on the grounds that had it proceeded, Patton would have been 'well on the way to the Straits of Messina, the enemy's line of reinforcement or retreat – whereby all the enemy forces in Sicily could have been trapped.' This, though, could only happen if the advance to the Straits was not prevented and since the landing would automatically have dispersed the Allied ground and air strength and the bulk of 15th Panzer Grenadier Division and two Italian mobile divisions were stationed in western Sicily, ideally placed to attack Patton from flank and rear, it seems highly probable that it would have been.

Far more convincing therefore is the testimony of General Eisenhower, who declared years later that even with the advantage of hindsight he still believed that the decision to land the Americans on Sicily's south coast was 'absolutely correct'. It was a judgement accepted by every other American authority and also, once they had got over their resentment of Montgomery's dictatorial attitude, by Cunningham and Tedder. The Official Naval Historian, Captain S.W. Roskill, declares in *The Navy at War 1939–1945* that: 'This change of plan which was pressed by General Montgomery undoubtedly reduced the risks of failure.' Tedder would claim, without a blush, that personally he 'had always favoured it'.

Apart from the plan's own merits, it replaced doubt and confusion with certainty and clarity and if Montgomery's way of achieving this was deplorable, he is surely entitled to respect for his moral courage in refusing to adopt a plan that he was convinced would lead to disaster. General Dempsey, a modest, retiring man who Ronald Lewin confirms was 'not given to over-statement', would declare that 'the part Montgomery played in evolving the final plan for HUSKY was his finest hour.'

Montgomery's superiors showed their own moral courage on 9 July. As the task forces headed for Sicily they were battered by gale-force winds and fierce seas. Yet Eisenhower, Alexander and Cunningham, all temporarily based on Malta, were assured by their weather experts that the storm would subside before the troops hit the beaches in the early hours of the 10th and united in deciding the operation must continue.

Their resolve was rewarded, for the storm did subside and in fact proved beneficial: the defenders thought the Allies would never invade in such conditions and relaxed their vigilance just when it was most needed.

In consequence, the soldiers landed on the right beaches at more or less the right time. They were much assisted by the industrial strength of the United States, from which large numbers of invasion craft were reaching the combat zone. These included Landing Craft Infantry (LCIs), Landing Craft Tanks (LCTs) and the larger 1,500-ton Landing Ship Tanks (LSTs), all of which could ground on a beach and then lower ramps, enabling men or vehicles as the case might be to swarm ashore. Also present were 'Ducks' – properly speaking DUKWs[1] – which were amphibious trucks that could carry men and equipment inland rather than unload them on the beaches.

With surprise achieved and the aid of their specialized invasion craft both the British and the Americans met far less resistance and suffered far fewer casualties than anyone had expected. Only in the skies where airborne troops preceded the naval landings did matters go badly. Part of 82nd US Airborne Division was to be dropped on high ground overlooking Patton's landing beaches, but the pilots of its Dakotas had had little training and that only in daylight. Hampered by the strong winds, they scattered their parachutists over some 50 square miles and these achieved no meaningful success. Worse still, when the rest of 82nd Airborne tried to reinforce the landing beaches late on 11 July, it was subjected to 'friendly' fire from ship and shore and almost 100 men were killed.

Montgomery's airborne warriors, who came from 1st (British) Airborne Division and were carried in 134 gliders, had a more definite objective. Far from being the slow, methodical leader portrayed in some accounts, Montgomery was eager to take two objectives as quickly as possible. The first was the port of Syracuse, through which supplies for both armies would pass. Then both Eighth Army's corps would race northward to Catania. Beyond this town, the coastal road, Route 114, was hemmed in by the slopes of Mount Etna, so there would only be room for XIII Corps to operate, but Montgomery was confident that if he could get to Catania before the defenders had had time to prepare, it would be able to reach Messina with the aid of bombardments from supporting warships.

The task of 1st Airborne Division was to speed up the capture of Syracuse by seizing a key bridge, the Ponte Grande, just south of the port. Its flight was assisted by Wellington raids on targets in the vicinity and attacks by night-intruder Hurricanes on any searchlights that might reveal it. Sadly, the great majority of its towing aircraft were manned by inexperienced American pilots and most of the gliders came down well away from the target area, a large number in the sea where most of their troops drowned. Only twelve, all towed by RAF crews, landed near the bridge and eight officers and sixty-five men secured it and held it against repeated enemy attacks until 1530 on 10 July when the nineteen survivors were joined by the advance troops of XIII Corps. Syracuse fell that evening.

It seemed that all Montgomery's hopes were on the point of being fulfilled. The whole Pachino Peninsula was in British hands and by 11 July, sappers were already restoring its airfield for use by British fighters spurred on by Montgomery, arriving in person that morning in a DUKW. The port facilities in Syracuse were intact and on 12 July, the more northern port of Augusta was taken as well. The American beachhead was also secure. Heavy attacks on it had been thwarted only by barrages from the supporting warships, but the Americans recovered their balance with remarkable speed and determination and by the 12th the danger had passed.

In his *Memoirs*, Montgomery states that once the Americans had gained experience they proved 'first-class troops', but apparently he had not appreciated how quickly they had learned from previous mistakes. By this time, they were already first-class and very mobile since they had more and better transport vehicles than the British. Montgomery, however, believed they would be pinned down in their beachhead, but would also pin down the Axis soldiers opposing them. These included the Hermann Göring Panzer Division and were about to be joined by the bulk of 15th Panzer Grenadier Division; the rest was facing the British north of Augusta. It therefore seemed to Montgomery that he had a splendid opportunity to cut off these forces and he changed his plans accordingly.

On 12 July, Montgomery signalled to Alexander: 'Intend now to operate on two axes.' Instead of advancing on Catania with both his corps, he would leave this task to XIII Corps alone. He would send XXX Corps

westward and then north-westward to the towns of Leonforte and Enna
and once it had reached them 'the enemy opposing the Americans will
never get away.'

It was another instance of Montgomery's quick-thinking flexibility,
but this one was ill-timed and unfortunate. In effect it sacrificed the
benefits that would have been gained by an early capture of Catania for
the sake of benefits that might be gained by XXX Corps, but in fact were
not. By an unkind trick of fate, this was mainly because the Americans
recovered so quickly and so well that they pushed their opponents out of
the trap before it could close. The Hermann Göring Panzer Division,
for example, retired to the important road junction of Vizzini where it
blocked the move by XXX Corps. This was only able to enter Vizzini in
the late afternoon of 14 July and only secured it next day and that with the
assistance of 45th US Infantry Division coming in from the south-west.

Once XXX Corps had been committed, however, it could not be
switched back quickly to the Catania area over Sicily's inadequate road
system. In order to compensate for its absence, Montgomery tried to
speed up XIII Corps' advance with a parachute landing by 1st Airborne
on the Prima Sole bridge that carried the main road to Catania over the
Simeto River. This was planned for the night of 13/14 July, but by that
time XIII Corps' opportunity had already disappeared.

For on 12 July, Kesselring had arrived in Sicily and ordered a regiment
of Germany's 1st Parachute Division to be flown in. That evening, he
watched as its men were dropped, most efficiently, south of Catania.
On the 13th, he confirmed a decision by Guzzoni that the main part of
Sicily should be abandoned and its defenders slowly withdrawn to a line
running from Catania westward along the Simeto and Dittaino rivers to
Leonforte and then northward to San Stefano on the north coast, from
which the line took its name. It was determined that these new positions
must be held as long as possible and to ensure this, reinforcements were
provided: the rest of 1st Parachute Division, two infantry battalions,
supporting artillery and, on 15 July, 29th Panzer Grenadier Division and
the HQ of XIV Panzer Corps under the one-armed General Hans Hube.

Consequently, XIII Corps' advance quickly ground to a halt. The
Dakotas carrying 1st Airborne's parachutists came under heavy 'friendly'
fire from Allied warships; many were shot down or turned back and the
remainder scattered their charges over a wide area. Only 200 men and a

few anti-tank guns reached the Prima Sole bridge in the early hours of 14 July and were savagely attacked by the German paratroopers. They were driven off the bridge that evening, but prevented their opponents from destroying it. Next day, XIII Corps' advance guard arrived and the bridge was finally secured on the 16th. By then, however, the enemy had received reinforcements and no further progress could be made.

On his western flank, Montgomery's flexibility was more beneficial. Though deprived of his chance to trap enemy forces, he continued to direct XXX Corps on Leonforte, from which he intended it should swing east to Adrano and from there pass Mount Etna and attack the defenders of Catania from behind. To guard his flank and rear, he wanted Bradley's II US Corps to advance northward on XXX Corps' left.

Though Montgomery had again underestimated the Americans – Bradley was capable of far more than a mere supporting role – this was another clever tactic, but typically Montgomery, as Leese would tactfully put it, was 'a bit impatient and hasty with others'. The best way to Leonforte was on a main road, Route 124, but Alexander had already allotted its use to Bradley. Yet Montgomery, without informing let alone asking permission from Alexander, Bradley or Patton, directed XXX Corps onto this road. Bradley, compelled to switch his advance further westward, was rightly displeased. His indignation was increased when XXX Corps passed east of Enna though this was its responsibility to capture, and thus exposed the flank of II US Corps which was left to take the town instead.

Fortunately Leese, XXX Corps' commander, liked and respected Bradley and their mutual good feelings prevented a major breakdown in Allied relationships. Nonetheless, Montgomery's attitude had made him disliked and distrusted by the Americans, which would soon cause further trouble. To make matters worse, XXX Corps was unable to reach Leonforte until 19 July or capture it until the night of the 21st. It therefore could not prevent the two Italian mobile divisions in western Sicily from retiring safely behind the San Stefano line, which they did on the 16th. Then when the corps turned towards Adrano, it met such strong resistance that Montgomery had to summon 78th (British) Division from North Africa to provide fresh troops with which to continue the advance.

Bradley's II US Corps, despite the loss of Route 124 and fierce opposition from 15th Panzer Grenadier Division, got further north than

XXX Corps and on 23 July reached the northern coast of Sicily, cutting both the coastal road from Palermo to Messina, Route 113, and the main inland road, Route 120. Bradley had always contended that he should then turn eastward to Messina and by now Montgomery had reached the same conclusion. On 19 July, he requested Alexander to direct an American division against Messina and, with unusual tact, declined Alexander's invitation that he command this. By the 21st, he was urging that the whole American strength should carry out the move. Unfortunately, it was not available to do so.

Lieutenant General George Patton had bitterly resented criticisms of American deficiencies in Tunisia and by the time Sicily was invaded it seems his judgement had become unbalanced. Before the landings he had told his Seventh US Army: 'When we meet the enemy, we will kill him. We will show him no mercy.' On 14 July, in two quite separate incidents, a sergeant and an officer of 45th US Division showed no mercy to Italian prisoners, some seventy of whom were shot in cold blood. When court-martialled, both pleaded that they were obeying Patton's orders. Sergeant West was sentenced to life imprisonment but released in just over a year. Captain Compton was acquitted and died in action later. There is no doubt that Patton had never intended this to happen but he showed little regret for it, telling a horrified Bradley to 'certify that the dead men were snipers or had attempted to escape or something.'[2]

Towards the end of the campaign, Patton on both 3 and 9 August violently assaulted shell-shocked men in hospital who he thought were malingering. He thereby exhibited not only brutality, as Eisenhower declared, but cowardice since the men in question could not retaliate without suffering severe punishment.[3] In between the shootings and the assaults came what American historians have called 'Patton's obsession with Palermo'. Patton understandably and rightly wished for a more important role in the campaign and on 17 July flew to Alexander's HQ to demand one. For some extraordinary reason, however, he wanted to operate against not Messina but Palermo in the north-west of Sicily.

It will cause little surprise that post-war critics blame Montgomery for Patton's action, saying that Seventh US Army needed a port since Montgomery had deprived it of one by sending it to southern Sicily. Yet it was getting adequate supplies through Syracuse and Augusta and, after 16 July, through the newly-captured Porto Empedolce on the Gulf of

Gela. Nor in any case would Palermo be of use as a port because the enemy had effectively blocked the harbour by sinking some forty ships in it. Eisenhower, Bedell Smith, Bradley and Major General Lucien Truscott whose 3rd US Infantry Division was detailed to take Palermo all agree it had not the slightest value; a view incidentally shared by Kesselring.

Nonetheless, Patton won the consent of Alexander who believed it was of the highest importance to soothe Patton's feelings for political reasons: for the sake of good inter-Allied relations. Unfortunately Montgomery, solely concerned with his men's welfare and never a politician – both good reasons why his troops trusted him – could not appreciate Alexander's wider responsibilities and wider vision and the incident marks the end of their former unity.

On 18 July, Patton duly set off for Palermo. The resistance he encountered is best expressed in the casualty lists: American killed and wounded 272; Italian killed and wounded 3,000; Italian prisoners 52,000. His achievements are best described by Bradley: 'The capture of hills, docile peasants and spiritless soldiers.' When Palermo was entered on 22 July, this was to the accompaniment of crowds shouting 'Long live America! Down with Mussolini!'

It may surprise some to learn that Montgomery sincerely admired the mobility and dash shown by the Americans. His complaint was that it had been directed against the wrong target. As he had already told Alexander, he wished it turned against Messina and in his usual high-handed way set about obtaining this. On 25 July, he met with Patton and urged that while XXX Corps resumed its advance on Adrano, the whole of Seventh US Army should strike at Messina, for which it would be given sole use of both main roads to the port: Routes 113 and 120.

Though this would virtually guarantee that the Americans would take Messina – Montgomery suggested they should then push southward to attack the enemy opposing XIII Corps at Catania from the rear – Patton showed none of the pleasure Montgomery had anticipated. Convinced that this was somehow a clever trick, he developed a new obsession: that there was a 'race' on for Messina and he must get there before Montgomery. His anxiety was increased because the need to reorganize his forces and bring them back from western Sicily meant that he could not attack before 1 August, whereas Leese began XXX Corps' advance on the night of 29/30 July.

Perhaps it mattered little. Dramatic political events – to be discussed later – had convinced Kesselring that Sicily could not be held much longer. Even Hitler, belatedly concerned about the number of Axis soldiers lost in Stalingrad and Tunisia, did not want to risk another mass surrender in Sicily. He therefore agreed on an evacuation in which the embarkation of men must be given priority over that of equipment.

A number of factors conspired to aid the Axis plans. Sicily tapers to a point in the vicinity of the intended embarkation area, so the further its defenders retired, the fewer men they needed to hold an increasingly shorter front line. Although Alexander, on the strength of Intelligence reports, had warned as early as 3 August that the enemy were considering an evacuation, Admiral Cunningham, as he would honestly admit, had given very little thought to preventing this. On the other hand, with their usual efficiency, the Germans had arranged a ferry service to Italy and Colonel Ernst Baade, appointed Commander Messina Straits by Kesselring on 14 July, had provided the protection of more than 500 anti-aircraft or coastal guns.

The rest of the campaign may be described briefly. Its finest achievement was that of 78th Division which could only approach Centuripe, the key to Adrano, through a single steep winding mountain road with deep ravines on each side. Nonetheless, after tremendous efforts, the division stormed Centuripe on 3 August and pressed on to take Adrano after dark on the 6th. Earlier on the 5th, the Germans had finally retired from Catania and XIII Corps could move forward, linking up with XXX Corps north of Mount Etna.

Further north still, the Americans were making steady if slow progress, taking Troina on the inland route on 6 August and San Fratello on the coastal road on the 8th. Both these little towns were voluntarily abandoned by an enemy concerned only with leaving Sicily. The first Axis soldiers set out for the Italian mainland after dark on the 11th. Night bombing raids by Wellingtons caused such damage that as from the 14th the men were carried out only in daylight when Baade's massive array of AA guns could keep the Allied airmen at bay.

Patton attempted to speed up his progress by amphibious flanking assaults in the early hours of 8, 12 and 16 August. The first found that the enemy had already retired. The second was engaged so fiercely that it lost all its tanks and artillery and was only saved from destruction by the main American advance along the coastal road. The third came ashore after the advance had already passed it. None of this prevented Patton from sneering at Montgomery for making no such imaginative moves. Those who agree with him are respectfully referred to Captain Roskill's Official Naval History where he points out that while Sicily's northern shore was suitable for such operations, 'to the north of Catania the coast becomes so precipitous, and the few beaches have such poor exits, that it was scarcely possible to land or deploy a substantial assault force.'

In fact, Montgomery did organize one seaborne landing on the eastern coast, but only because beyond Taormina, which was taken on 15 August, the coastal road had been demolished so thoroughly that the only way round the devastation was by sea. Therefore on the night of 15/16 August, a force built round 40th Commando Battalion came ashore at Scaletta, 8 miles south of Messina. It found that the Germans had already retired, but followed them up and entered Messina early on the 17th, behind the 7th US Infantry Regiment of 3rd US Division which had got there on the previous evening but just ahead of Patton who made a personal entry so ostentatious that the modest Bradley declined to take part in it.

Patton naturally made much of having beaten Montgomery in the 'race' for Messina. There had never been such a race, but if one must use that expression, then the winner was already in Italy, to which, as he informed a relieved Hitler, had been carried some 39,500 Germans, 62,000 Italians, 47 tanks, 94 guns, 9,600 lorries and 17,000 tons of other military equipment. He was Field Marshal Albert Kesselring.

It was a disappointing end to the campaign in Sicily, but it cannot detract from that campaign's achievements. It had cost the Allies some 22,800 casualties, about 8,400 of them fatal, but the German casualties were much the same, plus 5,500 more who had been taken prisoner, and the Italian losses were at least 130,000, most of whom had surrendered. Moreover, the first bastion of 'Fortress Europe' with all that this meant to both sides had fallen in just thirty-eight days.

All the Allies' strategic hopes had also been fulfilled. The Mediterranean was now completely secured; so much so that Axis troops abandoned Sardinia and Corsica without a fight on 8 and 12 September respectively. The news from Sicily had caused Hitler on 13 July to cancel an offensive he had launched on Kursk. It was never resumed. On the 15th, the Russians counter-attacked. By 4 August, the Germans had been driven out of their own salient that threatened to outflank Kursk and had suffered such huge tank losses that in future they could never do more than delay successive Russian advances that would end only in Berlin.

Best of all, the campaign in Sicily had had dramatic political repercussions that two months after its closure would deprive Hitler of vastly more soldiers than those he had lost in Stalingrad, in Tunisia and in Sicily all put together.

Notes

1. These were the code-letters used in the factories producing them. 'D', the fourth letter of the alphabet, indicated the fourth year of hostilities; 'U' stood for utility; 'K' for front-wheel drive; and 'W' for wheels, of which each vehicle had six.
2. Full details of this episode can be found in *Hitler's Last General: The Case Against Wilhelm Mohnke* by Ian Sayer and Douglas Botting. Mohnke was a SS officer whose troops were twice involved in the murder of Allied prisoners. The Sicily shootings are described in the course of an examination of the responsibility of senior commanders for the acts of their subordinates.
3. Despite Patton's notorious dislike of Montgomery, it should be noticed that Montgomery was never vindictive or hostile towards Patton. When these incidents were described in *Eighth Army News* and *Crusader*, Montgomery strongly rebuked Warwick Charlton, editor of both these newspapers – daily and weekly respectively – saying that he didn't think the reports were correct and that 'Patton was a good man'.

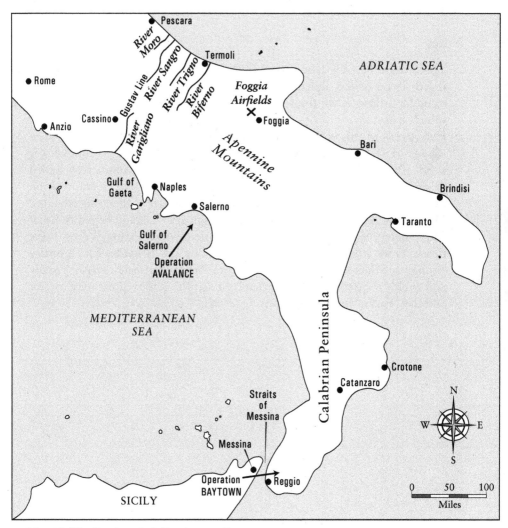

Map 12: The Southern Italy Battleground.

Chapter Six

River of Blood

On 24 July 1943, Benito Mussolini, dictator of Italy, was fiercely attacked by the formerly docile Fascist Grand Council, which demanded a dramatic reduction of his powers. Senior officers in the Italian Supreme Command were already working for Mussolini's overthrow and had gained the support of King Victor Emmanuel III. So when the dictator reported the Grand Council's action to the palace, the king told him curtly that he was the most hated man in Italy and called for his resignation. On his refusal, he was taken into custody, officially for his own protection.

A new government was formed by Marshal Pietro Badoglio, a long-time critic of Mussolini's regime. Badoglio assured Hitler, Kesselring and anyone else who would listen to him that Italy would remain loyal to the Axis Pact, but his real aim was to end a ruinous war as soon as possible. However, he had no wish to gain peace at the price of a German takeover of Italy. He therefore wanted Italy to join the Western Allies as a co-belligerent, which might enable the Germans to be driven out quickly and spare Italy from having a war fought out all over her territory.

Badoglio's outlook presented the Allies with immense opportunities, but only if they moved promptly. Kesselring, who had always got on well with the Italians, accepted their promises that they would not desert the Germans, but Hitler did not believe them for a moment. In a cold, unforgiving rage, he began to plan a military occupation of Italy, code-named with rather ghastly irony Operation ACHSE, the German for AXIS.

Before Italy's change of sides could be arranged, the terms for this had to be agreed. Unfortunately at the Casablanca Conference, Churchill and Roosevelt had announced that the Axis powers would not be offered any terms at all; only their 'unconditional surrender' would be accepted.

Although some historians have argued that this doctrine had no adverse consequences, this was not the view of the Allies' military leaders. It found no favour with the United States Joint Chiefs of Staff or Eisenhower or Alexander or indeed Montgomery who would call it a very great mistake and a tragic one. As Admiral Chester Nimitz, the US C-in-C, Pacific, points out in *The Great Sea War*, 'Not even Napoleon at the height of his conquests ever so completely closed the door to negotiation. To adopt such an inflexible policy was bad enough; to announce it publicly was worse.'

Its adoption led to August 1943 being passed in a miasma of hypocritical negotiations that could not officially be called negotiations. In these, the Allies tried to convince the Italians that if they surrendered 'unconditionally', they would in practice receive favourable terms, while the Italians most wanted reassurance that the Allies would save them from German vengeance. Ultimately, some required conditions were indicated, chiefly the withdrawal of all Italian forces from foreign territory, the free use of Italian ports and airfields and the surrender of the Italian navy and air force. These terms were not unexpected and on the basis of them Italy surrendered 'unconditionally' on 3 September, though the news was kept secret for the moment so as not to warn the Germans.[1]

However, while the Allies and the Italians argued, Hitler acted. On 1 August, Germany's 44th Infantry Division arrived at the Brenner Pass between Italy and Austria, supposedly to help oppose any Allied invasion. General Vittorio Ambrosio, who had become Italy's chief of staff in February 1943, dared not be obstructive until negotiations with the Allies had been complete. He therefore made no objection to the division's entry into Italy or to its promptly securing the pass, through which poured strong German reinforcements. He also allowed the 2nd Parachute Division of General Kurt Student's XI Parachute Corps to land at the Rome airfields on the pretence that it was on its way to join 1st Parachute Division in Sicily.

As a result, by 3 September there were eight German divisions in north Italy, formed into Army Group 'B' under the command of Rommel. In the Rome area, Student, under Kesselring's overall control, took charge of his 2nd Parachute Division, 3rd Panzer Grenadier Division and a tank battalion from 26th Panzer. Also under Kesselring came the German forces in southern Italy. When the ones in Sicily were withdrawn, these numbered eight divisions, to which a ninth from Sardinia was soon to be added. On 17 August, with the evacuation from Sicily completed, they became the German Tenth Army under General Heinrich Gottfried von Vietinghoff.

Allied preparations were much more confused. The 'Trident' Conference in Washington in May 1943 had decided that the knockout blow against Germany must be delivered from Britain, striking first at France, then as soon as possible at the Ruhr, Germany's economic heart, the capture of which would make final victory only a matter of time. It was provisionally agreed that the invasion of France, code-named Operation OVERLORD, would take place on 1 May 1944.

By contrast, the Mediterranean would become a secondary theatre. No reinforcements would be sent there and by 1 November 1943 at the latest, three British and four American divisions plus the bulk of the area's landing craft, troop-carrying aircraft and medium bomber units would leave for Britain. In these circumstances, there was little enthusiasm at first for a landing on the Italian mainland. By August, though, the occupation of Sicily, the fall of Mussolini and the possibility of Italy joining the Allies suddenly made this attractive.

Near at hand was an important strategic prize: the Foggia airfields on Italy's Adriatic coast. Their capture would enable Allied heavy bombers to attack targets, previously out of reach, in southern Germany, Eastern Europe and the Balkans, in particular the Rumanian oil-fields. More distant was an equally important political prize: Rome. Its capture would strike a tremendous blow at the morale of the Axis powers, especially that of Hitler's minor European satellites. Everyone could see the value of these prizes, but the Americans feared that achieving them might delay the build-up for OVERLORD. They made it clear that there could be no question of postponing the removal of Allied strength from the Mediterranean area.

Inevitably, Eisenhower came under pressure from his military and political superiors to gain these objectives as soon as possible. He responded, as he would do later in North-West Europe, by urging all his subordinates to keep advancing all the time in all circumstances; this led to the appearance of a mass of hastily-prepared and often unrealistic plans.

As in Sicily, responsibility for the land operations fell on Alexander's Fifteenth Army Group, which would again control one American and one British army. The former was now Fifth US Army led by General Mark Wayne Clark. This officer had successfully handled difficult staff appointments in the past, was forceful and determined and would shortly earn a Distinguished Service Cross by his personal gallantry. He had, however, no experience of commanding even a division in action. The British army was the Eighth, whose commander was very experienced but whose previous offensive behaviour now returned to haunt him.

Montgomery believed that one clear plan should be prepared and was disgusted by the vague, ill-considered and constantly altered ideas of his superiors. Nor was he happy about the role proposed for Eighth Army, which was originally intended to make a series of widely-separated landings on the Calabrian Peninsula, the 'toe' of Italy: a dispersal of strength that Montgomery instinctively disliked.

In late July, however, it was decided to speed up the advance into Italy by securing the valuable port of Naples. This would be achieved by Operation AVALANCHE, a landing by Clark's Fifth US Army in the Gulf of Salerno, south of Naples. Most of the landings on the Italian 'toe' were now cancelled, leaving only Operation BAYTOWN, an attack directly across the Straits of Messina.

It has been suggested by some that Montgomery was opposed to AVALANCHE. In fact he expressed his approval in principle to Brooke on 27 July, and was full of ideas as to how it could best be carried out, none of them exactly over-cautious. For a start, he wished the landing made in the Gulf of Gaeta, north of Naples. Here the beaches were not as good as those at Salerno, but they were not overlooked by surrounding hills like Salerno, and the country between them and Naples was far easier to cross. Their main disadvantage was that they were outside the range of shore-based single-engine fighters, so would have to be defended by carrier-based aircraft and twin-engine Lockheed Lightnings. Even this, though, would give the advantage of surprise, since Kesselring already suspected that Salerno would be a target.

Nor did Montgomery oppose the reduction of the landings on the Italian 'toe'. On the contrary, he felt that even BAYTOWN was pointless because it was unlikely to divert Axis forces from Salerno: rearguards and the dreadful terrain would easily check any advance from the 'toe'. He preferred a concentrated assault on Naples by both Fifth and Eighth armies, leaving any enemies on the Calabrian Peninsula to 'wither on the vine'.

Unfortunately, neither Eisenhower nor Tedder was prepared to risk a landing in the Gulf of Gaeta or to abandon BAYTOWN. Alexander did appreciate the strength of Montgomery's arguments, but remembering the damage done to inter-Allied and inter-service relations by Montgomery's dogmatic demands before and during the Sicilian campaign, it is understandable that he was reluctant to provoke further trouble by supporting Montgomery on this occasion.

In any case, the Allies were increasingly handicapped by a growing shortage of landing-craft. This made it impossible to land Fifth and Eighth armies together at Salerno as Montgomery wished; they would have had to go in separately with an interval between them. Indeed, there were insufficient landing-craft to enable AVALANCHE and BAYTOWN to be executed on the same day, and enough for the latter were only provided after Montgomery had made strong representations.

BAYTOWN was launched first in the early hours of 3 September. Its objectives were to obtain a bridgehead that would secure the Straits of Messina and assist AVALANCHE by engaging any enemy encountered. These were small aims for the famous Eighth Army, but then only a part of it – Dempsey's XIII Corps – would be involved. Its X Corps had been transferred to Fifth US Army, as incidentally had Montgomery's Director of Operations, Brigadier Richardson, who became Clark's deputy chief of staff (British).

To strengthen XIII Corps' landing, Montgomery had laid on a massive artillery bombardment, which proved unnecessary because the enemy had prudently retired from the area. The port of Reggio was captured almost undamaged and 3,000 Italian prisoners taken, but naturally Montgomery's critics have ridiculed this waste of metal and pointed out that Intelligence reports had suggested only weak opposition would be encountered. So they had but small reconnaissance landings on the Italian mainland had failed to confirm this, and remembering past Intelligence inaccuracies, Montgomery was not prepared to risk wasting a more precious commodity: the lives of his soldiers.[2]

Once ashore, XIII Corps moved up the Calabrian Peninsula, 5th (British) Division following the western coastal road and 1st Canadian the eastern one. These, the only possible routes northward, were hemmed in by steep cliffs, crossed rivers cutting through deep ravines, and contained so many hairpin bends that it took them 250 miles to cover a distance of 100 miles as the crow flew. The Germans took full advantage of these conditions, blowing up the overhanging cliffs to fall across the roads and demolishing all the bridges. Small amphibious landings on 3/4 and 7/8 September helped very little, but by the 10th, after tremendous efforts, the British and Canadians had reached their immediate objective, Catanzaro, where the width of the peninsula shrank to some 30 miles: a feature known, with scant regard for anatomical accuracy, as the 'neck' of the 'toe'.

By that time, much had occurred elsewhere. Since AVALANCHE was planned for the early hours of 9 September, Eisenhower warned Badoglio on the 8th that the Italian capitulation must now be revealed. When Badoglio, who had not expected this so soon, protested, Eisenhower, fearing treachery, announced it anyway at 1830. Badoglio, well aware that Hitler would never believe Italian denials, reluctantly followed suit. Then he and most of his senior army officers together with King Victor Emmanuel hurried to Pescara on the Adriatic coast to be carried behind the Allied lines in an Italian warship. The main Italian fleet sailed for Malta as ordered, losing its flagship, the battleship *Roma* to a Luftwaffe attack the next day, while some 300 Italian warplanes were flown to Allied aerodromes and surrendered.

Any hope that the Italians would actively assist the Allies was quickly dashed, however. When visited by Alexander at Reggio on 5 September, Montgomery declared: 'When the Germans found out what was going on, they would stamp on the Italians.' He was soon proved right. In Rome, Kesselring warned that unless the Italians handed over their weapons and defensive positions forthwith, their lovely city would be bombed without mercy, but promised that any troops who were disarmed would be allowed to return home. Von Vietinghoff followed his example and by the end of 10 September, the Germans were masters of central and southern Italy.

They were masters of northern Italy too, but here Rommel with stupid brutality wasted time and manpower capturing as many Italian soldiers as he could and sending them to Germany. Those who escaped retired to the hills, taking their weapons with them, later to become the basis of a savage resistance movement. The Germans also had to round up Italian soldiers in southern France, Russia, Greece, Albania and Yugoslavia and some of these handed over their arms to local guerrilla forces or became guerrillas themselves.

On 13 October, Italy officially declared war on Germany, but few of her soldiers or airmen showed much desire to fight for the Allies. On the other hand, the Allies would have 1.5 million fewer Axis soldiers to fight against, since only a few die-hard Fascist units were still prepared to support the once mighty Benito Mussolini.[3]

This was a direct though delayed consequence of the Allies' campaign in Sicily, not the one in Italy which quickly ran into trouble. The AVALANCHE landings came under heavy fire from coastal batteries; a situation made worse by Clark's having forbidden a preliminary bombardment in the hope of gaining surprise, thereby illuminating Montgomery's refusal to risk dispensing with one at BAYTOWN. Once ashore the attackers were fiercely engaged by von Vietinghoff's Tenth Army and for several days there seemed a real danger of their being driven into the sea. Fortunately, Alexander called for aid from every available aircraft and covering fire from every available warship and this risk was eventually averted.

On the evening of 10 September, Alexander asked Montgomery to push forward as soon as possible to threaten the Axis forces at Salerno. This was easier asked than achieved because, apart from the difficulties caused by the terrain and German demolitions, AVALANCHE had been given every priority over BAYTOWN in the provision of supplies. As a result, XIII Corps was short of petrol, ammunition and spare parts for motor vehicles which, if they broke down, had to be sent to Egypt for repair.

Despite these problems, on 11 September Montgomery captured the port of Crotone north-east of Catanzaro and, more importantly, airfields in its vicinity. To these, fighter-bombers from the Desert Air Force, as it was still called, were hastily transferred and from them, they joined in the heavy air attacks on von Vietinghoff's Tenth Army. Its War Diary also confirms the increasing anxiety it suffered from 'the slow but steady approach of the Eighth Army.' Montgomery's advanced troops reached the right flank of Fifth Army at 1400 on 16 September. That evening, von Vietinghoff recommended a withdrawal from the battle area; Kesselring agreed and the Germans fell back next day.

It would be incorrect to say that Eighth Army had saved the day at Salerno, and Montgomery never suggested that it had. In his *Memoirs*, in fact, he expressly states: 'I reckon General Clark had got it [the situation] well in hand before we arrived.' It must, however, be regretted that some critics have condemned the time it took Eighth Army to reach Salerno. It would seem they were ignorant of the physical nature of the Calabrian Peninsula. Those who were not have proved more generous. Clark congratulates Montgomery on 'the skilful and expeditious manner in which your Eighth Army moved up to the north.' De Guingand reports that Montgomery responded to Alexander's request 'wholeheartedly and with speed'.

On 16 September, Eighth Army also made contact with and subsequently took over British forces moving up from the 'heel' of Italy. On the 9th, the 'dismounted' 1st Airborne Division had captured the port of Taranto virtually intact. The Germans had accepted the loss of the 'heel', so 1st Airborne, though lacking tanks and artillery and short of petrol and transport vehicles, was able to take Brindisi on the 11th and Bari on the 14th. These ports proved of considerable value to Montgomery who now arranged to receive supplies through them; he also received reinforcements in the form of Lieutenant General Charles Alfrey's V Corps containing 78th (British) and 8th Indian divisions.[4]

Meanwhile, despite his supply problems, Montgomery pushed light forces forward and while Fifth US Army did not reach Naples until 1 October, Eighth Army troops occupied the crucial Foggia airfields, some 40 miles further north, on 27 September. On 1 October, Flying Fortresses of the United States Army Air Force took off from Foggia to strike at aircraft factories in Wiener Neustadt, Austria, previously out of range of such assaults.

Then on 4 October, Hitler intervened. He always hated giving up territory and had been much heartened by Kesselring's optimistic confidence and the fight that had been put up at Salerno. He commanded that Rome be held and promised reinforcements. Rommel would leave Italy for France and his former divisions become Germany's Fourteenth Army. This joined Tenth German Army in Army Group 'C' under Kesselring, formally appointed C-in-C, South West on 21 November. Hitler's decision ultimately benefited the Allies by diverting troops who would otherwise have faced the Russians or opposed OVERLORD, but in the short term it resulted in the Allied soldiers in Italy suffering months of hardship and frustration.

Kesselring accepted that southern Italy was lost, but he had always been reluctant to give up Rome without a fight. He ordered his engineers to construct a series of defences, known as the Gustav Line, running across the narrowest part of the Italian peninsula from the mouth of the River Garigliano in the west to the mouth of the River Sangro in the east. South of this, other delaying positions were constructed and the Germans took full advantage of Italian geography, particularly the central Apennine mountain range. All roads over it were systematically wrecked, committing the Allies to separate advances on its Mediterranean and Adriatic sides. Each of these in turn faced the natural barriers of a succession of swift rivers rushing from the mountains to the sea.

The first river to confront Montgomery was the Biferno. He responded on the night of 2/3 October with a neat pincer movement by 78th Division, now under XIII Corps' control, and a Commando landing at Termoli just north of the river's mouth. The port was captured intact and a brigade of 78th Division crossed the river next day. On the following night another brigade came ashore at Termoli, but Kesselring, though he had not expected these moves to come so quickly, personally ordered that the bridgehead over the Biferno be eliminated forthwith.

On 4 and 5 October therefore, enemy forces centred on 16th Panzer Division, previously held in reserve, and supported by Luftwaffe raids, did their best to oblige. They came close to succeeding, but the British held out until, during the night of 5/6 October, sappers completed a crossing for tanks over the river and 78th Division's third brigade landed at Termoli. On the 6th, the Germans fell back to the next river barrier, the Trigno. The British followed up quickly, but the bridge carrying the coastal road over the Trigno was blown up just in time to prevent its capture and Eighth Army's advance was temporarily halted.

At this time, Montgomery began to be increasingly hampered by the weather. Heavy and persistent rain made movement difficult even on roads. On the night of 22/23 October, 78th Division, now back under V Corps' control, secured a small bridgehead over the Trigno, but rain and mud foiled all attempts to expand it. So on the night of 29/30 October, XIII Corps – 5th (British) and 1st Canadian divisions – attacked in the foothills of the Apennines. It had to cope with bad weather, difficult terrain, demolitions and later the opposition of 26th Panzer Division, but it pushed on slowly yet steadily.

This move diverted attention from and tied down troops who might otherwise have opposed a major assault over the Trigno by V Corps on the night of 2/3 November. On the coast, 78th Division got over the river and for once the weather proved fine, allowing the Desert Air Force and bombardments from Allied warships to give support during two days of vicious fighting against 16th Panzer Division. On 78th Division's left flank, 8th Indian Division also crossed the Trigno, but was held up by fierce resistance from the German 1st Parachute Division.

On 4 November, 16th Panzer, after suffering heavy casualties, reluctantly withdrew and 78th Division followed up to reach the next river obstacle by the 8th. The less experienced 8th Indian Division joined them only on the 19th, when all the soldiers of V Corps could gaze across the ominously named Rio Sangro – River of Blood – at the fortifications of Kesselring's Gustav Line on the Li Colli Ridge just beyond its northern bank.

By this time, the Allied formations earmarked for OVERLORD, including 7th Armoured and 1st British and 82nd US Airborne divisions, were leaving Italy or preparing to do so, just as German reinforcements were starting to arrive. The rain became ever heavier, turning the ground into a sea of thick, clinging mud, and ever more cold as snow and sleet mingled with it, while biting winds swept down from the mountains. During December, 5 men from 78th Division froze to death and there were 113 cases of exposure.

Since Fifth US Army, despite immense efforts and high casualties, was advancing considerably less rapidly than Eighth Army,[5] any further immediate progress could only be made across the Sangro. Montgomery, as usual, had considered this problem already. As General Jackson tells us in *The Battle for Italy*: 'The Eighth Army staff had designed all its preliminary moves in the advance from Foggia northwards with this battle in mind.' The plans for it were all ready and again were scarcely those of a cautious methodical commander.

Montgomery, as before Tripoli and as in southern Tunisia, had in fact decided on a continuous series of forward moves. First the Sangro would be crossed and the Gustav Line breached. Then Eighth Army would advance to the next river, the Moro, cross this also and take the port of Pescara and the town of Chieti, some 10 miles inland to the south-west. Beyond Pescara spurs of the Apennines with rivers between them came

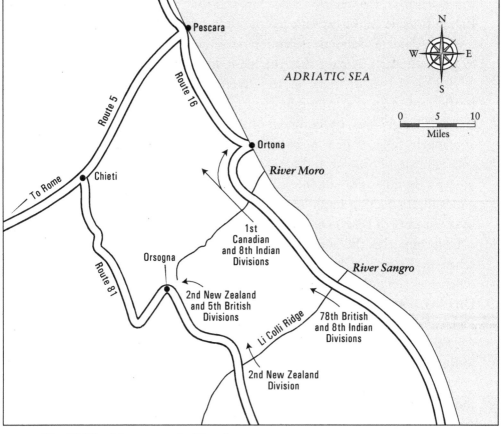

Map 13: The Advance over the River Sangro.

right down to the sea, making further progress north impossibly costly, but that did not matter. Both Pescara and Chieti were on Route 5, the main road over the Apennines, and this Eighth Army would follow to its destination on the Mediterranean coast: Rome.

To carry out the first move, V Corps' 78th (British) and 8th Indian divisions would attack along the coastal road, Route 16. They would be supported by 4th (British) Armoured Brigade, the appearance of which should take the enemy by surprise, for aerial reconnaissance had shown that the Germans had placed no anti-tank guns on the Li Colli Ridge, believing it would prove too steep for British armour. Meanwhile the veteran New Zealand Division had rejoined Eighth Army and, under direct army control, was ordered to advance along Route 81 to Chieti. In a further attempt to gain surprise, the New Zealanders' arrival was concealed from the Sangro's defenders and they assembled behind 19th Indian Brigade on the extreme left of 8th Indian Division's position.

As at Alamein, elaborate deception measures were adopted attempting to persuade the Germans that the main assault would be delivered by XIII Corps' two divisions in the Apennine foothills. False wireless traffic indicating that Montgomery's tactical HQ had been moved to the XIII Corps' area, concealment of ammunition dumps, gun positions and motor vehicles in the coastal zone and deliberately less effective concealment of similar military items – their numbers considerably increased by dummies – further inland were all employed. The Royal Navy joined in, conducting amphibious exercises and delivering bombardments in the vicinity of Pescara to suggest possible landings in this area.

Unfortunately, the atrocious weather effectively ruined all these schemes. Kesselring knew that major advances would be impossible other than along Routes 16 and 81. These he guarded with 1st Parachute Division, 65th Infantry Division and the admittedly rather battered 16th Panzer Division. He also ordered forward 26th Panzer Division from the Mediterranean coast and 90th Panzer Grenadier Division, a reincarnation of Rommel's famous '90th Light', from the north.

Montgomery was equally well aware that he was committed to using those two main roads. He has been condemned for doing so, but apart from calling off his offensive altogether, which might have appealed to an ultra-cautious commander but not to Montgomery, he had no choice in the matter. His preliminary moves went well. Bridgeheads over the Sangro were obtained by V Corps in the early hours of 20 November, and by 19th Indian Brigade acting as an advance guard for the New Zealanders on the night of the 22nd/23rd. Further dreadful weather, though, prevented either being expanded.

Then on 23 November, disaster threatened. It had rained heavily in the mountains and the Sangro rose suddenly and dramatically, sweeping away the three bridges the Royal Engineers had built over it. For the next four days, Eighth Army had no interest in further advances but was fully occupied in ferrying over as many men and weapons as possible to prevent their now perilous bridgeheads from being overrun.

Not until the 27th would the rain relent, but when it did, Eighth Army took full advantage of this. More infantrymen and about 100 tanks of 4th Armoured Brigade were moved over temporary bridges on this and the following day, while the Desert Air Force, flying some 450 sorties on both days, pounded the defenders. Late on the 28th, covered by massive artillery bombardments, both V Corps and 2nd New Zealand Division delivered major assaults. On the 29th, 4th Armoured Brigade's tanks followed by 78th Division's infantry climbed onto the Li Colli Ridge. By nightfall on the 30th, the whole section of the Gustav Line north of the Sangro was in British hands and the German 65th Division was retiring in confusion, having lost more than 1,000 men as prisoners.

Montgomery followed up and although some critics have said he should have done so faster, they forget that his soldiers as well as by now being very tired were faced with counter-attacks by the fresh, newly-arrived 26th Panzer and 90th Panzer Grenadier divisions. Even so, they had secured the south bank of the River Moro by 3 December and the New Zealanders pushed beyond it next day to enter Orsogna on the way to Chieti, only to be thrown out again by 26th Panzer. Montgomery's main concern, however, was to ensure he had a secure supply line over the treacherous Sangro. On 6 December, he got this when the tireless sappers completed a high-level flood-proof crossing called the 'Montgomery Bridge'.

Thereafter, Montgomery quickly adjusted his order of battle. In the coastal area, he transferred 1st Canadian Division to join 8th Indian in V Corps while an exhausted 78th Division retired to rest and refit. Further inland, the New Zealanders joined 5th (British) Division in XIII Corps. With his reorganization completed, Montgomery renewed his assault and on 8 December, Eighth Army crossed the Moro. Its immediate aims now were to recapture Orsogna and to gain the little port of Ortona on the way to Pescara.

Sadly the weather and the fresh German formations had other ideas. The New Zealanders made three full-scale divisional attacks on Orsogna, but 26th Panzer was unyielding and the attempts were finally abandoned in pouring rain on Christmas Day. The Canadians, resolutely opposed by 90th Panzer Grenadier, only reached Ortona late on 20 December and then had to engage in ferocious street-fighting with units of 1st Parachute Division garrisoning the town. It was not secured until the 28th. Neither on the coast nor inland had Eighth Army reached Route 5 leading to Rome, and Alexander, on Montgomery's advice, broke off the offensive.

This was Montgomery's last battle in Italy and, it is hesitantly suggested, his least successful of the Second World War. In the past, he had been thwarted at Enfidaville but had responded magnificently by releasing Horrocks and heavy Eighth Army reinforcements to capture Tunis. In the future, Operation MARKET GARDEN would fail to achieve his desired crossing of the Rhine, but would gain valuable territory from which he would launch a successful offensive in the Rhineland. The Sangro battle would never have beneficial consequences. There would be no advance on Rome from the Pescara area. Instead Eighth Army's part in the eventual capture of Rome would come only after and because it had been transferred from that area. Kesselring and his ally the weather had been too much to overcome.

It may be that Montgomery realized this. The Sangro battle is the only large one not mentioned in his *Memoirs* and these clearly show his unhappiness with the Italian campaign as a whole. Luckily, his fortunes were about to change dramatically. On 10 December, Eisenhower had been appointed OVERLORD's Supreme Commander and Montgomery now learned he was to command Twenty-First Army Group, OVERLORD's land forces. On 30 December, Leese arrived to take over Eighth Army and Montgomery made a formal farewell to its officers. He left Italy in his Dakota the next day.

This was also the end of the partnership between 'Alex' and 'Monty' that had seen the turn of the tide in the Second World War. Of late their relationship had become less happy. Montgomery had got used to Alexander obliging him and was not pleased when his superior was unable to do so for reasons of politics or inter-Allied solidarity, as when he allowed Patton to make for Palermo instead of Messina or rejected Montgomery's proposed conduct of the Italian campaign. In his frustration, Montgomery made a typically impulsive and unfair judgement: that Alexander lacked decision and 'did not understand the conduct of war'. He even told first Patton and later Clark that if they did not agree with Alexander's instructions, they should not hesitate to protest.

Montgomery's action was inexcusable and one would like to think that on reflection he was ashamed of himself. Certainly while his *Memoirs* are not lacking in criticism of others, there is none of Alexander who he emphasizes he liked and respected: 'I could not have served under a better Chief.' For his part, Alexander would understand and forgive his troublesome and inconsiderate lieutenant: 'I always like him best when I am with him.'

More importantly, Alexander never allowed Montgomery's faults to mask the latter's abilities. He was Montgomery's 'great supporter throughout'. This was perhaps especially the case when the post of C-in-C, Land Forces for OVERLORD was under consideration: Alexander recommended to Brooke that Montgomery be appointed.

Montgomery was delighted and reinvigorated by his new role. On his way home, he called at Marrakesh in Morocco where Churchill was recovering from a bout of pneumonia. The prime minister had his doubts and anxieties about OVERLORD and was 'gratified and relieved' to find Montgomery eager for the great task ahead of him. Bursting with suppressed energy, he insisted on walking up a hill to a famous viewpoint instead of accompanying the rest of the party in a car. 'He leaped about the rocks like an antelope,' relates the amused Churchill, 'and I felt a strong reassurance that all would be well.'

Notes

1. On 15 August 1945, Japan made an 'unconditional surrender' on the conditions laid down in the Potsdam Declaration previously issued by the United States, Britain and China – with Russia later concurring – and on the conditions subsequently agreed regarding the status of her emperor and Imperial system. This perhaps makes the final comment on the political and strategic folly of that idiotic slogan.
2. Intelligence reports had also indicated there were no German divisions covering the Salerno area. When the AVALANCHE troops landed, they were immediately opposed by 16th Panzer Division controlling some eighty Mark IV Special tanks, forty mobile guns and four battalions of infantry.
3. On 12 September Mussolini, then being held in a hotel in the Apennine Mountains, was rescued by a German force led by SS Captain Otto Skorzeny. He was flown to Germany where he was set up as head of a puppet North Italian Republic. He was, however, broken in body and spirit and Hitler, who genuinely liked him, was horrified to see the wreck he had become.
4. Alfrey and his V Corps had previously served in North Africa as part of Anderson's First British Army.
5. Not until January 1944 did Fifth US Army finally reach the Gustav Line defences.

Chapter Seven

'Neptune's General'

While at Marrakesh, Montgomery had been asked by Churchill to have his first look at the plan for Operation OVERLORD. Montgomery had bluntly stated that the command organization was bad, the proposed bridgehead too narrow and the whole plan 'impracticable'. Eisenhower had already expressed doubts so, since he had to return to the United States on 1 January for consultation, he instructed Montgomery to review every aspect of the plan as his representative.

On 2 January, Montgomery moved into the Headquarters of Twenty-First Army Group at St Paul's School, Kensington, of which he had once been a pupil. He at once began replacing the army group's existing staff. The previous day had seen the arrival of de Guingand, Williams and Major General Miles Graham, formerly senior administrative officer in Eighth Army, who Montgomery valued so highly that he cheerfully ignored a War Office refusal to allow Graham's transfer. Brigadier R.F.K. 'David' Belchem, Eighth Army's Head of Operations in Italy, was quickly added, while in March, Richardson, sporting the ribbon of the United States Legion of Merit, became Head of Plans.

It was not unreasonable for Montgomery to appoint officers with battle experience, which most of the existing staff lacked, but his abrupt, insensitive attitude inevitably aroused criticism, then and later. For instance, Field Marshal Viscount Slim in his *Defeat into Victory* sneers at 'travelling circuses' of staff officers 'grouped round particular generals' and prides himself that when he went to his Fourteenth Army he was 'without a following and took over the complete staff as I found it'. He then rather spoils the effect by saying that he promptly introduced 'some officers of my own choosing'.

In fact Montgomery had previously taken over the existing staff of Eighth Army and acknowledges the debt he owed to them far more than

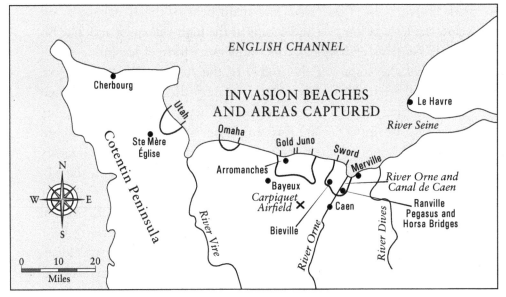

Map 14: The D-Day Landings.

Slim does. For their part, they were grateful to have a commander who, unlike Auchinleck with his dependence on his 'evil genius' Dorman-Smith, made proper use of their talents. Joined by a small, extremely able American team under Colonel Charles Bonesteel, they set about preparing for the greatest operation of the Second World War.

How difficult the operation was can be seen from the problems it would have to overcome. The German fixed defences on the coast of France, though given the dramatic title of the 'Atlantic Wall', had not been highly regarded by the Commander-in-Chief, West, Field Marshal Gerd von Rundstedt, who felt they stifled initiative and flexibility. However, on 31 December 1943, Hitler in effect supplanted him by appointing Rommel head of Army Group 'B', controlling the German Seventh Army south of the River Seine and Fifteenth Army north of it. Von Rundstedt remained C-in-C, but as he later complained without undue exaggeration: 'My only authority was to change the guards in front of my gate.'

Rommel did believe fixed coastal defences could prevent any invaders from getting ashore. He set to work with furious determination, strengthening existing positions, building new ones, adding anti-tank ditches, laying almost 6 million mines, placing anti-airborne obstacles in every suitable field within 7 miles of the sea and covering the beaches with obstructions. There were four main belts of these, starting at 6ft below the level of low tide and ending at the high-tide mark and, like his 'Devil's Gardens' at Alamein, containing every form of hazard.

Rommel also improved the calibre of the Atlantic Wall's defenders. Hitherto these had only been 'static' infantry divisions which, as their name indicates, lacked motor transport. They were of limited quality also, even containing 60,000 Russian prisoners who had chosen or been compelled to fight for the Germans. Rommel brought 'mobile' infantry divisions forward and had hoped to get panzer divisions. This, though, was not well received by von Rundstedt or General Freiherr Leo Geyr von Schweppenburg who commanded Panzer Group West; both of them wished to hold the tank formations in reserve ready to counter-attack.

There is no doubt that Rommel was very concerned by the losses inflicted on the ground by Flying Fortress assaults on the German aircraft industry and in the air by long-range P-51 fighters, newly given Merlin engines and the splendid name of Mustangs. He was convinced that the Luftwaffe could offer little resistance to the RAF's Second Tactical Air Force and the US Ninth Air Force, both of which were directed to support OVERLORD's ground forces by Eisenhower's Air C-in-C, Air Marshal Sir Trafford Leigh-Mallory. These would therefore, Rommel contended, be certain to cause heavy casualties and lengthy delays to armour moving up to the front.

There were, however, fatal flaws in Rommel's argument. Since he had an immense length of coast to defend, if his panzer divisions were to give close support, they would have to be widely dispersed. When the invasion took place, the majority of them were bound to be in the wrong place and would have to be hurried to the right one. While doing so they would be just as vulnerable to air attack as those coming forward from reserve. Also he could attack at full strength only after lengthy delays that would give the invaders time to secure their beachhead, or if he engaged immediately, he could do so only by committing his tanks piecemeal as they arrived.

These flaws were not overlooked by von Rundstedt or Geyr von Schweppenburg and Hitler, faced with his generals' conflicting views, decided on a compromise that made matters worse. He left three of the six available armoured divisions – 2nd, 21st and 116th Panzer – under Rommel but placed the other three – 1st SS, 12th SS and Panzer Lehr[1]

– in Panzer Group West. This, though, was to be under the direction of *Oberkommando der Wehrmacht* (OKW), the German Supreme Command. In practice, this meant the direction of Hitler who thus had the impossible task of controlling his armour from a great distance.

Of course it would not have mattered had the Allies been stopped on the Atlantic Wall as Rommel intended. The duty of preventing this had, on 1 April 1943, been given to Lieutenant General Frederick Morgan, a very experienced staff officer but one who had seen no combat since the fall of France. His title was 'Chief of Staff to the Supreme Allied Commander (Designate)', no supreme commander having yet been appointed. This he shortened to COSSAC and it became the name for his organization that prepared the initial invasion plan.

Since the COSSAC planners would be strongly criticized – not only by Montgomery – it is right to emphasize that they had laid down some basic rules that were gratefully accepted by everyone. They rejected landing in the Pas-de-Calais – it was too obvious – proposing instead Normandy where the beaches sloped more gently, were better sheltered from the elements and were likely to be less strongly defended. They were also responsible for the creation of the two famous 'Mulberry' artificial harbours and PLUTO, the 'Pipe Line Under The Ocean' that would supply the invaders with oil.

It was in the details of the invasion that the COSSAC planners could be faulted. They envisaged an initial assault force of just three divisions. It has been argued that this was imposed on them by a shortage of resources, particularly landing craft, but since their senior members fought hard against later proposals for an increase in strength, it appears that they disapproved of a larger assault force even if the necessary equipment was available.

Moreover their three divisions would come in on only two of the beaches later used: those code-named GOLD and JUNO. Subsequent reinforcements – British, American and Canadian – would all land on these same beaches. Since their area was comparatively limited, the probability of massive 'traffic jams' and administrative confusion was very high.

It was here that Montgomery's intervention was vital. The naval landings, as a crucial aspect of OVERLORD, had their own code-name: Operation NEPTUNE. So important were the changes made by Montgomery that Ronald Lewin hails him as 'NEPTUNE's General'.

Montgomery bluntly declared that 'it must be a five-division front or no show' and that front 'the widest possible'. He extended the NEPTUNE area westward as far as the River Vire at the base of the Cotentin (or Cherbourg) Peninsula: this added OMAHA beach to those of GOLD and JUNO. He decided to land on UTAH beach on the east of the peninsula, although this had been rejected by the COSSAC planners since it was separated from the main invasion force by ground the Germans had deliberately flooded. On the eastern flank of the NEPTUNE area he added SWORD beach, taking it up to the mouth of the River Orne.

Montgomery thus had five beaches for his seaborne landings. He decreed that each was to be the target for one of his five assault divisions and all reinforcements of men or matériel for any beach must be sent to that particular beach and in no circumstances land on another one. This, he rightly concluded, would reduce the chances of delay and confusion inherent in the COSSAC plan.

To execute his own invasion plan, Montgomery, as head of Twenty-First Army Group, had First US Army led by Bradley and Second (British) Army led by Dempsey, and his attitude towards them was very different. With Bradley, his role was one of supervision and suggestion. In an address to senior officers as early as 13 January, he declared that 'American doctrine' was their 'own affair'. In view of Montgomery's notorious lack of tact, it should be noted that Bradley would later record that he 'exercised his Allied authority with wisdom, forbearance and restraint' and that he (Bradley) 'could not have wanted a more tolerant or judicious commander'.

By contrast, in his address on 13 January, Montgomery stated flatly: 'The British and Canadians will do as I say.' He would direct Second Army's strategy and tactics, give advice on its formations and sometimes deal directly with Dempsey's subordinates. However, Peter Rostron, a former instructor at the Army Staff College, reports in his biography of Dempsey[2] that while never a figurehead and quite prepared to state his disagreement with any of Montgomery's ideas, Dempsey was very ready to accept this situation since he believed his chief was 'our finest military brain'. He was also grateful for the help Montgomery had given him when he had commanded a corps in Sicily and Italy.

August 1942. Top: Montgomery explains his plans to officers of 9th Australian Division. Note his own Australian slouch hat. Bottom: Lieutenant General Horrocks, appointed to lead XIII Corps at Montgomery's request, addresses his new command.

The Battle of Alam Halfa. Top: In July 1942, the American Grant tank had a more powerful gun and thicker protective armour than any German tank. Bottom: At Alam Halfa Rommel had the Panzer Mark IV Special, superior in all respects to the Grant and indeed the later American Sherman.

The Battle of Alam Halfa. Montgomery rejected previous plans for a fluid, mobile battle and repelled Rommel's attacks from fixed positions.

The Battle of El Alamein. Top: Montgomery relaxing with the crew of his command tank from whom he acquired his famous black beret. Middle: The Qattara Depression blocked any outflanking movement. Bottom: The preliminary artillery bombardment.

The Battle of El Alamein. Top: The British 6-pounder gun with which the Rifle Brigade on the 'Snipe' position knocked out fifty-seven Axis tanks or self-propelled guns. Bottom: Montgomery reflects on his successes and on the tasks still ahead of him.

The capture of Tripoli. Top: Just three months after the start of Montgomery's offensive, British soldiers stand in the main square of Libya's capital. Bottom: Churchill and Brooke join Montgomery in celebration.

The Mareth Line. Top left: The Wadi Zigzaou: inability to get equipment over this wrecked Montgomery's frontal assault. Top right: His flanking movement through the Tebaga Gap relied on air support, spearheaded by Hurricane 'tank busters'. Bottom: The end of the 'left hook': Horrocks enters El Hamma in his command tank.

Sicily and Italy. Top left: First Sicily: British troops go ashore. Top right: Allied successes caused the replacement of Mussolini by Marshal Pietro Badoglio. Bottom: Then Italy: Montgomery enters Reggio.

Italy. Top: Montgomery was most happy among his soldiers. Middle: Bad weather and the resulting mud bogged down the lightest vehicle. Bottom: 'Alex' and 'Monty'. A magnificent team in North Africa, but in Sicily and Italy their relationship was less happy.

D-Day. Top: The landing barges are loaded. In the foreground is a 'Firefly' – a Sherman tank with a 17-pounder gun – a conversion for which Montgomery was personally responsible. Bottom: The landing barges head for the beach.

Formidable foes. Top left: Field Marshal Rommel. Top right: Field Marshal von Rundstedt. Bottom left: Field Marshal Model. Bottom right: Field Marshal Kesselring.

The Battle of Normandy. Top: After more than a month of effort, a Canadian tank stands amid the ruins of Caen. Bottom: Despite all disappointments, Montgomery never failed to stimulate the determination of his troops.

The Battle of Normandy. Top: British armour advances. In the foreground is a 'Crab' flail-tank, one of the 'Funnies' of which Montgomery made good use. Bottom: The destruction inflicted by rocket-firing Typhoons in the Falaise pocket.

The Battle of Normandy. Top: Another great team: Bradley, Montgomery and Dempsey. Bottom: The fruits of victory: the citizens of Brussels celebrate the city's and their liberation.

MARKET GARDEN. Top left: General Student, Montgomery's chief opponent. Top right: The planning was entrusted to Lieutenant General Browning, seen here with Air Chief Marshal Tedder. Bottom: Men of Browning's I Airborne Corps move through Arnhem. They did not land 'a bridge too far' but not near enough to the bridge.

Final triumphs. Top: Montgomery's soldiers cross the Rhine in amphibious craft. Bottom: Montgomery, with Colonel Joe Ewart as interpreter, confronts General Admiral von Friedeburg and receives the surrender of North Germany, Holland and Denmark.

For the NEPTUNE landings, Montgomery gave control of those at UTAH and OMAHA to Bradley and those on the three eastern beaches to Dempsey. His army commanders would also have responsibility for airborne landings which Montgomery had decided to make on both flanks of the NEPTUNE area. These had originally been suggested by the COSSAC planners but only with airborne brigades, whereas Montgomery wanted full airborne divisions. He was particularly anxious to be strong on his eastern flank.

The provision of SWORD beach would bring Montgomery's troops closer to Caen, a vitally important road and rail centre, the strategic importance of which, already emphasized by the COSSAC planners, was fully appreciated by Montgomery. He had therefore wished to extend the NEPTUNE area further east, right up to the River Seine. This proposal, however, was firmly vetoed by Eisenhower's Naval C-in-C, Admiral Sir Bertram Ramsay.

There was good reason for Ramsay's attitude. A seaborne landing near the Seine would come under intense fire from powerful shore batteries in the vicinity of Le Havre. It would also, though Ramsay could not know this, have encountered units of 12th SS Panzer Division which von Rundstedt on his own initiative, contrary to Hitler's orders, had sent to this area. Yet Montgomery realized that if Allied forces could move only as far as the River Dives, some 5 miles east of the Orne, this would still give him a base from which he could more easily deliver pincer movements on Caen to bring about its early capture. He therefore intended that while 101st US Airborne Division supported UTAH, both 82nd US and 6th (British) Airborne Divisions would operate east of SWORD.

Having established the basic requirements of Operation NEPTUNE to his satisfaction, Montgomery turned his attention to aids for his seaborne invaders. He urged that naval support be as strong as possible and entirely approved a suggestion by the COSSAC planners that small vessels should provide close covering fire to the landing craft. In fact, he improved on this by ordering that those craft coming just behind the infantry with tanks or artillery pieces on board should be so loaded as to enable some of these to fire on the beaches as they approached them. By contrast, he totally rejected COSSAC's refusal to allow a preliminary air bombardment and insisted on 'heavy air bombing' both before and during the landings.

Next Montgomery looked at ways in which the hazards his men would have to face might be reduced. He decided that 'H-Hour', the moment when the initial wave would touch down on the beaches, would be between high and low tides, some three or four hours before high water. This should reduce the casualties caused by Rommel's underwater obstacles, but not give the soldiers too great a distance to cover across open ground. Since high tide would come at different times on different beaches, H-Hour would have to be 'staggered' from west to east with UTAH attacked first and the unlucky SWORD troops most likely to face an aroused and prepared enemy.

As his men would inevitably come under enemy fire while crossing the beaches, Montgomery looked for assistance from 79th Armoured Division. Since March 1942, under the command of Major General Sir Percy Hobart, who by a strange quirk of fate was Montgomery's brother-in-law, this unit had been preparing a number of unusual vehicles, collectively called 'Funnies', for just this purpose. Sadly and rather surprisingly, it seems that the Americans regarded the Funnies as illustrations of typical British caution and showed interest only in Hobart's DD (Duplex Drive) amphibious tanks, and even these they did not use properly.

Montgomery, though, as we have seen, was always ready to employ new weapons and was delighted with the Funnies. There were 'Crabs', minefield-clearing flail-tanks which were a great improvement on the 'Scorpions' used at Alamein; 'Crocodiles', tanks equipped with a hideously effective flame-thrower; armoured bulldozers; AVREs – the initials stood for Armoured Vehicle Royal Engineers – incredibly versatile machines that could carry men, guns or equipment for filling ditches, crossing tank-traps or scaling sea-walls as required; and of course DD tanks, which in a moment of inspiration Montgomery decreed should touch down with the first wave of infantry.

Another activity that met with American indifference but gained Montgomery's steadfast support was Operation FORTITUDE. Conducted by Colonel John Bevan, an Intelligence officer and by an odd coincidence a brother-in-law of Alexander, this was an attempt to convince the Germans that the assault would be delivered in the Pas-de-Calais. As Montgomery had done before Alamein and before the River Sangro, Bevan relied on false wireless traffic and dummy tanks, vehicles, ammunition dumps, headquarters etc., but he also used deliberate indiscretions in diplomatic circles, inaccurate reports by 'double agents' and carefully staged air attacks.[3]

So successful was FORTITUDE that even after the full strength of the Normandy landings had been revealed, the Germans still believed this was only a preliminary invasion and a larger one would come later. Accordingly, their Fifteenth Army remained north of the Seine on guard against an attack that never came, while south of the Seine their Seventh Army was slowly bleeding to death.

The success of FORTITUDE, however, would only become apparent after the Normandy landings had taken place and in the days leading up to these Eisenhower, Montgomery and their subordinates had plenty of reasons for concern. Chief of these was the refusal of US Fleet Admiral Ernest King to release more landing craft to join the 2,500 already allocated for OVERLORD, though he had kept more than 28,500 for use in the Pacific. Montgomery and Ramsay therefore persuaded Eisenhower to postpone Operation ANVIL, a landing in the south of France intended to coincide with that in Normandy, and commandeer its landing craft. They also got the benefit of an additional month's production of these by delaying the launching of OVERLORD from May to June.

Unfortunately on 2 May, Hitler's intuition warned him that the Allies might land in Normandy. He demanded an immediate improvement of its defences. Rommel obliged and among other actions sent 21st Panzer Division from north of the Seine to Caen, 91st Infantry Division to the Cotentin Peninsula and the very experienced 352nd Infantry Division to OMAHA beach.

Reports of these developments naturally alarmed Bradley, who urged that 82nd US Airborne Division be transferred from the Caen area to join 101st Airborne in the Cotentin. This would much reduce Montgomery's chances of an early capture of Caen, but as usual he was prepared to lose a tactical advantage for the sake of a strategic gain and in this case inter-Allied unity. He accepted Bradley's request and when Leigh-Mallory warned that casualties in the Cotentin would be prohibitively high, replied that if so he and not Bradley would 'assume full responsibility'.

It was a great pity that Montgomery did not show such a generous spirit more often, for his dictatorial manner infuriated many people and though the majority swallowed their resentment out of respect for his dynamic leadership, two did not. Lieutenant General Morgan never forgave the arrogant contempt with which he had dismissed many of COSSAC's plans. Despite his title, Morgan did not become chief of staff to Eisenhower who retained Bedell Smith, but as deputy chief of staff (British) he never ceased to criticize Montgomery and blame every setback on Montgomery's changes to his ideas.

Montgomery also made clear his disapproval of Eisenhower's close relationship with Lieutenant Kay Summersby, an attractive Irish divorcée, who was his car-driver, constant companion and possibly – although this is disputed – his mistress. In particular, Montgomery deplored Eisenhower's sharing of important military secrets with her. She responded with venomous hatred, repeatedly telling Eisenhower that Montgomery should be 'put in his place' and calling him a 'woman-hating little martinet'.

It was scarcely a balanced judgement. No one who has read Montgomery's heart-broken – and heart-breaking – account of the tragic early death of his beloved wife Betty can ever believe that he was a woman-hater. No one who considers Montgomery's unconventional attire or learns that he did not rebuke Australian and New Zealand troops who waved to rather than saluted him as Slim among others demands but instead waved back, can ever believe he was a martinet. Not that Kay Summersby was interested in balanced judgements and unfortunately she had the ear of the supreme commander and into it she steadily dripped her poison.

Unaware of the problems he was creating for himself and somehow unwearied by the demands of preparing the NEPTUNE plans, Montgomery also set about instilling confidence in the minds of his fighting men. By mid-May, he had talked to more than a million soldiers as well as the civilians who would support them, especially factory workers producing their weapons and equipment. Eisenhower and Bradley tried to follow his example, but generously accepted that they were not nearly so successful.

Probably Montgomery was least successful with 7th Armoured and 50th and 51st Infantry divisions that had fought for him previously. They were physically and mentally exhausted, badly needed a long rest that Britain's acute shortage of manpower made impossible, and were inclined to consider it was time that others bore the brunt of the fighting. He did, however, undeniably stimulate the highly-trained but inexperienced divisions that had not left the United Kingdom: Alan Moorehead, the

Australian war correspondent, declares in his *Eclipse* that the effect he had was 'magic'. He also won over the Americans, not least because they were astonished that so senior an officer had bothered to talk to them, and Bedell Smith heartily congratulated him on the confidence he had inspired.

Montgomery's last duty as 'NEPTUNE's General' came in early June. In order to obtain the best conditions for the landings, they had to be made on the 5th, 6th or 7th or be put off for another month. On 4 June, with a furious storm raging, the senior Allied commanders held anxious meetings to decide on their course of action. At one of these early that morning, Montgomery resolutely declared that he was in favour of defying the weather and proceeding on the 5th as planned.

This was not a cautious attitude, but not a wise one either. The weather would have played havoc with the landings and dramatically reduced the essential aerial support. It was probably fortunate therefore that Ramsay, Leigh-Mallory and Tedder, who had been appointed Eisenhower's deputy, all disagreed and the supreme commander rightly decided to postpone the operation for twenty-four hours.

At a further conference that evening, however, the Chief Meteorological Officer, Group Captain Stagg, reported the likelihood of an unexpected break in the bad weather on the 6th. Ramsay and Bedell Smith now felt that the gamble should be taken, but others were understandably hesitant and had Montgomery as Land Forces Commander been unwilling, there seems little doubt that the invasion would have been postponed until July. Yet when Eisenhower asked him if he saw any reason for not invading on the 6th, Montgomery instantly replied: 'I would say – Go!' Tuesday, 6 June 1944 would be known ever after as 'D-Day'.

Now all the decisions taken and plans prepared by Montgomery, Ramsay, Leigh-Mallory and their staffs would be put to the test against Normandy's immensely strong fixed defences. Their hard work was deservedly rewarded by one stroke of good fortune. The Germans knew that invasion was imminent, but the bad weather had convinced them that it would not be coming just yet. Among those in error was Rommel who, as at Alamein, was absent from his post at the crucial moment, visiting his wife in Germany.

The bad weather, though, had not discouraged Leigh-Mallory's airmen and Allied aircraft, painted in huge black and white stripes for identification purposes, were there in swarms. The preparatory bombardment by heavy bombers stunned many of the defenders and 'kept their heads down' at the crucial moments when the invaders were disembarking. Fighters, chiefly Spitfires and Mustangs, provided protection, while Typhoons, destined to prove the most valuable aircraft in the Normandy fighting, swept down to launch their rockets at strongpoints on the beaches or known targets inland.

Among the modern warplanes, a squadron of now elderly Hawker Hurricanes fitted with long-range tanks circled monotonously overhead. It was there to spot fall of shot for the Allied warships directly and most effectively supporting the land forces. At GOLD beach, for instance, HM light cruiser *Ajax* of River Plate fame knocked out a battery of four 6in guns by putting two of her own 6in shells through the narrow embrasure from which the Germans fired.

Nor did the bad weather deter the airborne forces, British members of which were the first Allied soldiers to reach Normandy when D-Day was only some twenty minutes old. These were sixty pathfinders who parachuted from ten RAF Albemarles to mark the dropping- or landing-grounds for the main body of Major General Richard Gale's 6th Airborne Division. This had the task of extending the eastern flank of the bridgehead to and beyond the River Orne and at 0045, 180 more of its men arrived in 6 Horsa gliders towed behind Halifax bombers. A few were sappers but most came from '2 Ox & Bucks' – more formally 2nd Battalion Oxfordshire and Buckinghamshire Light Infantry – commanded by Major John Howard.

Much to the credit of the men of the Glider Pilot Regiment, five of the six Horsas came down almost on top of their objectives: a pair of bridges that carried the only road in the area over the Orne near the village of Ranville and over the Canal de Caen that ran parallel to the river half a mile to the west. Only ten minutes later, both had been secured at minimal cost to be renamed respectively 'Horsa Bridge' after the gliders and 'Pegasus Bridge' after the mythical winged horse that was the emblem of Britain's airborne warriors.

Rough weather did impede the rest of 6th Airborne's men who were dispersed over a wide area. Nonetheless a group from 9th Parachute Battalion under Colonel Terence Otway, at the cost of sixty-seven dead and some thirty badly wounded, captured a strongly fortified battery at

Merville near the coast and destroyed its four heavy guns which could have delivered a devastating fire onto SWORD beach.[4] Other units secured good defensive positions and sappers provided further protection by wrecking four bridges over the Dives and one over a tributary. When daylight came, Gale had set up his headquarters at Ranville and been joined by his staff, an Australian war correspondent named Chester Wilmot and a handsome chestnut horse that he intended to ride later.

At 0130, the two American airborne divisions began their assault on the Cotentin Peninsula. High winds again scattered the parachutists, but they captured an important road junction at Ste Mère Église, attacked any enemies they encountered and distracted attention from the landing on UTAH beach.

This was the target of VII US Corps led by Lieutenant General Collins, a veteran of the Guadalcanal campaign nicknamed 'Fighting Joe', who incidentally was much admired by Montgomery. The sea proved less fierce, the tide less high and the fixed fortifications and their garrisons less strong than on any other beach. The landing was also greatly assisted by DD tanks, twenty-eight out of thirty-two of which 'swam' ashore safely at the same time as the infantrymen. By nightfall, the beachhead was sizeable and secure.

All the other four landing-beaches were cursed by high winds that blew waves 4ft high over them a good half-hour earlier than normal. This effectively frustrated Montgomery's intention to land before high tide and so avoid Rommel's underwater obstacles. These caused heavy losses of landing craft, the wrecks of which provided further obstructions to formations arriving later. On the three beaches that were the responsibility of Dempsey's Second Army, however, once the troops were ashore, they received immense assistance from the Funnies of 79th Armoured Division.

Unfortunately, on OMAHA beach, the target of Lieutenant General Leonard Gerow's V US Corps, the Americans had rejected Hobart's specialized armour apart from the DD tanks, and they were launched either not at all or 4 miles offshore, as a result of which all except two sank. Thus deprived of support, the soldiers were pinned down all morning and only in the afternoon, when their enemies had been shelled by destroyers from close range, did they respond to the indomitable example of 1st US Division's commander, Colonel George Taylor, who proclaimed: 'Two kinds of people are staying on this beach, the dead and those who are going to die. Now let's get the hell out of here.'

By nightfall the Americans had gained a foothold, but this was everywhere less than 2 miles deep and they were still without tanks and short of supplies, equipment and ammunition. It was a small return for the horrors they had endured. Contrary to general belief, the First US Army had committed fewer soldiers on D-Day than the Second (British) Army, yet it had suffered many more casualties.[5] The slaughter the Germans inflicted on OMAHA demonstrates clearly what would have happened had the assault forces been less powerful, less well-prepared or less well-supported than Montgomery had ensured they should be.

On the eastern part of the NEPTUNE area, Dempsey's Second (British) Army had committed I and XXX Corps. The latter, led by Lieutenant General Gerald Bucknall, who had commanded a division in Sicily and Italy, went ashore on GOLD beach. The infantrymen of its 50th Division were preceded by some of 79th Division's Funnies and although the fierce seas prevented the DD tanks from being launched, they were brought right up to the beach before being unloaded to provide close support. Thus assisted, by nightfall 50th Division had secured the beach, captured the port of Arromanches, the planned location for a Mulberry harbour, and moved up to the road from Caen to Bayeux.

In the course of this action, Company Sergeant Major Stanley Hollis of 6th Green Howards charged a pillbox and killed its defenders with sub-machine-gun fire and a hand-grenade. He then raced towards another pillbox, but the garrison wisely preferred not to resist and he took twenty-five prisoners. He was awarded the first Victoria Cross of the OVERLORD campaign.

Both JUNO and SWORD beaches were the responsibility of I Corps under Lieutenant General John Crocker who had commanded a corps in First (British) Army in Tunisia. He had not previously served under Montgomery, but would soon win Montgomery's unqualified admiration. He entrusted JUNO to 3rd Canadian Division and though this time the Funnies were delayed by high seas, they did follow the footsoldiers closely, while ten DD tanks of 1st Canadian Hussars 'swam' ashore to land with them. The Canadians responded with the longest Allied advance on D-Day. By nightfall they had joined up with troops from XXX Corps, had come close to Carpiquet airfield west of Caen, and were only some 3 miles north-west of Caen itself.

SWORD beach was left to 3rd (British) Division, accompanied by the Commandos of 1st Special Service Brigade under Brigadier Lord Lovat. Their assault was preceded by an especially heavy aerial bombardment and accompanied by an equally heavy naval one from battleships *Warspite* and *Ramillies* and monitor *Roberts*; the 16in guns that all these carried inflicted massive damage, including the elimination of three major shore batteries. The attackers were preceded by twenty of the twenty-four DD tanks of 13th/18th Hussars and accompanied by the usual Funnies. Thus supported, they overran the beach with reasonably slight casualties and effectively shattered the defending German 716th Infantry Division.

Thereafter the Commandos effectively broke through to reinforce Gale's 6th Airborne Division, but 3rd (British) Division was unable to fulfil its aim of taking Caen. For this, naturally certain critics blame Montgomery, accusing him of underestimating the difficulties and consequently not providing the SWORD forces with sufficient strength.

It is difficult to support this contention. It was Montgomery who had provided the particularly heavy air and naval support already discussed. It was Montgomery who had added to 3rd Division's three infantry brigades, the tanks of 27th Armoured Brigade and the self-propelled guns of 7th Field Regiment, Royal Artillery. Moreover in any case the problem with SWORD was not the troops allocated to it, but its own geography. Though rarely shown on maps of the invasion, outcrops of rock imposed a 5-mile gap between SWORD and JUNO and limited the width of the former to just 3 miles.

As a result, 3rd Division's brigades had to land in turn, one after the other, causing a steadily growing 'traffic jam'. This prevented one infantry brigade and most of 27th Armoured's tanks from getting ashore at all until mid-afternoon and delayed all forward movement until the Germans had had every chance to recover their balance. Giving SWORD increased numbers of troops would not have solved this problem and indeed would presumably have increased the delays and confusion.

In these circumstances, it was certainly optimistic of Montgomery to set Caen – and incidentally Bayeux and the Carpiquet airfield – as D-Day objectives. Yet de Guingand, Dempsey and Crocker all warned that taking Caen would not be easy, but all still approved of Montgomery setting objectives well inland, hoping that this would prevent any relaxation of effort once the beaches had been gained. Sadly, as its officers would honestly admit, 3rd Division would not fulfil this hope and its forward progress lacked determination and urgency. At about 1600, its advanced troops reached the village of Biéville some 3 miles from Caen, only to be halted by counter-attacks from German armour.

There were in fact two panzer formations within striking distance of the beaches, but 12th SS Panzer Division, stationed south-east of Caen, was in the reserve and could not be moved forward without Hitler's consent. Von Rundstedt, alarmed by the airborne operations, requested this as early as 0400, but no one dared to disturb Hitler who had taken a strong sleeping draught and retired to bed. He finally approved von Rundstedt's request in the early afternoon, but by then it was far too late. Only at midnight did 12th SS Panzer reach the Caen area, only to find that Allied fighter-bombers had destroyed the petrol dump from which it was supposed to refuel.

That left 21st Panzer Division which, being in Rommel's Army Group 'B', did not need Hitler's permission. However, as we saw, Rommel was in Germany, his staff hesitated to act in his absence and the Divisional Commander, Major General Edgar Feuchtinger, at first directed his attention to 6th Airborne Division. Not until 1030 was 21st Panzer ordered to oppose 3rd (British) Division which had now been recognized as a far more dangerous threat.

Feuchtinger attempted to comply, but his quickest route to the combat zone lay through Caen and his movements were seen and reported. Montgomery therefore ordered a heavy bombing raid on the city. This has been criticized on the grounds that it would have made Caen easier to defend had 3rd Division reached it. Montgomery, though, was again willing to lose a tactical advantage for the sake of a strategic benefit: he was prepared to risk being unable to take Caen quickly but not to risk any chance of the panzers driving his soldiers into the sea.

His action proved justified. Heavy casualties were inflicted on two of 21st Panzer's mobile infantry battalions and on its flak battalion – and sadly but inevitably on French civilians – and its armour was so hampered and disorganized that it did not get clear of Caen until 1500 or begin to counter-attack 3rd Division for another hour. At the same time, however, Feuchtinger made a much more dangerous move, sending an advance guard of both tanks and infantrymen under the magnificently-named Colonel Hermann von Oppeln-Bronikowski into the weakest link in the British line, the gap between the SWORD and JUNO forces. It reached the coast at about 2000.

For a moment the situation appeared serious, but luckily Montgomery's aerial assault reinforced by continual strikes from rocket-firing Typhoons had shaken 21st Panzer. At about 2100, a formation of 250 aircraft towing gliders appeared. This was, in reality, carrying light tanks and artillery pieces to reinforce 6th Airborne Division – which it did successfully – but the Germans concluded that it was intended to cut off the advance group. This therefore fell back in haste to its main body and 21st Panzer, which during the day had lost fifty-seven tanks to Typhoons or anti-tank guns, made no further forward move.

Thus when on 7 June, Montgomery crossed the Channel on HM destroyer *Faulknor* to confer with Dempsey and Bradley, he could be satisfied that if his men had not made all the gains he had hoped and had suffered distressingly high casualties on OMAHA, there was little danger of their being unable to hold their bridgehead. Operation NEPTUNE had succeeded.

'NEPTUNE's General' could be – and since he was Montgomery no doubt was – very proud of the part he had played in achieving this. In the weeks before D-Day right up to the moment of the final decision to invade, he had been the only leading figure, civil or military, who, free from all doubts and hesitations, had remained steadfast in his conviction that all would be well. His exalted if sometimes exasperating assurance had given his soldiers confidence in themselves and everyone else confidence in the soldiers.

This was a remarkable achievement and as Ronald Lewin relates in *Montgomery as Military Commander*, one that could have been accomplished by no one else except Churchill, 'certainly not Brooke, certainly not Slim, certainly not Paget, and certainly, for all his skills, not Mountbatten'. With great respect to Lewin, certainly not even Churchill at this particular time for, haunted by nightmare visions of the English Channel awash with bodies, the prime minister had lost most of his usual fire.

Still more commendable was the way in which Montgomery had justified the confidence he had created by his military skill. In view of the quarrels and misunderstandings that would arise in the future, it is particularly pleasant to note that this was perhaps most appreciated by the Americans. Bradley would declare that Montgomery's 'incomparable talent for the "set" battle – the meticulously planned offensive – made him invaluable in the OVERLORD assault'. 'I don't know if we could have done it without Monty,' reflected Bedell Smith. 'It was his sort of battle. Whatever they say about him, he got us there.'

Notes

1. *Lehr* means 'Training' and Panzer Lehr had been given its name because it was originally formed from demonstration units at training schools. By 1944 it was probably the most powerful of the German armoured divisions.
2. Its full title is *The Military Life & Times of General Sir Miles Dempsey GBE KCB DSO MC: Monty's Army Commander.*
3. Full details may be found in *The Intelligence and Deception of the D-Day Landings* by Jock Haswell.
4. The Germans had intended to install 150mm-calibre guns at Merville but had not yet done so. On D-Day, the guns destroyed were 'only' 75mm weapons.
5. The figures are disputed and probably impossible to determine exactly. In round numbers, 75,200 British and Canadian soldiers invaded from the sea, plus 7,900 from the air. Of these, 4,300 were killed, wounded or reported missing. The Americans sent in 57,500 by sea plus 15,500 by air. Their total casualties were about 6,000, almost half of these suffered on OMAHA beach.

Chapter Eight

The Battle of Normandy:
Trials and Tribulations

The Battle of Normandy began on D+1 (7 June), but it had been planned well in advance by Montgomery. He had revealed his basic intentions as early as 21 January and on 7 April in a presentation to Churchill, Brooke, Eisenhower, Ramsay, Leigh-Mallory, Bradley, Dempsey and the Allied corps commanders, he set these out in detail.

Montgomery correctly assessed Rommel as a determined but impulsive character who would 'hurl his armour into the battle' as soon as possible. Intelligence reports had revealed that the three German armoured divisions in Normandy – 21st Panzer, 12th SS Panzer and Panzer Lehr – were all south-east of Caen, with the next nearest north of the Seine. Their first assault therefore must fall on the east of the Allied bridgehead. Montgomery accordingly intended that, having captured Caen, Carpiquet aerodrome and perhaps other airfields south of Caen, Dempsey's Second (British) Army, joined on 23 July by Lieutenant General Henry Crerar's First Canadian Army, should stand on the defensive and prevent the panzers from interfering with Allied operations elsewhere.

These would be carried out by Bradley's First US Army, which would capture Cherbourg, then turn south to take the crucial road centre at St Lô and then the port of Avranches at the base of the Brittany Peninsula. Patton's Third US Army would then be introduced to capture the Brittany ports and thereafter guard the flank of First US Army on the River Loire while this raced north-east for Paris.

This division of labour was another example of Montgomery's trait of using formations in roles that best suited them. The British were noted for their stubbornness in defence, whereas the Americans had not only limitless equipment but an instinctive ability to use this in swift movements over long distances.

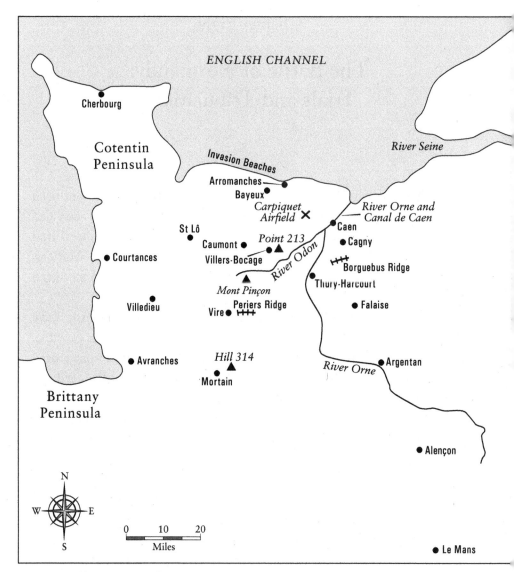

Map 15: The Normandy Battleground.

Montgomery illustrated his presentation with a Phase Line Map showing estimated developments until D+90 when he anticipated the Allies would have reached the Seine. Bradley, de Guingand and Richardson all thought this undesirable and Montgomery was unwise to have ignored their opinions since, inevitably perhaps, the lines he intended as a general guide were regarded by many as exact guarantees of progress. Yet it should be noted that even the Phase Line Map showed that after its initial gains, Second Army was to advance no further for nearly three weeks and only some 10 miles eastward for a further fortnight.

Montgomery reaffirmed his basic scenario in a Final Presentation of Plans on 15 May, in repeated messages to Brooke and Eisenhower, and in conferences on 22 and 30 June and 10, 21 and 30 July. That it was clearly understood by de Guingand and Bradley is made plain in their memoirs, *Operation Victory* and *A Soldier's Story* respectively. Indeed it seems extraordinary that it could ever have been misunderstood, although it would be, both then and later.

At first, Montgomery's hopes were mainly fulfilled. Even on D-Day, 3rd Infantry and 6th Airborne divisions had protected the Americans from 21st Panzer. On D+1, 12th SS Panzer entered the fight but was forced onto the defensive by 3rd Canadian Division. Panzer Lehr was attacked by Typhoons on its way to the front, losing five tanks and numerous other vehicles; it was then engaged by 50th Division which had previously taken Bayeux, the first French town to be liberated and one of the few to escape serious damage in the process.

Although the panzers checked Allied advances, they were quite unable to prevent Allied consolidation of the bridgehead. In the east, the SWORD and JUNO forces linked up. The situation of 6th Airborne Division remained perilous for a time, but an assault on the evening of 12 June, though at heavy cost, captured a crucial ridge and it was never endangered again.

In the west, the troops on GOLD and OMAHA made contact on 8 June and on the 12th the Americans, recovering with remarkable resilience from the horrors of D-Day, linked up with the UTAH forces and began a steady but relentless advance on Cherbourg, which was reached on the 27th. On the 12th also, they advanced 20 miles southward to capture the little town of Caumont. On learning this was threatened, General Erich Marcks, commander of LXXXIV Corps – the Seventh Army's infantry formations – went forward to stiffen the defences. His car was strafed by American fighter-bombers and Marcks, who had lost an eye in the First World War and a leg on the Russian front in the Second, was unable to get out in time and was killed.

Marcks was not the only important officer lost by the Germans at this time. Also on the 12th, Major General Fritz Witt, CO of 12th SS Panzer, was killed by naval shellfire. Previously on the 10th, the Headquarters of

Panzer Group West, its location 12 miles south of Caen betrayed by Ultra intercepts, was hit by sixty-one Mitchell bombers and forty rocket-firing Typhoons. Geyr von Schweppenburg retired to hospital in Paris and no fewer than eighteen senior staff officers died.

Montgomery, meanwhile, had gone ashore on 8 June to set up his Tactical Headquarters in the grounds of a château east of Bayeux. He had with him a small, hand-picked group of brilliant young liaison officers that he used to obtain first-hand news from all parts of the battlefield. His presence so near the front line sharing at least some of his soldiers' dangers strengthened his bond with them and provided a great boost to morale.

Only one important flaw marred Montgomery's initial success. Caen had not been taken and a direct assault on it would clearly prove costly. Montgomery, though, was not dismayed; on the contrary, he thought he saw an opportunity to take Caen and also destroy the panzer divisions in its vicinity. This, as he wrote to de Guingand on 9 June, would 'checkmate the enemy completely'.

To effect this, Montgomery intended to use his veteran 7th Armoured and 51st Highland divisions that had now arrived in Normandy. The former was to strike south, taking important high ground at Villers-Bocage and outflanking Caen from the west; the Highlanders to thrust at Caen from the bridgehead east of the Orne; the 1st (British) Airborne Division to be dropped south of Caen, completing its encirclement. Sadly Montgomery was over-optimistic. Leigh-Mallory refused to allow the airborne drop, fearing it would suffer heavy casualties, and neither of the pincers made real progress. That by 51st Highland was abandoned on 13 June, but Montgomery decided to take advantage of the Americans' southward advance by sending 7th Armoured in the direction of Caumont, then swinging it eastward to Villers-Bocage.

On 13 June, 7th Armoured Division entered Villers-Bocage and its leading tank squadron, accompanied by the half-tracks of its supporting infantry, pushed on, halting near a rise of ground called Point 213. Suddenly, down this roared a single Tiger tank commanded, it was later learned, by Captain Michael Wittmann of 501st SS Heavy Tank Battalion who had won an enviable reputation on the Russian front.[1] This raced along the halted column pouring 88mm shells and machine-gun fire into it and continued on to Villers-Bocage where it caused further havoc.

Wittmann then retired to join up with four other Tigers and completed the slaughter at Point 213. That evening, 7th Armoured withdrew from Villers-Bocage, having lost twenty-five tanks and twenty-eight other armoured vehicles.

This shameful setback had all manner of unhappy consequences. Tedder and Air Marshal Sir Arthur Coningham, head of the Allied Second Tactical Air Force, were worried by Second Army's failure to capture Caen and the airfields beyond it. Yet British and American construction wings would eventually create thirty-one and fifty airfields respectively in the Allied bridgehead. These were certainly jammed close together, but neither Broadhurst whose 83 Group worked directly with Second Army nor his US counterpart Major General Elwood 'Pete' Quesada ever expressed concern about their cramped conditions.

Unfortunately, Tedder and Coningham were personally hostile towards Montgomery. Tedder had never forgiven him for having opposed his (Tedder's) strategy in North Africa and Sicily and worse still having been proved right to do so. Coningham was frankly jealous. Chester Wilmot in *The Struggle for Europe* describes an outburst by Coningham to a group of war correspondents: 'It's always "Monty's Army", "Monty's Victory", "Monty Strikes Again". You never say "Coningham's Air Force".'

So on 14 June, Tedder and Coningham claimed that a 'dangerous crisis' had arisen. Richardson, who Montgomery had sent to Allied Air Forces HQ as his liaison officer, maintained that the overall situation was satisfactory, but an alarmed Leigh-Mallory flew to Normandy to check this. Montgomery reassured him and next day he announced that Richardson had given 'a truer picture' of the position and talk of a crisis was unfounded. Richardson was suitably gratified, but Tedder and Coningham continued to complain.

Admittedly the failure at Villers-Bocage had indeed ended any chance of an early capture of Caen. Montgomery, though, saw that this would not be fatal as long as the Germans continued to direct their armour against Dempsey and allowed the Americans to conduct the lengthy manoeuvres with which he had entrusted them. He must have been greatly encouraged to learn that strong reinforcements, including 2nd Panzer Division summoned by Rommel from north of the Seine, were in fact attacking Dempsey. It has been argued that this was just good luck and reflects no credit on Montgomery, but surely he deserves some for having correctly anticipated the results of Rommel's eager impulsiveness.

Montgomery was not unaware that the failure to take Caen had made Dempsey's task harder. It deprived him of a strong protective shield, the use of a valuable road and rail centre and all the advantages of fighting on the defensive. As late as 7 July, Montgomery would tell Brooke that 'we cannot be 100 per cent happy on the eastern front until we have got Caen.'

It was therefore singularly stupid of Montgomery to insist in later years and repeat in his *Memoirs* that everything had gone exactly according to plan. By doing so, he has deprived himself of credit for once again having displayed quick-thinking flexibility under pressure and of sympathy for that pressure having been increased by a factor outside his influence: the weather.

On 19 June 1944 – D+13 appropriately enough – with the minimum of warning, the worst June storm for forty years descended on Normandy. For three days, strong winds from the north-east hurled a succession of waves 6 to 8ft high against the Allied landing beaches, smashing everything in their path. The Mulberry harbour off OMAHA was almost completely destroyed and what was left had to be used to help complete the one off Arromanches; this was done by early July. More vessels were sunk by the storm than by enemy action throughout the whole campaign. Some 800 were blown ashore, although about 600 of these were later repaired and refloated. The Allied build-up of reinforcements – men and matériel – was also wrecked. Dempsey alone received three fewer divisions than anticipated and 140,000 tons of stores and 20,000 vehicles failed to arrive.

Worse still, the storm grounded the Allied airmen. Able at last to move in daylight without fear of attack from the sky, the Germans rushed in reinforcements. From Belgium came 1st SS Panzer Division; from the south of France came 2nd SS Panzer; from the Russian front 9th and 10th SS Panzer were on their way. These SS formations were larger and better equipped than the regular German army divisions and were manned by the pick of the Hitler Youth, veterans of the Russian campaigns, brave, ruthless, callous, fanatically loyal and ready to fight to the death for their Führer.

Their moves were faithfully reported by Ultra, as was the alarming news that Hitler intended to use them against the Americans. This would have wrecked Montgomery's plan. The only way to prevent it was by resuming the offensive on his eastern front, compelling the Germans to devote all their efforts to holding back Dempsey, but it would be an offensive every aspect of which would favour the defenders.

For a start, the British and Canadians and indeed the Americans further to the west had to fight through the 'bocage' country. This lay between Caen and the River Vire, stretching southwards endlessly it seemed. The word means 'grove' or 'coppice', but this is a very inadequate description of an area of small fields separated by thick hedges and high banks of earth covered with a profusion of trees and bushes that strictly limited visibility. Furthermore it was crossed by no proper roads, only overgrown sunken lanes. These conditions largely neutralized the Allied superiority in artillery and mechanized transport. The desert veterans, used to fighting in the open, particularly hated the bocage's claustrophobic atmosphere.

To make matters worse, the Germans had better anti-tank guns, the 88mms that had already proved deadly killers in the desert; better mortars, the 'Moaning Minnies'; and especially, as the Villers-Bocage episode had shown, better armour.

Both the British and the Americans used Sherman tanks. These had long since solved their 'teething troubles' and were now extremely reliable, easy to produce and easy to maintain. Since February 1944 they had also been armed with an improved high-velocity 76mm gun. The British tanks in Normandy were less satisfactory. The Churchills could be hideously effective when fitted with a Crocodile flame-thrower, but were rarely risked against enemy armour. The Cromwells had a 75mm gun, strong armour plate and a faster speed than any German tank, but they had been designed for rapid movement in desert conditions, not for close combat in the bocage. The Comets, revised versions of the Cromwells, had a high-velocity 77mm gun with a greater penetrative power than that of the Cromwells or Shermans, but they would appear only in later campaigns.

Sadly, in any case none of these tanks could match their German opponents in either the protection afforded by their armour or the range and penetration of their guns. There were the Mark IV Specials with a long-barrelled 75mm gun that had first appeared at Alam Halfa. There were the Mark V 'Panthers' with a 75mm gun, 80mm armour and a speed of 28 mph: an ideal mixture of firepower, protection and rapidity. Finally, there were the Mark VI 'Tigers' mounting a lethal 88mm gun and carrying 102mm armour plate.

Since Montgomery had to deal with this problem, it might be thought that he was deserving of sympathy. This has rightly been extended to his soldiers, but his later critics note only that he prohibited 'alarmist reports' about the Allied armour's inferiority and so contrast him very unfavourably with Eisenhower who, we are told, nobly explained the whole position to General Marshall, the US Army's Chief of Staff.

Certainly Montgomery did discourage 'alarmist reports' and was quite right to do so; he had not forgotten how similar rumours had once badly damaged Eighth Army's confidence even though they were untrue. The complaints this time were correct but, as Sir Max Hastings points out in his *Overlord*, they were futile because 'there was no hope of quickly changing' the situation: new weapons could not be designed, tested, developed and produced in large numbers without a lengthy lapse of time.

In fact, during June and July, Montgomery did report the situation to the War Office, either directly or by way of de Guingand, stating bluntly that he was 'very disturbed' about the calibre of the Allied tanks and that the Cromwell must be replaced.[2] For the reason already stated, this had no useful result. Neither did Eisenhower's approach to Marshall for that matter, but whereas Eisenhower was content to report the problem, Montgomery attempted to mitigate it by taking action.

At the Battle of Medenine, Montgomery had made good use of 'Pheasants', this being the innocuous name for British 17-pounder anti-tank guns. On his own initiative he now arranged for Second Army's Shermans, the turrets of which were larger than those of the British-designed tanks, to be converted to carry a Pheasant. These tanks – they were called 'Fireflies' – were superior to Panzer Mark IV Specials, and at least less inferior to Panthers and Tigers than any of their predecessors.

Some 600 Fireflies were ultimately produced and since, unfortunately, the conversions took a long time, Montgomery spread them equally among all his Sherman-equipped units. He also offered Fireflies to the Americans, but they showed no interest in them at first. Not until late August did Eisenhower, apparently on the urging of Bradley, belatedly feel that perhaps it would be desirable to have Fireflies after all. He then requested that 700 Shermans should be converted, but this proved impossible because of a lack of facilities.

Montgomery also attempted to counter the superiority of the German armour by making maximum use of the Allied superiority in the air. With the ready co-operation of Broadhurst and Quesada, close support by the Allied airmen was brought to a quite exceptional degree of efficiency, particularly in the ground-attack role in which the eighteen squadrons of Hawker Typhoons were outstanding. This had been Montgomery's policy when in command of Eighth Army and he now began to consider other ways in which Allied warplanes might be of assistance that would be put into practice later.

Montgomery further tried to ease the burden on his men by entrusting Operation EPSOM on 26 June – his first major assault after the great storm – to fresh troops. Though I and XXX Corps put pressure on the flanks, the main advance was made by the newly-arrived VIII Corps containing 15th (Scottish) and 43rd (Wessex) Infantry divisions, 11th Armoured Division and the independent 31st Armoured Brigade with Crocodiles. Its task was to cross the River Odon, a tributary of the Orne, then the Orne itself and threaten Caen with encirclement by cutting the road to Falaise. This should compel the SS panzer divisions to protect Caen instead of engaging the Americans.

Command of VIII Corps was given to Lieutenant General Sir Richard O'Connor. He had been taken prisoner in Rommel's first desert offensive and was only able to resume his military career in November 1943 following the collapse of Italy. Prior to his capture, he had conducted a brilliant campaign that had all but annihilated the Italian forces in Cyrenaica. This much impressed Montgomery, who had strongly urged that O'Connor be appointed one of his corps commanders. Sadly, though, O'Connor found well-trained and well-equipped German soldiers very different from Italians; he was felt by Roberts, now commanding 11th Armoured Division, unable to co-ordinate his infantry and his armour; and his tactical decisions were considered by Dempsey to be very unfortunate. Montgomery, forced to admit that O'Connor's appointment was a mistake, reflected that perhaps captivity had 'taken its toll'.

The upshot was that VIII Corps, hampered by bad weather that prevented aerial support, did not even reach the Odon on 26 June. It did seize a bridge over the river on the evening of the 27th and made further advances on the 28th, but very high casualties were suffered, particularly by 15th (Scottish) Division, and Dempsey decided not to attempt the Orne but to go onto the defensive and resist the counter-attacks that Ultra had revealed were already being planned.

Throughout 29 and 30 June and 1 July, the SS panzer divisions made repeated assaults on VIII Corps. This was forced to abandon its advanced positions, but the German armour suffered savage losses to the ubiquitous Typhoons, to British artillery fire and to British armour, for the close-quarter nature of fighting in the bocage nullified the longer range of the German tanks' guns. So effective was the British defence that Dempsey was able to withdraw his own armour over the Odon but still hold his bridgehead on the far side.

Though critics at the time and later would sneer at the minimal territorial gains made by Operation EPSOM, it had in fact entirely achieved Montgomery's main aim of getting the SS panzers embroiled on his eastern flank, leaving the way clear in the west, and had severely mauled them into the bargain. To no one was this clearer than to General Bradley who would declare that the inability of EPSOM to take Caen was unimportant and that: 'Monty's success should have been measured in the panzer divisions the enemy rushed against him.' Bradley had every reason to appreciate that success. In mid-June there were 70 German tanks opposing the Americans and 520 opposing the British or Canadians. By the end of EPSOM, Bradley faced 140 German tanks while 725 held Dempsey back from Caen.

Operation EPSOM had also greatly added to the problems of Normandy's defenders, as Chester Wilmot describes:

> By his timely thrust Montgomery compelled them to commit their armoured reserves piecemeal and in haste; then by assuming the timely defensive he was able to inflict on the SS Panzer Divisions a costly defeat; and finally by withdrawing his armour into reserve at the height of the battle, he re-created the threat of a major offensive in the Caen area.

If Montgomery's achievements were not understood by his critics, they were horribly clear to his professional opponents, on whom the strain was becoming unbearable. On 28 June, General Friedrich Dollmann, the luckless head of Seventh Army died, possibly having committed suicide by taking poison, probably having suffered a heart attack; in either case, a victim of worry. On the same day, von Rundstedt and Rommel were summoned to a conference at Berchtesgaden on the 29th. At this, Hitler categorically refused their requests to be allowed to retreat. On their return to their headquarters on the 30th, however, they were greeted by reports from Geyr von Schweppenburg back at the head of Panzer Group West and SS General Paul Hausser, formerly head of II SS Panzer Corps – 9th and 10th SS Panzer divisions – and now appointed Dollmann's successor, both urging the abandonment of Caen and retirement to the south.

Although desperately unhappy, Rommel was not prepared to defy his Führer. Von Rundstedt, though, had had enough. On his own initiative, with considerable courage, he ordered preparations to be made for a retreat from Caen, sent the reports from Geyr von Schweppenburg and Hausser to OKW, and fully supported them in a covering letter. Hitler, of course, would not agree and the withdrawal plans were cancelled. On the evening of 1 July, however, von Rundstedt telephoned Keitel, the OKW Chief of Staff, to inform him that all German counter-attacks had failed. 'What shall we do? What shall we do?' Keitel wailed. 'Make peace, you fools,' snarled von Rundstedt. 'What else can you do?'

Hitler's reaction was milder than might have been anticipated: next day von Rundstedt received a fresh decoration and 'a nice letter' telling him he had retired on the grounds of ill health. His post of C-in-C, West was not given to Rommel, much to his humiliation, but to Field Marshal Günther von Kluge who Hitler mistakenly believed was completely loyal. On 4 July, Geyr von Schweppenburg was replaced as head of Panzer Group West – soon to be renamed Fifth Panzer Army – by General Hans Eberbach. Both von Kluge and Eberbach are said to have been in a confident mood, but if so, it would be of short duration.

Montgomery's own cheerful confidence never wavered, at least on the surface. His main concern at this time was First US Army. He had hoped it would expand its bridgehead well to the south at the same time as it secured the Cotentin Peninsula, but American attention, understandably, was fixed on the capture of Cherbourg. With this taken, however, Bradley was willing to oblige and on 3 July began a major assault southwards. To divert German attention away from this, Montgomery proposed another attack on Caen. Operation CHARNWOOD, as this was entitled, would be made by I Corps, employing 3rd and 59th British and 3rd Canadian divisions supported by 79th Division's Funnies.

Dempsey fully agreed that the Germans must be tied down in the east, but was worried about the casualties likely to be inflicted on his infantry, and with good reason. The defences around Caen had been steadily increased to a peak of effectiveness. They were based on a number of villages from which the inhabitants had been removed and the buildings turned into strongpoints. Connected by anti-tank ditches, minefields and cleverly camouflaged communication trenches, these formed a barrier 3 miles deep, held by three panzer divisions backed by infantry and artillery. Dempsey therefore felt strongly that new tactics must be introduced if these formidable obstacles were to be overcome.

Dempsey therefore revived a suggestion, originally put forward by Leigh-Mallory, that Allied heavy bombers might blast a way through for his footsoldiers. Montgomery, always eager to try a new trick in his offensives, promptly agreed and Richardson and Canadian Brigadier Charles Mann were sent to London to obtain this aerial assistance. Finding Tedder and Coningham unenthusiastic, they went directly to Air Marshal Sir Arthur Harris, Bomber Command's formidable leader, who willingly gave his consent.

The use of the 'heavies' has been the subject of much dispute. Ronald Lewin who took part in Operation CHARNWOOD as an officer in 59th Division considers it was 'probably the best arrangement' that could be made. By contrast, Major General J.F.C. Fuller in *The Second World War 1939–1945* agrees that the planning of the Normandy campaign, the actual invasion and the use of the air forces to impede German movement were all 'brilliant', but calls the 'colossal cracks', as Montgomery described the heavy bomber strikes, 'asinine' as they were inaccurate and if anything hampered the forward movement of the ground troops.

This was not an unfair assessment of the weaknesses of high-level bombing. It was acknowledged to be inaccurate and therefore a 'safety margin' was proposed and the bombing directed not at the fortifications nearest to the British lines but at those further back, near or even in Caen. This would mean damage for the city and death and injury for its helpless inhabitants, but it was hoped it would prevent the Germans from getting reinforcements and supplies to their forward troops. Dempsey accepted this decision, the more readily because, as Chester Wilmot tells us, he judged the destruction of enemy matériel less important than the lift in morale that the strikes would give to his watching soldiers.

A more serious disadvantage was caused by the Allies' old enemy: the weather. It was intended that the ground attack would begin at 0420 on 8 July, with the air strike delivered immediately prior to this. Sadly, unfavourable weather forecasts caused the strike – by 467 Lancasters and Halifaxes – to be brought forward to 2150 on the 7th. There was no time for Dempsey to change his own plans and the defenders were thus given more than six hours in which to recover their balance.

Nonetheless, the air-raid did make a valuable contribution to the operation. Quite apart from the harm it inflicted, it did raise the morale of the attackers and lowered the resolution of the defenders. Dempsey's men, despite high casualties, did break through the immensely strong defences. They entered Caen on the morning of 9 July but, it must be said, found that the bombing, as de Guingand admits, had caused 'too much disruption'. However, if this slowed their advance, it also prevented any possibility of a German counter-attack. By next morning Caen, except for its suburbs on the far bank of the Orne, and also Carpiquet aerodrome, were at last in Allied hands.

Despite all the criticisms made against it, Operation CHARNWOOD had been a success. As for later accusations that the bombing of Caen was morally wrong, its much-tried inhabitants clearly considered that the removal of the National Socialist yoke justified the grim price paid. The man who had first requested the use of heavy bombers was General Dempsey. The man who had approved the inclusion of Caen in their attack was General Dempsey. The people of Caen hailed General Dempsey as their 'glorious liberator' and made him an honorary citizen.

Montgomery, though, was still anxious about First US Army. When this had begun its southward thrust on 3 July, so much enemy strength had been attracted to the Caen area that the Americans had a superiority of three to one in infantry and eight to one in tanks. Like the British and Canadians before them, however, they quickly found that German defensive positions in bocage country presented formidable obstacles. On 10 July, they had to check their advance in order to reorganize and renew their supplies, especially of ammunition; their initial objective, the crucial road centre of St Lô, was still out of reach.

To his immense credit, Montgomery uttered no word of reproach or blame or impatience. In a conference with Bradley and Dempsey on 10 July, as Dempsey confirms, he refused to harry Bradley into premature action, saying: 'Never mind. Take all the time you need, Brad.' Then he instructed Dempsey to keep attracting German strength, particularly

German armour, onto Second Army 'so as to ease the way for Brad'. Dempsey privately suggested that he should make the decisive break-out, but Montgomery thought this would cost too many casualties and repeated his desire that it should be done by the Americans.

It was therefore decided that Bradley should take St Lô as soon as possible to provide the base from which he would make that decisive break-out. On 16 July, a diversion would be caused by pressure in the Odon area from the newly-arrived XII Corps commanded by Lieutenant General Neil Ritchie.[3] On the 18th, Dempsey would deliver a major attack to the east of Caen, code-named Operation GOODWOOD, to fix German armour and German attention in the east. Finally on the 19th would come Bradley's major assault, the code-name for which was Operation COBRA.

Montgomery directed Dempsey to capture the Bourguébus Ridge that lay across the road running south-east from Caen to Falaise and in the process cause as much damage as possible to the Germans, particularly their armoured divisions. Having given these basic instructions, however, Montgomery left Dempsey to plan the details of Operation GOODWOOD. This was unusual, for he is often accused of merely using Dempsey to pass on his orders to the corps commanders, but perhaps he had come to accept the truth of the accusation. More probably, though, it was because his main attention was directed towards First US Army. As he told Brooke in a letter of 14 July, it was 'in the west that I want territory'.

To carry out his task, Dempsey proposed to rely on his armour, which unlike his infantry had so far suffered no serious losses, supported again by heavy bombers. The left flank of his offensive would be protected by I Corps; on its right the newly-formed II Canadian Corps – 2nd and 3rd Canadian divisions – would take those suburbs of Caen lying beyond the Orne, which it did successfully. The principal striking force of Operation GOODWOOD would be O'Connor's VIII Corps which was to pass east and then south of Caen towards the Bourguébus Ridge. To strengthen it, Dempsey transferred 7th Armoured and Guards Armoured divisions which with its existing 11th Armoured Division gave O'Connor 750 tanks.

Heartened and encouraged by these reinforcements, Dempsey believed that he could advance well beyond Bourguébus and reach Falaise or even Argentan, threatening the rear of the enemy facing Bradley. His optimism secured the eager support of senior air force officers who believed they would finally obtain the long-desired airfield sites between Caen and Falaise. It seems that Montgomery also felt he might now gain these and silence some of his critics. In his letter to Brooke of 14 July, he declared that: 'The possibilities are immense' as with a tank force of more than 700, 'anything may happen'.

After the war, Montgomery's stupid obsession with maintaining that all had gone exactly according to plan led him to state that 'never at any time' did he entertain such ideas. By doing so he underrated his own ability. As General Sir David Fraser points out, considering all possibilities 'was surely good generalship, to be declared rather than disavowed.... He was a better general than autobiographer.'

In fairness to Montgomery, he quickly abandoned his optimism and had good reason to do so. It became clear that the Americans were not going to make a rapid capture of St Lô; they only occupied its shattered ruins on 18 July and would then have to spend several days getting reorganized. There would thus be no possibility of Operation COBRA commencing on 19 July and GOODWOOD and COBRA giving each other mutual support.

Worse still, British Intelligence gave warning that the Germans were vigorously strengthening their defences in the area where Dempsey proposed to launch GOODWOOD, having discovered the time and place of this. Credit for the defences has usually been given to Rommel, but Sir Max Hastings has shown that this really belongs to General Eberbach.

Rommel, however, was naturally interested in the progress of the defences and on 17 July visited Eberbach's headquarters for a final update. The 'Desert Fox' was returning to his own headquarters when his staff car was strafed, almost certainly by a Spitfire of 412 Squadron Royal Canadian Air Force flown by the appropriately named Flight Lieutenant Charles Fox. Rommel's driver was fatally wounded, the car crashed, and the field marshal, unconscious and with a fractured skull, was taken to a nearby village called by another strange coincidence Sainte Foy de Montgomery, the Sacred Faith of Montgomery, named after an ancestor of Rommel's deadliest opponent.

Eberbach's defences were in fact the strongest encountered in the Battle of Normandy, consisting of five interconnected fortified lines stretched out over 10 miles and containing infantry, armour, anti-tank guns, artillery and mortars. Although the full details of these were not known to the Allies, enough had been revealed to quench any undue hopes. As early as 15 July, Montgomery reminded Dempsey and O'Connor that their job was to gain the Bourguébus Ridge and destroy enemy forces. On the 17th, Dempsey ordered O'Connor to ensure he could 'establish' his armour in the Bourguébus area; he made no mention at all of moving on to Falaise.

With these limited objectives before it, Operation GOODWOOD opened at 0530 on 18 July with a massive aerial bombardment by more than 1,000 heavy bombers. The lessons of CHARNWOOD had been learned and they attacked German positions on both flanks of the line of advance, but not those in front of this so as to avoid causing obstacles and delays. They were followed by some 400 American 'medium' bombers that did attack positions directly opposing the advance but only with anti-personnel bombs.

Although a number of strongholds, tanks and anti-tank guns inevitably escaped serious harm, this bombardment belied the criticisms of 'colossal cracks' previously recorded. It inflicted heavy casualties of men and equipment, stunned and confused many of the defenders and, incidentally, so appalled Field Marshal von Kluge that thereafter he would be frankly and unalterably defeatist. The air strikes ceased at 0745 and, again learning from CHARNWOOD, the ground attacks followed immediately under cover of a heavy artillery barrage.

At the head of the advance was Major General Roberts with 11th Armoured Division's 29th Armoured Brigade. At first matters went reasonably well and Roberts advanced 6 miles, capturing a large number of prisoners dazed by the bombing. North-east of Bourguébus, however, he was held up by the fortified village of Cagny which had escaped the aerial strikes. It seems that O'Connor again failed to co-ordinate his armour and his infantry, and despite strong verbal and written protests had deprived Roberts of his 159th Infantry Brigade which instead of being used to take Cagny had been sent against a pair of strongholds well to the west of the line of advance. Roberts was eventually compelled to bypass Cagny, but continued his advance until brought to a halt by a strong group of anti-tank guns just short of the Bourguébus Ridge.

O'Connor had also not controlled the movement forward of 7th Armoured and Guards Armoured divisions at all well. These had had to cross the bridges over the Orne and the Canal de Caen and then pass through a minefield laid to protect the bridgehead east of the Orne. O'Connor had been urged to lift this, but would only make lanes through it. They proved inadequate in number and width and caused massive 'traffic jams'. The Guards Armoured finally got through, but it too was checked by the Cagny stronghold. This it attacked but could not subdue it until 1600. The 7th Armoured only reached the front line at 1800.

Yet that evening, a totally inaccurate Intelligence report informed Montgomery that the Bourguébus Ridge had been taken. This would have been much earlier than anticipated and perhaps thinking – though he would never admit this – that he might get the airfield sites between Caen and Falaise after all, he badly overreacted. He dramatically informed a press conference that Second Army had 'broken through' and he was 'well satisfied with the progress made'.

Montgomery did admit later that he was 'too exultant'. That was putting it mildly. During the night of 18/19 July, the Germans rushed reinforcements of armour and infantry to the Bourguébus Ridge and for the next two days, Second Army tried vainly to capture it. Some fortified villages on its northern slope were taken and 8th Battalion, the Rifle Brigade captured 400 SS troops, not normally ready to surrender. However, while the Germans lost only 120 tanks, the British total rose to more than 400. As at Alamein, these were not all permanent losses: about two-thirds were ultimately repaired. Also, mercifully, casualties among their crews were astonishingly light, making later talk of a 'death ride' rather ridiculous.

Nonetheless it was all very depressing after all the high hopes and dramatic announcements, and on the afternoon of the 20th, a violent thunderstorm reduced the battlefield to a sea of mud and brought Operation GOODWOOD to its inglorious end. It was Montgomery's worst moment in the Battle of Normandy.

Notes

1. Wittmann would be acknowledged as the most successful tank commander on either side in the Second World War, credited with destroying an eventual total of 138 tanks or self-propelled guns and 132 anti-tank guns.
2. Churchill was also harried by awkward questions in the House of Commons about the Allied tanks' poor performance. Unable to deny this, he was reduced to accusing his inquisitors of 'spiteful curiosity' or 'lack of patriotism'.

3. Ritchie had been appointed by Auchinleck to lead Eighth Army in November 1941 despite his protests that he lacked experience of high command or operations in a desert. Auchinleck subjected him to constant interference and then put on him all the blame for subsequent defeats. Luckily for Ritchie, Montgomery appreciated he had been placed in 'an impossible position' and accepted him as a corps commander. 'He did very well,' Montgomery confirms.

Chapter Nine

The Battle of Normandy: Triumph

While the soldiers of Second (British) Army strove to carry out their leaders' plans by capturing the Bourguébus Ridge, two other plans were reaching their culmination. One came in a conference room at Hitler's Headquarters in Rastenburg, East Prussia. Colonel Count von Stauffenberg had planned to kill the dictator by leaving a briefcase containing a time-bomb under the table. This did kill four staff officers, but Hitler escaped with superficial injuries, triumphantly declaring he had been protected by providence and savagely promising to take vengeance on the plotters against him 'in the way that we National Socialists are accustomed'.

That, as might be imagined, was horrifyingly brutal and among its victims was Erwin Rommel. He had been in contact with the conspirators, but had never moved from talk to action, although that did not save him. He was in effect sentenced to death, but since he was probably Germany's most popular field marshal, it was decided that his formal condemnation would cause trouble. He was therefore allowed to take poison, his family was not harmed and it was given out that he had died of wounds suffered in Normandy. To preserve the illusion, he received a state funeral.

The other plan also materialized at a headquarters: that of General Eisenhower. The chief plotter was Tedder and his target was Montgomery; however, not his death but his dismissal was desired. Late on 18 July, Tedder telephoned the Allied Supreme Commander, raging against Montgomery for having 'stopped his armour' – really done by German resistance, much against Montgomery's wishes – and for having wasted the heavy bomber attacks: '7,000 tons of bombs for 7,000 yards.'

Tedder followed up with other telephone calls and though their contents have been disputed, they certainly did not favour Montgomery. There is no argument that on 21 July, Tedder wrote to Eisenhower, urged him to take over as Land Forces Commander at once and made it clear

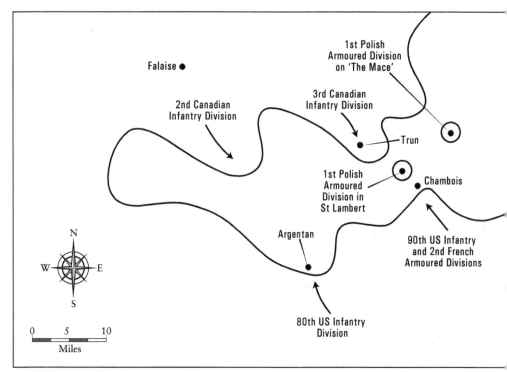

Map 16: The Falaise Pocket, 18 August 1944.

that as Eisenhower's 'immediate British subordinate', he would support
any action Eisenhower might 'consider the situation demands'.

It has been suggested that Montgomery had not kept Eisenhower
properly informed, but de Guingand, on whom this duty was placed,
reports that Eisenhower was told full details of Montgomery's intentions.
The trouble was that he did not like Montgomery's attempts to throw the
Germans off balance, leaving them helpless against a decisive assault at
the right time in the right place. These took time to come to fruition and
Eisenhower longed for quick results.

Nor did Eisenhower really approve of a single decisive assault. As
in Italy, he wished to see every unit under his command attacking all
the time regardless of the situation, and thus presumably regardless
of casualties. Bedell Smith called his attitude that of 'a football coach
exhorting everyone to aggressive action.'

It is easy to understand Eisenhower's frustration at what seemed to
him maddening obstinacy on Montgomery's part. Subjected as he was
to the constant carping of Morgan and Kay Summersby, Eisenhower's

anxieties were brought to a head by Tedder's outburst. He complained to Churchill about the lack of progress and it seems from his later reactions that he might not have been sorry if the prime minister had turned on his difficult Land Forces Commander.

Churchill had been totally pessimistic about the prospects in Normandy, telling Eisenhower that if by winter the Allies had been able to secure Cherbourg and Brittany, he would 'consider it a victory'. It might therefore be thought that he would be unwilling to harry Montgomery. In fact, by early July he also had become impatient and was complaining to Brooke about Montgomery's management of the battle.

After the war, Montgomery would declare that Churchill, who he admired immensely, was 'chief among all my friends'. He deceived himself. Churchill was a friend when Montgomery was successful. When Montgomery was in trouble, Churchill did not hesitate to disown him. As Brooke would wryly note, 'Monty was always "my" Monty when he was out of favour.' He was very much out of favour in mid-July 1944. He had tried to prohibit any visitors as he considered them a distraction, but Brooke showed him this attitude was unwise. Yet with Eisenhower arranging to come on the 20th and Churchill on the 21st, his position was perilously insecure.

In these circumstances, Montgomery's conduct was truly admirable. As Sir Max Hastings points out, he could have continued Second Army's assaults regardless of casualties and thereby 'stave off the political demands made of him'. He did not and, says Hastings, he 'is entitled to the gratitude of his country, as well as of his soldiers for declining to yield to the temptation'.

Then again, as Dempsey's biographer Peter Rostron states: 'To maintain his own position, Montgomery could have thrown the blame [for GOODWOOD] on Dempsey. It was Dempsey's plan after all.' Dempsey's over-optimism and O'Connor's poor handling of the offensive had not helped either. Of course as Montgomery had ordered Dempsey to prepare the plan and had insisted on O'Connor being a corps commander, ultimate responsibility must be his. Yet many a commander has 'passed the blame down'. Montgomery was not one of them. As Dempsey would expressively and gratefully recall: 'He did not rat.'

Montgomery therefore deserved some good fortune and it came in the form of Ultra intercepts revealing that GOODWOOD had been a great success in Montgomery's most important objective: that of directing German attention and German strength away from Bradley. The enemy had intended to transfer 2nd and 116th Panzer divisions to the St Lô area, but GOODWOOD caused them to be retained in the east, to which were also sent five of the six fresh German infantry divisions to reach the battle-zone in July. This, as he would confirm after the war, was all that Bradley had expected from it.

Montgomery could thus demonstrate to Eisenhower and Churchill that his plan was proceeding satisfactorily and all would soon be resolved. He won Churchill over completely. When the prime minister arrived, according to Montgomery's staff, he was 'still very grumpy'. He left with his own morale renewed, and a bottle of brandy as a parting present. Eisenhower was less happy, grumbling that Montgomery had 'obviously sold Winston "a bill of goods"'. It was perhaps in this sour mood that he wrote to Montgomery urging how necessary it was that Dempsey should keep up the pressure required to 'pin down' enemy reserves.

Since every British and Canadian operation from D-Day to GOODWOOD inclusive had been designed to do just that, Montgomery was not impressed. With his usual hasty rush to judgement, he impulsively concluded that Eisenhower had never understood his intentions. This was perhaps excusable as an immediate reaction, but Montgomery would repeat his opinion on every possible inappropriate occasion, ultimately losing Eisenhower's friendship and causing much trouble for himself.

For the moment, though, Montgomery's attention was firmly fixed on First American Army. Its coming offensive, Operation COBRA, would, he felt certain, win the Battle of Normandy and justify his previous actions. He had revealed the general outline of the operation as early as 13 June, declaring that after taking St Lô the Americans should capture the following in sequence: Coutances near the coast west of St Lô; Villedieu south of St Lô and north-east of Avranches; and Avranches itself at the base of the Brittany Peninsula. This outline Bradley would faithfully follow.

Montgomery had also indicated Bradley's basic tactics. Dempsey confirms that at the conference of 10 July, Montgomery, 'putting two fingers on the map' to emphasize his point, urged Bradley to concentrate his forces for one solid punch. This was much as he had advised Alexander before the capture of Tunis and, like Alexander, Bradley would be richly rewarded for following the advice.

Bradley had one further advantage. Though the Americans had regarded Hobart's Funnies as evidence of undue British caution, they now produced a tank modification of their own. This involved fitting eight steel 'teeth' to the front of hundreds of Shermans, enabling them to bulldoze their way through the thick banks of the bocage with a minimum of delay. The 'Rhinos', as they were called, could thus manoeuvre across country as they pleased while the panzer units were restricted to using the roads.

Nothing, however, could overcome Montgomery's usual bad luck with the weather. This prevented any possibility of an offensive until 24 July and on that day visibility only improved temporarily before the clouds closed in again. The Americans had already despatched a preliminary raid by heavy bombers and although most were recalled, some did not receive the signal and dropped their bombs blindly through the clouds. Horrifying to relate, they hit 30th US Division, inflicting more than 150 casualties.

Quite apart from his grief over the mistake, Bradley was greatly concerned that the Germans would have been warned of his impending assault. Montgomery, however, to Bradley's relief, ordered an attack on the Bourguébus Ridge by II Canadian Corps commencing at 0330 on 25 July. Though this made few gains, it did succeed in convincing the Germans that the American bombing was a diversion and the main Allied offensive would come in the east.

As a result, during 24 and early 25 July, German units including some armoured formations were to be found moving eastward away from the area west of St Lô where Operation COBRA was about to strike. At 0940 on the 25th, it did strike and its bite was soon to prove fatal.

The first day of the offensive was one of mixed fortunes. The Americans had again arranged massive heavy bomber strikes, but it appears that, unlike Bomber Command, the US Eighth Air Force did not allow a 'margin for error'. Tragically, US bombs killed more than 100 US soldiers including Lieutenant General McNair and wounded almost 500 others. Fortunately, the harm – mental and physical – that they inflicted on the enemy was far greater. In particular, Panzer Lehr Division, the only armoured formation opposing Bradley, suffered a 70 per cent personnel casualty list and lost thirty-six of its forty-five tanks. Moreover, so much German armour had been moved out of the area that only five reserves were able to reach Panzer Lehr and it had been wiped out completely by 27 July.

By then, two US corps, with infantry riding on tanks and Thunderbolt fighter-bombers acting as 'flying artillery' were everywhere breaking through a collapsing enemy. At last the German commanders escaped from the mental chains that Montgomery had riveted on them and ordered 2nd and 116th Panzer divisions to move to the threatened area, but it was too late. This 'relief force' only came into action on the 28th, when it was easily repulsed. Coutances fell on 28 July, Villedieu and Avranches on the 30th, and on 1 August American soldiers entered Brittany.

On 1 August also came long-planned changes in the Allied Order of Battle. Crerar's First Canadian Army had joined Twenty-First Army Group on 23 July. Now Patton's Third US Army was activated. It joined a new Twelfth Army Group led by Bradley, who controlled Patton's men and those of his old First US Army under his former deputy, Lieutenant General Courtney Hodges.

Montgomery's plan was at last coming to fruition, but sadly the delight felt by everyone at the time would not be reflected by some later commentators. These suggest that Montgomery had delayed bringing Third US Army into action as long as possible to prevent the creation of Twelfth US Army Group which would make Bradley 'independent' of him.

It is a suggestion as inaccurate as it is mean. For a start, a glance at the Phase Line Map shows that Montgomery wished to reach Avranches and thus let Patton enter Brittany on 26 June, more than a month earlier. Moreover, as early as 7 July Montgomery, in a letter to Brooke, confirmed it had been agreed that until the Battle of Normandy was over he would retain 'operational control' of Twelfth US Army Group and be responsible for the 'tactical co-ordination' of all Allied Land Forces. It was a decision that pleased Montgomery and was willingly accepted by Bradley.

Captain Liddell Hart, while not stooping to traduce Montgomery, does feel that he should have followed Dempsey's advice to deliver his decisive thrust down the road to Falaise and Argentan. Since, however, the Germans could meet an attack here with the bulk of their armour and the strongest defences in Normandy, there can be no certainty that it would have succeeded and every certainty that it would have resulted in massive casualties that Montgomery was not prepared to accept.

Moreover if Dempsey had reached Argentan, this would not have been decisive. Liddell Hart claims that Dempsey would have taken all the bridges over the Orne between Caen and Argentan and so trapped the Germans 'more effectively than any American break-out on the Western flank could have done'. Yet of the seven panzer divisions facing Dempsey, the whole of five and most of a sixth were east of the Orne so would not be trapped. German forces facing Bradley would be threatened from the rear, but they had an easy withdrawal route south of Argentan, the one the Americans used to trap them after the 'break-out on the Western flank'.[1]

Liddell Hart also complains that 'the outdated pre-invasion plan' of liberating Brittany should have been disregarded and Third US Army turned not westward but eastward. In fact another glance at the Phase Line Map shows that Montgomery envisaged an Allied move westward to capture Alençon, Le Mans and Angers before the liberation of Brittany was completed. He now put this intention into practice. He did not halt Third US Army's move into Brittany entirely as Liddell Hart believed he should have done – and was no doubt wise as one shudders to think of Patton's reaction – but at 1030 on 1 August, he instructed Bradley to let only Patton's VIII US Corps enter Brittany while his XV and XX Corps made a 'wide sweep' south and then east.

Thereafter events moved with bewildering speed. As with the dash to Palermo, all Patton's forces were lucky enough to find, as Chester Wilmot puts it, 'neither natural obstacles, nor prepared defences, nor organized forces to staunch the flow of armoured and motorised troops.' Even so, it is impossible not to admire the way in which the Americans took advantage of their good fortune. The two corps making the 'wide sweep' set out on 4 August and by the 8th had already taken Le Mans and Angers. By that date also, VIII US Corps had overrun the whole of Brittany except its main ports, the garrisons of which held out at Brest until 18 September and at Lorient and St Nazaire until the end of hostilities.[2]

While Third US Army was making rapid progress against minimal opposition, Lieutenant General Hodges and his First US Army were fighting large numbers of determined enemies in difficult conditions as they strove to widen the gap torn in the German lines. They made a number of useful gains including on 2 August the important crossroads at Mortain, and to assist them Montgomery arranged another offensive, this time not south-east down the road to Falaise but south-west.

The details of Operation BLUECOAT, as it was called, were relatively simple. While XII (British) Corps kept the area between Caen and Caumont secure, XXX Corps would capture Villers-Bocage, then move on to the steep-sided 1,200ft-high Mont Pinçon some 18 miles west of Caen, dominating the entire district. At the same time, VIII Corps would thrust between XXX Corps and the Americans to protect First US Army's left flank. The attackers' task was no easy one, for the terrain over which they had to move was bocage of the very worst kind. Indeed, Montgomery had personally warned of its difficulties, but his advice had been ignored or, more probably, forgotten.

Consequently, when BLUECOAT began on 30 July, it did so in an air of unjustified optimism that would result in a great deal of disappointment, not least for Montgomery personally. Already he had realized that 51st Highland Division was no longer 'battleworthy', and this was mainly his own fault. He had recommended as the division's commander Major General Charles Bullen-Smith who had served in his 3rd Division at the time of Dunkirk, but had seen no action since and, worse still, was a Lowland Scot from a Lowland regiment.

How Montgomery, the senior officer most aware that all divisions had different strengths, weaknesses, requirements and needs, could have made such a mistake is inexplicable. On 26 July, he rectified it by replacing Bullen-Smith with Major General Thomas Rennie who had served for many years in the Highland Division. Poor Bullen-Smith, whose failure was not caused by any want of effort, was heart-broken. Lieutenant Colonel 'Kit' Dawnay, Montgomery's Military Assistant, confirms that 'Monty himself was deeply moved' but was adamant, explaining: 'If I don't remove you Charles, men will be killed unnecessarily.'

Dempsey had agreed with Montgomery about Bullen-Smith, and had also expressed doubts over two more of Montgomery's selections: Lieutenant General Bucknall, the XXX Corps Commander, and Major General Erskine, CO of 7th Armoured Division. The early events of BLUECOAT decided him. By 2 August XXX Corps had made virtually no progress and Dempsey had had enough. He had warned Montgomery – as had Brooke – that Bucknall, although he had led 5th Division with success in Sicily and Italy, was not a suitable corps commander. He now recommended that Bucknall be replaced and Montgomery complied, openly admitting that his choice of Bucknall had been a mistake. Next day, Erskine was also dismissed, as were three other senior officers of 7th Armoured.

Fortunately VIII Corps did much better, especially its 11th Armoured Division. Roberts had personally ensured full co-ordination of its different arms and its 29th Armoured Brigade now contained infantry battalions and its 159th Infantry Brigade included tank regiments. By 2 August, 11th Armoured Division had advanced some 12 miles, made contact with the Americans, severely mauled a detachment from 21st Panzer Division – the only one in the area – and was approaching Vire, another important road junction. Scouting armoured cars reported that Vire was only weakly defended, but it had been allotted to the Americans and both Montgomery and Bradley were sensitive on the subject of inter-Allied boundaries after the unhappy incidents in Sicily. Roberts was therefore ordered not to advance any further.

Naturally, later critics have suggested that Montgomery had lost a great opportunity because 11th Armoured in Vire could have threatened the rear of the enemy facing First US Army. However, they omit to mention that as a result of the failures of XXX Corps, 11th Armoured in Vire would also be at the end of a long narrow salient with lengthy supply lines, unsupported by Allied artillery and very vulnerable to the counter-attacks that Allied Intelligence was already predicting. At the time, Roberts was disappointed that he had been halted, but with a greater knowledge of the facts, he would later declare that he had 'looked at Vire several times since the war and have been rather thankful that we were not allowed to take it'.

For that matter, 11th Armoured Division had already achieved BLUECOAT's main aims. General Eberbach had determined to send his Fifth Panzer Army to the western sector of the battle-front and in addition to 21st Panzer that was there already, had gathered together 9th SS and 10th SS Panzer divisions, part of 116th Panzer, a motor brigade and three battalions of Tiger tanks. This formidable force, however, was not directed against the Americans, who were thus able to capture Vire on 6 August. Nor was it directed against XXX Corps; indeed during 4 and 5 August Eberbach, to shorten his defensive front, abandoned to this corps a number of advanced positions including the ravaged remains of Villers-Bocage.

It was against 11th Armoured Division that Eberbach threw his armour and happily this had retreated from the vicinity of Vire to a good defensive position on the Périers Ridge where it was joined by Guards Armoured Division and could be supported by Allied artillery. The panzers suffered considerable damage from Allied fighter-bombers, particularly Broadhurst's inevitable Typhoons, before they even reached the ridge and when they did, both sides had high losses, but the panzers were so deeply committed that they could not be used elsewhere and by the end of 6 August, all their attacks had been repelled.

On 6 August also, XXX Corps' attack reached a dramatic and successful culmination. To replace Bucknall Montgomery had selected Horrocks, now recovered from the serious wounds inflicted by a strafing German warplane during rehearsals for the landings planned in Italy. Horrocks at once set out to restore morale by Montgomery's methods of visiting as many units as possible to explain the situation and future plans. He made little progress with 7th Armoured for the dismissal of its senior officers was much resented and it hated fighting in the bocage, but he did better with 50th Infantry Division and better still with 43rd (Wessex) Division. Under the determined, ruthless and some said brutal leadership of Major General Ivar Thomas, 43rd (Wessex), despite heavy casualties, had already gained a deserved reputation which it was shortly to confirm.

At about 1800 on 6 August, after bitter fighting all that day and the previous one, the 5th Battalion of the Wiltshire Regiment from the division's 129th Brigade, though reduced to only sixty unwounded men, reached the western foot of Mont Pinçon. Here the slopes were particularly steep, but the supporting tanks of the 13th/18th Hussars found a narrow track leading to the summit that the enemy had neglected to guard. Under cover of a smokescreen, seven of them were able to reach the top. As darkness was falling, the brigade's reserve battalion, 4th Wiltshires, scaled the same track and prevented any counter-attack. Next day, reinforcements drove the Germans off Mont Pinçon and Horrocks arrived to congratulate all concerned on 'a remarkable feat of arms'.

On 7 August, the most important move was made by Hitler. The gap torn at Avranches was still only 25 miles wide and the Führer felt sure that his soldiers could break through this and cut off all Allied forces further south. He ordered von Kluge to attack through Mortain to Avranches with every tank he could find and supported by the entire available strength of the Luftwaffe.

This was a good idea on paper, but not in reality. To Hitler's fury, the Allied air supremacy was so pronounced that the Luftwaffe made no useful contribution. Von Kluge was unable to extricate the panzers tied down in the Caen area or on the Périers Ridge and his great assault in the early hours of 7 August was made by 1st SS, 2nd, 2nd SS and part of 116th Panzer divisions only, containing 185 tanks or mobile guns. Warned by Ultra intercepts, Bradley, Hodges and their men were fully prepared to meet it.

Consequently, though Mortain itself fell, 30th US Infantry Division retained vital high ground to the north and north-east. Part of its 120th Regiment (the American equivalent of a brigade) was cut off on a knoll called Hill 314, but despite heavy casualties held out with the aid of supplies dropped from the air. Nor did Hitler's offensive hamper Third US Army's advance; in fact it assisted it. The 9th Panzer Division from southern France had just arrived in the area of Le Mans, but on 8 August it was sent to that of Mortain and would later be all but wiped out there.

Actions elsewhere also aided First US Army. On the night of 6/7 August, three British battalions had crossed the upper Orne in the vicinity of Thury-Harcourt, north-east of Mont Pinçon. Here during 7 and 8 August they were fiercely attacked by Tiger and Panther tanks, but drove these back. Their gallantry was symbolized by Captain David Jamieson of 1st Battalion, Royal Norfolk Regiment whose inspiring leadership, undaunted by wounds to eye and leg, earned him a Victoria Cross.

A far bigger move was made on the night of 7/8 August: Operation TOTALIZE, another attempt to take Falaise by First Canadian Army's II Corps. Led by Lieutenant General Guy Simonds, this contained 4th Canadian Armoured and two Canadian Infantry divisions and was supported by a rejuvenated 51st Highland Division, 33rd (British) Armoured Brigade and the newly-arrived 1st Polish Armoured Division. Simonds, like Montgomery, was keen to use new weapons: they included

'Crab' flail-tanks, 'Priests' – armoured vehicles carrying infantrymen – and searchlights shining on clouds to produce so-called 'Monty moonlight'.

Aided by these and by extremely accurate night attacks by Bomber Command on the flanks of the line of advance, the Canadians, British and Poles broke over the formidable Bourguébus Ridge and by morning were heading down the Falaise road. Tragically, however, at about 1250 when US Flying Fortresses appeared intending to deliver a supporting attack, they mistook their targets and hit 4th Canadian Armoured's tanks and its infantry formations as well, causing more than 300 casualties.

This resulted in the advance losing all its impetus and gave the Germans a chance to recover from the shock inflicted by the night assault and night bombing. Both the Canadian and the Polish Armoured divisions had more eagerness than experience and proved no match for veteran enemy armour and anti-tank guns. By 10 August they had lost about 150 tanks and were brought to a halt still 7 miles short of Falaise.

Yet TOTALIZE had not been wasted. When it was launched, 12th SS Panzer Division with forty-eight tanks and 101st SS Heavy Tank Battalion with nineteen Tigers were just moving away to the west and forty 88mm anti-tank guns that had just reached the Falaise area were intended to follow them. The panzers were hastily recalled, the 88mms were hurried to the front line and though it was these units that halted TOTALIZE, they were unable to participate in the Mortain fighting as von Kluge had planned.

In addition, on 8 August Captain Michael Wittmann, Germany's greatest tank 'ace' and hero of the action at Villers-Bocage, had lost his life. There have been many claimants of responsibility, but it seems most probable that the destroyer of Wittmann's Tiger – and two others – was Gunner Joe Ekins of 1st Northamptonshire Yeomanry from 33rd Armoured Brigade, whose own tank was a Firefly, one of the Shermans fitted with a 17-pounder gun on Montgomery's personal direction.

Assisted and encouraged by these events, Bradley and Hodges repulsed all assaults on 8 August and began to make counter-moves threatening the enemy's flanks. Mortain was recaptured on 11 August and next day, the heroic defenders of Hill 314 were relieved. Even before that, however, Bradley had noticed that huge numbers of German troops from both Seventh and Fifth Panzer Armies were now in a vast salient, under pressure from all sides: a situation of which he wanted to take full advantage.

It had always been Montgomery's intention that the Americans should reach the Seine in the Paris area, and then make a 'long hook' northwards to catch the Germans as they tried to escape over the river. Bradley's idea was to send his Third US Army on a 'short hook' from Le Mans to Alençon and on to Argentan where it would meet the Canadians advancing from Falaise and trap the Germans in what would later be called the 'Falaise pocket'.

At first Montgomery hesitated, perhaps remembering how faulty Intelligence had caused him to 'tap in' too quickly after Alamein. De Guingand, though, strongly supported Bradley and Montgomery's usual flexibility of thought reasserted itself. He insisted that the Americans should not halt their 'long hook' to the Seine so they could catch any Germans who had escaped from or had never been in the pocket, but agreed they should make the 'short hook' to Alençon as well. Since this was the main enemy supply base, both Montgomery and Bradley thought it would be strongly defended and that the Canadians would reach Falaise and then Argentan first. They therefore fixed the boundary between the two armies at just south of Argentan.

In fact, von Kluge's transfer of 9th Panzer Division from Le Mans to Mortain gave Patton's XV Corps under Major General Wade Haislip a clear run to Alençon, which it captured on 12 August. Next day, however, it was halted just short of Argentan by orders from Bradley. Allied Intelligence had wrongly indicated that the Germans were in full retreat and Bradley was afraid they would trample down Haislip's men in their efforts to escape; he 'much preferred a solid shoulder at Argentan to the possibility of a broken neck at Falaise.' Bradley makes it clear in *A Soldier's Story* that Montgomery was in no way responsible for this order – by an unintentional error he was not even notified of it – though this would not prevent his being blamed for it by Patton and certain later critics.

Only on 14 August did von Kluge really begin to retire. He sent 9th SS and 10th SS Panzer divisions well to the east of Falaise and Argentan as a back-up force and gradually withdrew from the western end of the pocket. This, though, was a slow business because German transport was not very modern. So much stress is laid on the mobility of German formations that it comes as a shock to learn that artillery pieces and the supply wagons for many infantry units were still being pulled by horses.

Withdrawals at any speed would not find favour with Hitler, but what sealed von Kluge's fate was the discovery of his dealings with the 'July plotters', although, like Rommel, he had talked but never acted. On 16 August, he was dismissed from his command and ordered back to Berlin. He set out on the 18th, but only as far as Metz where he committed suicide by poison. 'He would have been arrested anyway,' was Hitler's cold reaction.

Von Kluge's successor as C-in-C West was Field Marshal Walter Model, a capable, ruthless officer genuinely loyal to Hitler. He was known as the 'Führer's Fireman' and 'The Saviour of the Eastern Front', but there was no possibility of his doing more in Normandy than reducing the scale of German losses. His difficulties were increased because on 14 August another major attempt, Operation TRACTABLE, had been made to capture Falaise and Argentan and seal the eastern end of the pocket.

This was again the responsibility of First Canadian Army, though it has been suggested that Montgomery should have strengthened it with Second Army units. There were, however, several reasons against this. The Canadians in general and their leader Crerar in particular had resented Montgomery doing this in TOTALIZE, thinking it indicated doubt in their abilities. Also Montgomery wished to avoid the probable confusion and certain delay that this reorganization would have caused,[3] desired to give the hard-worked Second Army a rest, and believed – as did Dempsey and Bradley – that the Canadians and Poles could manage TRACTABLE on their own.

So they could and perhaps would have but for a couple of tragic incidents. The day before the offensive, a Canadian officer in a scout car was killed and the Germans discovered that, contrary to every standing order, he had been carrying a copy of the TRACTABLE plan. Then on 14 August, a lack of liaison with Bomber Command resulted in the RAF 'heavies' for the only time in the Battle of Normandy hitting their own troops; they inflicted almost 400 casualties, mainly on 1st Polish Armoured Division. Even so, on 16 August, 2nd Canadian Infantry Division entered Falaise and by the end of the day had killed or captured the last fanatical fighting men of 12th SS Panzer.

Meanwhile, Montgomery and Bradley had been wrongly informed by Allied Intelligence that the bulk of the enemy forces had already escaped beyond Falaise and Argentan. They therefore decided to seal off the pocket between the villages of Trun and Chambois and sent 3rd Canadian Infantry and 4th Canadian and 1st Polish Armoured divisions to the former and 90th US Infantry and 2nd French Armoured divisions, the latter under Eighth Army's old friend General Philippe Leclerc, to Chambois.

On 18 August, the Canadians took Trun and a small detachment from 4th Canadian Armoured – 175 men, 15 tanks and 4 anti-tanks guns under Major David Currie of the South Alberta Regiment – pushed on to the village of St Lambert lying between Trun and Chambois, capturing its northern half but not the road running through it. The 1st Polish Armoured Division also moved forward with 1,500 men and 80 tanks to seize a ridge north-east of St Lambert, officially known as Mont Ormel but 'The Mace' to the Poles from its shape. From these advanced positions, a merciless fire from the units' own guns and more distant supporting artillery was poured onto every enemy force sighted causing ghastly losses, especially among the horse-drawn transport.

Above them, the Allied fighters and fighter-bombers, as they had done for the previous four days, caused still more havoc with their pilots flying as many as six sorties a day. The poor horses presented a particularly vulnerable target and hundreds of them were found dead in their traces. The panzers were not forgotten either and by now the Typhoons, through long practice, could dive on and destroy individual armoured vehicles.

For their part, the Germans within the pocket and 9th SS and 10th SS divisions from outside it made continuous attacks on the advanced Allied forces. Those at St Lambert, although few in number, repulsed every assault; Major Currie being awarded a Victoria Cross in recognition of his leadership, his courage and that of every one of his men. The Poles were stronger in manpower and fire-power and though entirely surrounded, they too held out. Both groups continued firing at or directing artillery onto Germans trying to edge past them. As a crowning horror, the SS tanks shelled their own infantry if these attempted to surrender. The stench of dead men and dead horses was apparent even to pilots flying high overhead and with closed cockpits.[4]

Early on 19 August, the Americans and Free French at last captured Chambois – grimly renamed 'Shambles' – and 80th US Infantry Division took Argentan. Then strong Allied attacks from north and south relieved the exhausted defenders of St Lambert and 'The Mace' and closed the jaws of the trap. Next day, 2nd Panzer Division, its unity and organization still intact, smashed past the Canadians, but the gap was then closed permanently and the troops left in the pocket had no choice but to surrender.

In the pocket the Germans lost 10,000 dead and 50,000 prisoners of war including Lieutenant General Otto Elfeldt, the commander of LXXXIV Corps which controlled Seventh Army's infantry units, who was captured by the Poles. Some 500 tanks, 200 guns and 7,700 other vehicles had been destroyed or abandoned. About 20,000 men originally in the huge Mortain Salient escaped but many were wounded, among them SS General Hausser who had lost an eye and most of his jaw and was carried out unconscious on the back of a tank. General Eberbach got clear, but was captured at Amiens on 31 August by 11th Armoured Division.

Many others who escaped from the pocket had been captured earlier. On 20 August, Third US Army reached the Seine and swept down it in Montgomery's 'long hook', taking thousands of prisoners. The Germans' situation was made worse because every bridge over the Seine had been destroyed by air strikes except one badly damaged rail bridge at Rouen. Some got across on hastily collected ferries or hastily prepared pontoons, but only at the cost of abandoning all their heavy equipment.

The Germans had committed some 3,000 guns and 2,200 tanks to the Battle of Normandy. Of these they could bring over the Seine just sixty guns and twenty-four tanks, one less than the British had got out at Dunkirk. The number of German prisoners taken in Normandy rose to 210,000, the total German casualties to half a million, almost twice those at Stalingrad. There was no possibility of their preventing the Allies crossing the Seine at several different locations. American units, led by Leclerc's 2nd French Armoured Division, liberated Paris on 25 August. The first British crossing – by 4th Wiltshires from 43rd (Wessex) Division at Vernon between Paris and Rouen – took place in the early hours of the 26th.

It was the greatest victory won by the Western Allies in the Second World War. For this, credit must first be given to the soldiers who achieved it in the face of a determined enemy aided by difficult conditions and in many respects far better weapons. The Allies, however, had enjoyed superior leadership, in particular that of Montgomery, Dempsey and Bradley.

For the basic plan that won the Battle of Normandy, credit can only be given to Montgomery. He altered tactical details at various times, but stuck to his fundamental intentions regardless of pressure from Churchill, Eisenhower or his enemies at Supreme Allied Headquarters. He never gave a sign of a loss of confidence; he showed no anger or impatience at setbacks or delays; he heartened his subordinates and his soldiers by his own constant resolution. His outlook and his actions proved more than justified: the first British troops crossed the Seine on D+81, nine days earlier than envisaged on his Phase Line Map.

Montgomery in turn received unfailing loyalty from Dempsey and Bradley. Both were kept fully informed of his intentions and fully approved of them. Both rejected the unfair and uninformed criticisms made at the time and later. Both also were in difficult positions. It could not have been easy for Dempsey to be given a hard, undramatic but essential task under the close – perhaps too close – direction of Montgomery, but he accepted this, as Bradley confirms, with tolerance and without jealousy.

Bradley, though treated with a tact astonishing for Montgomery, was perhaps in a still more awkward situation: an American answering to a British superior. Yet de Guingand reports he was always 'co-operative and charming' and took no notice of the carping of some of his countrymen.

It is sad to record that the mutual respect and loyalty between Bradley and Montgomery would later be soured and that this was almost entirely Montgomery's fault. However, it was Montgomery's service in the Battle of Normandy that was remembered on a cold 1 April 1976 when the Allied Land Forces Commander was laid to rest. There were more than eighty wreaths from British or Commonwealth sources; only one from America but perhaps Montgomery would have appreciated this one most of all. 'Dear Monty' read its brief and rather touching inscription, 'Goodbye and thanks. Brad.'

Notes

1. Of course Hitler might have forbidden his soldiers to withdraw, but then their escape would have been prevented by a German mistake and not because they had been trapped by an Allied action.
2. The German garrisons in the British Channel Islands which had been occupied in the summer of 1940 also surrendered only at the war's end. It had been thought preferable to leave the islands in German hands rather than cause the destruction that recovering them by force would have entailed.
3. When Bradley had halted XV US Corps on 13 August, he had sent two of its divisions to rejoin Patton's main strength, but the other two had been transferred to First US Army's V Corps. The delay this caused prevented First US Army from making any further advance in this area until late on 17 August.
4. A vivid description of the sickening scenes in the pocket can be found in Alan Moorehead's *Eclipse*. He ends it by saying: 'The beaten Wehrmacht is a pitiable thing.'

Chapter Ten

The Race to the Rhine

Montgomery's rift with Bradley arose from a series of meetings on 23 August. Earlier on the 17th, Montgomery, as usual thinking 'one battle ahead', had suggested that once the Seine had been crossed, his own Twenty-First Army Group and Bradley's Twelfth US Army Group should form one 'solid mass of forty divisions', be given all possible resources and deliver 'one powerful full-blooded thrust' into the Low Countries and thence across the Rhine to the Ruhr. This provided Germany with one half of her coal and steel, without which she could not go on fighting for more than three months.

Bradley readily agreed, thereby convincing Montgomery that his command of the Allied Land Forces would continue as before. Later that day, however, a curt signal from General Marshall informed Eisenhower and Bradley that American public opinion would no longer tolerate a British officer in control of US forces and Eisenhower should become his own Land Forces Commander forthwith.

This was in fact inevitable. While British divisions were being broken up to fill the gaps in other formations, American reinforcements were pouring into France, a new Ninth US Army was being built up in Brittany and, on 15 August, Operation DRAGOON (ANVIL renamed for security reasons) had seen the Seventh US Army land in southern France and move up the Rhône Valley against minimal resistance. The American preponderance would grow until eventually Eisenhower commanded seventy-two US divisions, while the British, Canadians and Poles between them could provide only twenty-one.

Since 1944 was a presidential election year, Eisenhower and Bradley had no choice. Montgomery, though, was no politician. He had never understood Alexander's need to consider political implications and he did not understand those of his American colleagues. When he learned on 23 August that he would cease to be Land Forces Commander on

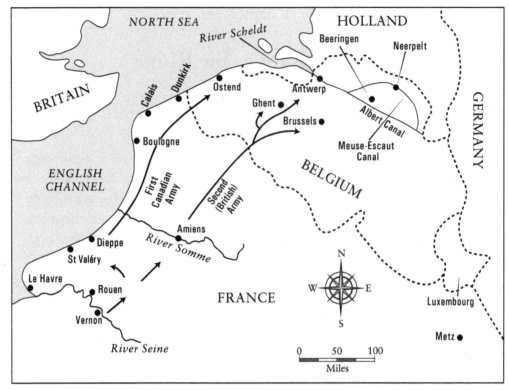

Map 17: The Advance from the River Seine to the Frontier of Holland.

1 September and worse still neither Eisenhower nor Bradley would support his assault through the Low Countries to the Ruhr, he reacted very badly. He was furious with Bradley for having 'reneged' on their agreement and towards the Supreme Commander he was dictatorial, patronizing, ill-tempered and ill-mannered. He would later confess that Eisenhower's patience and forbearing had been remarkable.

It was the abandonment of his plan that most concerned Montgomery and he was not mollified by Eisenhower and Marshall making it clear at press conferences that his replacement was in no way a reflection on his ability. Even his promotion to field marshal on 1 September amid a chorus of praise he regarded as no more than a 'consolation prize'.

On how to replace Montgomery's plan, Eisenhower and Bradley had different views. Bradley admired the suggestion of 'one powerful full-blooded thrust', but this could not be made through the Low Countries without stopping the advance of Third US Army into Lorraine, which was something else that Americans would not tolerate. Bradley therefore wanted the thrust to come from Lorraine towards Metz and the industrial Saar area.

Eisenhower, as in Italy and Normandy, did not like the idea of a single thrust anywhere. He instructed all his forces to advance on a broad front and gain the whole length of the Rhine from the North Sea to Switzerland. This decision appalled Montgomery, who believed the Allies would then not be strong enough to break through anywhere and the war would drag on into the spring of 1945.

Inevitably, Montgomery's later critics would suggest that his plan was designed to increase his importance. Yet on 23 August, he showed himself to be totally unselfish. He preferred Bradley's thrust to a broad front advance and declared that if Eisenhower should favour it, Bradley must have all the support needed and he (Montgomery) would accept a subsidiary role. He believed his own thrust was better still and if it would appease American public opinion, he was willing to serve under Bradley, an offer he would repeat more than once subsequently.

Eisenhower courteously but firmly insisted on his broad front policy, but Montgomery was not prepared to abandon his plan just yet. On 29 August, he sent Second (British) and First Canadian Armies into northern France, ordering them to make a 'swift and relentless' advance that, by showing they could move just as fast as Patton's men, might change Eisenhower's mind.

This was a tall order, for at this crucial moment Montgomery was again handicapped by equipment failure: a design fault was discovered in the engines of 1,400 of his British-built lorries and all replacements of the same type. He therefore had to ground most of his artillery and the bulk of VIII Corps. Roberts and his 11th Armoured Division and Major General Allan Adair's Guards Armoured Division, however, were transferred to XXX Corps, which under the forceful Horrocks became the spearhead of the thrust.

General Hodges and his First US Army advanced on XXX Corps' right. Hodges was hampered because to provide Eisenhower's broad front, he had to disperse his forces widely across the gap between the offensives of Montgomery and Patton. He did, however, provide a firm protection of XXX Corps' flank and capture more than 25,000 Germans fleeing from XXX Corps' armour. The left flank of XXX Corps was held by XII Corps which also provided a link with First Canadian Army which, strengthened by Crocker's I (British) Corps, advanced up the Channel coast.

Despite his urgency, Montgomery had not forgotten that his divisions were different and individual. He arranged that 51st Highland Division, now one of Crocker's formations, should capture St Valéry where its predecessor had surrendered in June 1940. He directed Dieppe as the target of 2nd Canadian Division in compensation for its sufferings in the raid of August 1942.

Montgomery's men rewarded his concern magnificently. They did not advance as fast as Patton's, they advanced faster. In the early hours of 31 August, 11th Armoured Division after a night dash of 40 miles captured Amiens, the main bridge over the Somme and two of three smaller ones. On 1 September, 2nd Canadian Division took Dieppe with its harbour installations undamaged. On 2 September, 51st Highland seized St Valéry before turning back to join another I Corps formation, 49th Division, which had cut off the Germans in the area of Le Havre. The two British divisions then closed in on Le Havre and on the morning of the 12th took the city, its submarine pens and 12,000 prisoners.

Also on 2 September, 2nd and 3rd Canadian Infantry, 4th Canadian Armoured and 1st Polish Armoured divisions broke over the Somme and raced through the Pas-de-Calais, isolating Calais, Boulogne and Dunkirk and overrunning the launch sites of the V1 flying bombs that had been pounding London. On the afternoon of 3 September, the Guards Armoured Division, having covered 250 miles in six days, entered Brussels amid scenes of wild celebration. On the afternoon of 4 September, 11th Armoured Division reached Antwerp, took 6,000 prisoners and with the help of Belgian resistance fighters secured its massive docks intact.

There had been only one disappointment in this amazing advance. The bridges over the Albert Canal had not been taken by 11th Armoured when it captured Antwerp. It has been said that Roberts should have received specific orders to do this, but he would honestly accept that he did not need them. He fully intended to take the bridges and believed he had done so, because he had been advised that the canal ran through Antwerp when in fact it ran just north of the city.[1] Ironically Montgomery, by winning the Battle of Normandy more quickly than anyone had expected, had caught out Allied Intelligence.

In any case, the days of rapid advance were ending as Hitler began to regain his grip on the situation. Patton was the first to learn of this. His Third US Army reached the Moselle River on 1 September, but supply problems prevented it from crossing until the 5th and when it did, Patton found his way to Metz and the Saar blocked by fixed defences manned by 3rd and 15th Panzer Grenadier divisions each containing two regiments (the equivalent of brigades) of infantry and one of artillery. Hitler had withdrawn these from Italy and he reinforced them with newly-created tank and infantry units to create a revived Fifth Panzer Army, which he entrusted to General Hasso von Manteuffel, a brilliant tank commander summoned from the Russian front.

Patton's attempts to break through the defences cost his Third US Army 41,000 casualties in four weeks; as many as those of the whole Twenty-First Allied Army Group in the six weeks after D-Day. This bloodbath is usually ignored except as an argument in favour of the broad front policy on the basis that without Patton's advance, his opponents would have been available to oppose Montgomery's full-blooded offensive.

Since the Saar industries were important, it seems probable that just a subsidiary move towards them would have pinned them in place. If they had been sent against Montgomery, they would have lost the protection of their fixed defences and they were not prepared for mobile warfare: their artillery was largely horse-drawn, their infantry was short of vehicles, and their tanks, having come straight from the factories, broke down with depressing regularity. It does not appear, therefore, that they would have presented much of a threat to Montgomery's intended forty divisions: an opinion shared by all those who would have had to oppose his assault.

After the war, Chester Wilmot and Liddell Hart interviewed von Rundstedt, who Hitler now reappointed C-in-C West – Model became head of Army Group 'B' and continued to direct the fighting in the Low Countries – his new Chief of Staff, General Siegfried Westphal; his former Chief of Staff, General Günther Blumentritt; von Manteuffel; General Kurt Student, the creator of Germany's airborne force and now head of First Parachute Army – of which more shortly – and General Hans Speidel, Rommel's former Chief of Staff in Army Group 'B'. Without a single exception all declared that the Allies had lost a great opportunity by rejecting Montgomery's proposed concentrated thrust through the Low Countries to the Rhine and the Ruhr: this must have succeeded, shortened the war considerably and saved 'tens of thousands of lives – on both sides'.

Montgomery's state of mind as he saw this great opportunity rejected can be imagined and explains if it cannot wholly excuse his insubordinate and confrontational attitude. It also explains why he clung to the hope that he might somehow regain the opportunity. This, though, he would have to do quickly as increasingly vile weather deprived the Allies of many of their advantages and German resistance began to stiffen ominously.

In the Normandy fighting, the German 85th Division had been severely mauled but its commander, Lieutenant General Kurt Chill, had made good its losses by recruiting the remnants of two other shattered infantry divisions and on 4 September, began to set up defences along the Albert Canal. Then on the 6th, his force was taken over by Student's First Parachute Army. This contained 20,000 paratroopers and 10,000 air crew made available by Göring, desperate to atone for the Luftwaffe's poor performance in Normandy. Few had been trained for land-fighting but all were young, ardent and, like the SS tank crews, fanatically loyal to and ready to die for their Führer.

It was therefore unfortunate that shortage of supplies should have forced Twenty-First Army Group to halt temporarily to 'refit, refuel and rest'. Captain Liddell Hart waxes indignant at this action, declaring that only Patton realized the importance of persistent pursuit, but since Patton had halted for supply reasons during both his sweep towards the Seine and his advance towards Metz, this was scarcely a fair judgement. Moreover Liddell Hart's assertion that the halt lasted from 4 to 7 September is simply incorrect.

In reality, Twenty-First Army Group did not halt on 4 September: as we have seen it was on that date that Roberts took Antwerp. There was a pause on the 5th, apart from reconnaissance sorties, but on the 6th the advance resumed, encouraged by Montgomery having arranged for 1,000 tons of supplies, especially petrol, to be delivered to Brussels every day by aerial transports.

On 6 September, both 11th Armoured and Guards Armoured crossed the Albert Canal. Counter-attacks drove the former back but at Beeringen, the Guards held their ground while sappers replaced a bridge the Germans had destroyed. On the 6th also, XII Corps captured Ghent. On the 9th, the Canadians took the Belgian port of Ostend. On the

10th, the Irish Guards' 3rd Battalion seized a crossing at Neerpelt over the Meuse-Escaut Canal, renaming it 'Joe's Bridge' in honour of their CO, Lieutenant Colonel Vandeleur.

Despite this continued progress, many have claimed that Montgomery should have abandoned his race to the Rhine and turned his attention to the estuary of the River Scheldt on which Antwerp stands. Some 50 miles long from the city to the sea, this was heavily mined and covered by coastal batteries that prevented Allied shipping from reaching Antwerp's docks. The batteries were situated south of the river around the little port of Breskens and north of it on the somewhat confusingly called South Beveland Peninsula[2] and the island of Walcheren, and were held by the Fifteenth Army of Lieutenant General Gustav von Zangen.

Von Rundstedt wished to increase his strength in southern Holland by withdrawing some of von Zangen's forces from the Scheldt's south bank which was naturally protected by canals, dykes and waterlogged ground. For two weeks a collection of freighters, barges and small boats, operating by night to avoid air attacks, carried a total of 65,000 men, 530 guns, 4,600 motor vehicles and 4,000 horses from Breskens to the port of Flushing on Walcheren. By no means all reached von Rundstedt, for the rest of their route by causeway from Walcheren to South Beveland and then to mainland Holland over a long narrow isthmus was made by day and suffered heavy casualties from Allied aircraft.

Nonetheless, von Rundstedt did receive an increase of strength and it has therefore been urged that Montgomery should have advanced a further 15 miles to the end of the isthmus and blocked this escape route. The trouble was that von Rundstedt only ordered the withdrawal on 6 September and the night crossings from Breskens to Flushing concealed the Germans' intentions from Allied Intelligence. By the time the situation was appreciated, Student and Chill could offer fierce resistance; how fierce would be revealed when the Canadians attempted to reach the isthmus on 1 October. They got there only on the 10th and it was another fortnight before the isthmus was sealed off.

It may indeed have been fortunate that the Germans had not decided on this withdrawal earlier. Had they done so and the Allies learned of it on say 4 September, 11th Armoured Division would probably have been sent to and blocked the end of the isthmus. Whether this could have been held against counter-attacks from all sides is another matter, but in any case both Horrocks and Roberts have confirmed that 11th Armoured lacked the strength to reach the isthmus and also seize Antwerp which would therefore have been bypassed. The Germans would thus have had plenty of time to wreck the docks and cause damage that Roberts later learned would have taken years to repair.

Even after this withdrawal, the Scheldt Estuary was strongly defended. The south bank was held by the 64th Division which the Canadians considered 'the best infantry we have met'. The 70th Infantry Division in South Beveland was less formidable, but had 170 artillery pieces. The island of Walcheren was strongly fortified and, except at its port of Flushing, protected by a massive dyke. To clear the Scheldt Estuary would take the full strength of Twenty-First Army Group, but many have argued this was what Montgomery should have done.

Montgomery's attention, however, remained fixed on achieving an early crossing of the Rhine and he was strongly supported by Dempsey and Horrocks. As Horrocks would later declare, while there was any chance of gaining this 'big prize', 'he [Montgomery] would have been wrong to deflect his resources to a subsidiary task.'[3] Instead, Montgomery looked to a new factor for help: the First Allied Airborne Army.

The First Allied Airborne Army under American Lieutenant General Lewis Brereton controlled XVIII American and I British Airborne Corps. The former contained 82nd, 101st and the newly-formed 17th Airborne divisions and was led by Lieutenant General Matthew Ridgway, who had commanded the 82nd on D-Day. The British Corps came under Brereton's deputy, Lieutenant General Frederick Browning, and consisted of 1st and 6th Airborne divisions and 1st Polish Parachute Brigade, plus 52nd Lowland Division once the corps had secured a suitable airfield.

It was agreed by everyone that the men of the Airborne Army were magnificent soldiers. Unfortunately, their high standard masked a number of serious flaws, particularly in 1st (British) Airborne Division. Neither Brereton nor Browning nor the division's CO, Major General Robert 'Roy' Urquhart – his real Christian names were Robert Elliott – nor most of its staff officers had any experience of airborne operations, its communications were poor, its wireless sets were unreliable and the relationships of many of its senior officers were not happy.

This was particularly the case with Browning. He and Brereton disliked and distrusted each other, as did he and Major General Stanisław

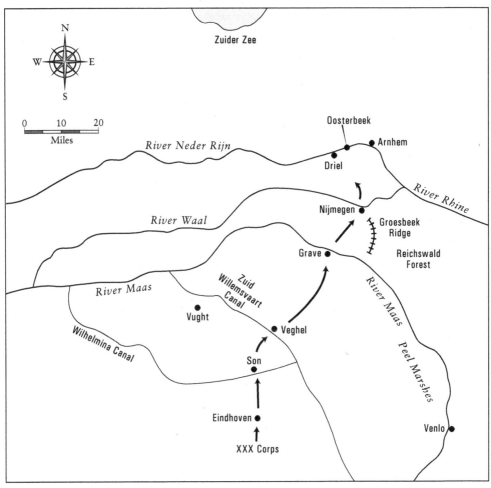

Map 18: Operation MARKET GARDEN.

Sosabowski, the very independently-minded commander of 1st Polish Parachute Brigade, who Browning considered 'an impediment to Allied harmony'.[4] Some of Browning's most experienced subordinates had no confidence in his leadership, including Sosabowski, Brigadier John (later General Sir John) Hackett, leader of 4th Parachute Brigade and Major Brian Urquhart – no relation to 'Roy' – Browning's Chief Intelligence officer.

Montgomery was unaware of these flaws because airborne troops had performed so splendidly on D-Day. He had hoped to use First Airborne Army to assist his advance from the Seine, but this had been so swift that all such plans proved unnecessary and were cancelled. He now hoped it could help him to cross the Rhine and regain the initiative.

There had originally been six water obstacles in Montgomery's path but as we have seen, Guards Armoured would reduce them to four. These reading from south to north were the Wilhelmina Canal, the Zuid Willemsvaart Canal, the River Maas – as the Meuse was called in Holland – and the Rhine. Montgomery knew that his engineers could quickly erect temporary bridges to replace any blown up over the canals but not over the rivers, which he intended to cross at Venlo and Wesel respectively. However, he remembered that on D-Day airborne troops had seized the bridges over the River Orne and the Canal de Caen before they could be destroyed and decided to call on airborne troops again to perform a similar service.

On 5 September meetings were held, first between Montgomery and Browning and then between Browning and Dempsey. It quickly became clear that the air force chiefs would never risk an airborne operation at Wesel, fearing their vulnerable transport aircraft would suffer prohibitively high losses from AA fire. Browning, desperate for 1st Airborne Division to see combat, therefore persuaded Montgomery and Dempsey to strike not north-east but north on a much wider sweep to the Ruhr.

This was Operation COMET and was prepared by Browning's planners, not those of Twenty-First Army Group. It had the advantage of bypassing the defences of Germany's Siegfried Line and the Peel Marshes near Venlo, but it meant seizing the bridges over three major rivers because on entering Holland, the Rhine separates into a main branch named the Waal and the more northern Neder Rijn. However, Browning's biographer, Richard Mead, in his *General 'Boy'* – this was Browning's nickname – confirms that Browning assured Montgomery that 1st Airborne Division plus 1st Polish Parachute Brigade could 'do the job alone'.

Browning also brushed aside protests by Sosabowski, Hackett and the two Urquharts that his available strength would be inadequate, cheerfully proclaiming that 1st Airborne and the Poles 'can do anything'. Montgomery, though, was increasingly concerned about growing German resistance and continuing shortages of supplies. COMET had originally been intended for 7 September, but Montgomery first postponed it and finally, on the evening of the 9th, cancelled it altogether.

Not that Montgomery had abandoned his desired northward thrust supported by airborne landings. Even if this might not take the Ruhr and end the war in 1944, it would still confer many benefits. It should reach the Zuider Zee, thereby cutting off not only von Zangen's men but all the Germans in southern and western Holland. It should overrun the sites from which the V2 rocket bombs that first fell on London on 8 September were being launched. It should cross the Rhine and prepare for an advance on the Ruhr later. It just might persuade Eisenhower to 'invest in success' and approve Montgomery's 'full-blooded' thrust.

Montgomery, though, realized that he must increase the strength of his airborne forces and the supplies of his ground forces. Eisenhower generously agreed that 82nd and 101st US Airborne divisions might support COMET and on 10 September, Montgomery, Dempsey and Browning met to sort out details of a strengthened Operation COMET II. There was still the question of supplies and when Eisenhower, though in pain from an injured leg, flew to meet Montgomery in Brussels, he was treated to an ill-tempered and abusive diatribe about the dangers of his broad front policy. Quietly but firmly, he retorted: 'Steady Monty! You can't speak to me like that. I'm your boss.' Montgomery then apologized.[5] He continued to ask for priority of supplies but in a restrained and dignified fashion, if apparently without result.

In fact, Montgomery had been more successful than he knew. When Eisenhower had had a chance to forget his lack of respect and consider his plan, its boldness and imagination so impressed him that he later declared he not only approved but insisted upon it. On 12 September, Bedell Smith flew to meet Montgomery and promised that the drive to the Saar would be halted, the transport of three US divisions and 1,000 tons of supplies a day would be sent to Twenty-First Army Group, and First US Army would also receive increased supplies and would support Montgomery's offensive.

On 17 September therefore, this began. It was now entitled Operation MARKET GARDEN, a good name since it consisted of two plans from different sources combined in one essential whole. Operation GARDEN was the responsibility of Dempsey's Second (British) Army which was to advance to the town of Eindhoven and thence over the water obstacles to the Zuider Zee. The main thrust would be by Horrocks and his XXX Corps, containing Guards Armoured Division, the independent 8th Armoured Brigade and the 43rd and 50th Infantry divisions. Its left and right flanks would be secured by advances by XII and VIII Corps respectively.

Operation MARKET was planned by I Airborne Corps. This was the seizure of the bridges that would speed up XXX Corps' progress. Those over the two remaining canals were at Son and Veghel: they were the objectives of 101st US Airborne. Those over the Maas at Grave and the Waal at Nijmegen were the targets of 82nd US Airborne. That across the Neder Rijn at Arnhem was the responsibility of 1st British Airborne and the Poles.

Montgomery was normally reluctant to have his operations planned by anyone but his own staff under his direction, yet he left MARKET to the airborne planners who he thought were experienced in such operations. It was a mistake for there were several flaws in MARKET, though in fairness many were outside the Airborne Army's control or resulted from sheer bad luck.

One was the weather that contradicted favourable forecasts by deteriorating badly after the first day of the battle. It particularly hampered aerial operations and General Student considered it a major cause of their failure.

Another was that the extra supplies and transport promised by Bedell Smith were not forthcoming because Patton's costly attacks on Metz were not halted and therefore his maintenance could not be reduced. As a result, Hodges could not mount an effective diversion and Dempsey could not use either XII or VIII Corps to support Horrocks. Instead XXX Corps had to operate on its own with its flanks and line of communication wide open to attack. Protection on its right flank was provided by 82nd US Airborne, but at the expense of an early assault on the bridges at Nijmegen.

A further one was that the Germans by pure chance had sent to the Arnhem area for rest and refitting units savaged in Normandy, in particular II SS Panzer Corps: 9th SS and 10th SS Panzer divisions. Montgomery, Dempsey and Brereton were all assured by their Intelligence staffs that these were unlikely to be a threat as they were 'battered', 'battle-scarred' or even 'broken', although Major Brian Urquhart did warn Browning that they were a danger. He was unconcerned, however, calling his Intelligence Officer a permanent pessimist and telling the other Urquhart, Major General 'Roy', that he would be unlikely to face more than a weak brigade group with perhaps a few tanks.

There were reasons for these views. In 1944 a panzer division officially contained 14,700 men and 100 tanks. On 17 September, 9th SS Panzer had about 2,500 men, 10th SS Panzer had about 3,000 and the two between them had some 20 Panther tanks, several of which were unserviceable. When battle was joined, part of 9th SS Panzer and the majority of 10th SS Panzer tried to hold the Nijmegen bridges but failed to do so. The remainder of II SS Panzer Corps was sent to recapture the Arnhem road bridge – the less important railway bridge had been blown up by the Germans – but took three days to overcome a mere 600 defenders.

This was scarcely the performance expected of any SS Panzer Corps and none of the German accounts of MARKET GARDEN consider it had a crucial effect. They lay more stress on yet another piece of ill fortune on 17 September. One of 101st US Airborne's gliders came down at Vught, west of Veghel, which was the site of Student's headquarters. In an American officer's briefcase he found details of the sites chosen for later air-lifts – to which he hastily sent AA batteries – and of 101st's part in the operation, and sufficient information to indicate all the other parts as well.

At 1300 on 17 September, Operation MARKET commenced, followed by Operation GARDEN at 1400, when British guns opened fire on enemy positions north of XXX Corps' start-line; the corps advanced at 1435, supported brilliantly by Broadhurst's Typhoons. Unfortunately it had become apparent that there were not enough aircraft to tow all the gliders and carry all the parachutists at the same time. Both Montgomery and Browning considered that this difficulty could have been solved by mounting two separate air-lifts on the 17th, but Brereton rejected the idea, fearing high casualties from pilot fatigue or insufficient aircraft maintenance and repairs.

Since the main aim of MARKET GARDEN was to get Second (British) Army beyond the Rhine, with the capture of the bridges only a means to this end, it was decided that 101st US Airborne, as the first formation able to help Horrocks, would be given its full strength on 17 September, but 82nd US Airborne only its two parachute regiments with its glider-borne regiment arriving the next day. Urquhart's 1st (British) Airborne Division would receive 1st Parachute Brigade and 1st Airlanding (glider-borne) Brigade on the 17th and 4th Parachute Brigade on the 18th. Finally on the 19th, 1st Polish Parachute Brigade would be dropped close to the south end of the Arnhem road bridge.

On the 17th, 101st US Airborne just failed to reach the bridge over the Wilhelmina Canal before it was blown up, but by next morning XXX Corps had reached Eindhoven and moved on to Son where the indefatigable Royal Engineers erected a new bridge in just twelve hours. At Veghel, 101st US Airborne captured not one but four bridges over the Zuid-Willemsvaart Canal intact.

Further north, the men of 82nd US Airborne landed on both sides of and duly captured the bridge over the Maas at Grave. They made no attempt on the Nijmegen bridges, however, because they also had to take the Groesbeek Ridge to the east of their line of advance that blocked an obvious path for a German attack from the Reichswald, a great forest on the Dutch-German frontier. On the 18th, the Germans did indeed surge out of the Reichswald, capturing the landing-area where the 82nd's glider-borne supplies and reinforcements were intended to arrive. Luckily, however, the Americans drove the enemy back just before these came in.

Finally on 17 September, 1st Airborne Division suffered no interference from the Germans, although it lost thirty-eight gliders that had snapped their tow-ropes. There was, however, a crucial flaw in its plans: one that tends to be concealed under an all-prevailing myth.

Everyone 'knows' that when early on 10 September, Montgomery and Browning – and Dempsey though he is rarely mentioned – met in conference, Browning warned that 'we might be going a bridge too far.' This pithy catchphrase has been endlessly repeated and become almost a summary of Operation MARKET GARDEN. Yet it was not even mentioned until 1958 when it appeared in Robert 'Roy' Urquhart's book *Arnhem*, and though made in all good faith, there are grave doubts as to its reliability.

In the first place, Browning was desperately anxious to bring 1st Airborne Division into action as soon as possible, believing that any more cancelled operations would lead to a collapse of cohesion and morale. If he expressed doubts in his division's ability to hold the Arnhem bridge, Montgomery might well cancel MARKET GARDEN as he had COMET. It is difficult to believe that Browning would have taken the slightest risk of this happening.

Nor was there any good reason why Browning should have had doubts. Urquhart says he was concerned by 'the distance that the Second Army would have to cover before it reached Arnhem.' Yet it was Browning who had convinced Montgomery to go for Arnhem in the first place. He had raised no objections when COMET was decided on 5 September and since then, Second Army had decreased the distance between its start-line and Arnhem, not much in terms of mileage but greatly in terms of difficulty by getting over two of the obstacles between them: the Albert and Meuse-Escaut canals.

Still further evidence that Browning made no 'bridge too far' comment at the 10 September meeting comes from Peter Rostron, who in his biography confirms that Dempsey had never been happy about directing Second Army towards Arnhem and expressed 'everlasting regret' that he had not at that meeting argued against this. It is inconceivable that he would still have remained silent if Browning had raised doubts.

In his biography of Browning, Richard Mead declares that Urquhart was one of the first people to see Browning on his return from Belgium and so is 'a good witness'. However, when Montgomery's biographer Nigel Hamilton interviewed Urquhart in 1983, Urquhart confirmed he had never personally heard Browning use the phrase 'a bridge too far'.

For that matter, Nigel Hamilton interviewed Hackett in 1985 and was told that Hackett had never heard this expression used by Browning either. The only person who has claimed to have done so is Brigadier Gordon Walch, Browning's Chief of Staff in I British Airborne Corps, in a statement lodged in the Imperial War Museum and quoted by Richard Mead. This differs from the version given by Urquhart stating that Browning told Montgomery the operation 'was possible' but perhaps was going 'a bridge too far with the air lift available.' Walch says he learned this 'immediately after' Browning's return to Britain following the conferences of 10 September.

Once again, though, there is little to support this contention. Whatever Browning may have said to Walch, it is difficult to believe that he would have raised any doubts with Montgomery for the reasons already stated, and again there were no good grounds for doubts. When he had prepared COMET on 5 September, he had looked to seize the Arnhem bridge with just one brigade; his initial air-lift on 17 September would give him two brigades and he would have all three by the end of the 18th.

Add to all this the fact that Browning could not possibly have warned Montgomery on 10 September that the air-lifts would cause problems since the details of these would not be decided until the 11th following a hectic night checking aircraft availability – Montgomery would only learn them on the 12th – and we can see that Walch's statement can inspire little confidence. It was, after all, prepared forty-five years after the incident described and Walch's memory may have tricked him.

The 'bridge too far' expression is also inaccurate and misleading in two respects. It does not give but it does disguise the real reason for failure at Arnhem. This, says Chester Wilmot, was that fearing heavy casualties if Urquhart's men came down in Arnhem, the airborne planners preferred to use the flat open areas west of the town for their dropping- and landing-zones. These, though, were 6 miles from their objective of the bridge, and when Urquhart's 4th Parachute Brigade arrived on 18 September, it too was dropped west of Arnhem and the site fixed for the delivery of supplies was further away still.

That this was the basic reason for failure has been confirmed by Urquhart, Hackett, Major General Gale whose 6th Airborne Division adopted different tactics on D-Day, Major General James Gavin, 82nd US Airborne's brilliant commander, General Student and Field Marshal von Rundstedt. Von Rundstedt, incidentally, also specifically stated in his official report to Hitler that the British had *not* 'selected a target too far in advance of the main defensive line'. 'A bridge not far enough towards' is far too clumsy to be a catch-phrase, but it does have the merit of being true.

Lieutenant Colonel John Frost, perhaps Urquhart's most experienced subordinate, was another of those confident that 1st Airborne Division would have taken the Arnhem road bridge easily with better planning. He demonstrated this by leading 500 men of his 2nd Parachute Battalion through Arnhem to seize the northern end of the bridge, although SS troops held on to its southern side. Unfortunately, attempts to move to his support broke down in the face of fierce resistance organized by Field Marshal Model, whose headquarters were located in an Arnhem suburb. No one reached Frost on the 17th and only 100 men on the 18th.

On 19 September, everything went wrong. Bad weather prevented 1st Polish Parachute Brigade from dropping south of the Arnhem bridge to help Frost's gallant band. The rest of 1st Airborne Division could not help them either, partly because it was trying to reach the planned supply-drop area. This it failed to do and its poor wireless equipment prevented it from informing its aerial transports, which braved ferocious AA fire to deliver the supplies only for them to fall into enemy hands.

This tragedy was illuminated by a remarkable display of skill and courage. A Dakota of 271 Squadron piloted by Flight Lieutenant David Lord had its starboard engine set ablaze but Lord flew on and, despite losing height and under continuous fire, circled twice over the dropping-zone to deliver his supplies with pinpoint accuracy. He then ordered his crew to bail out, remaining at the controls to give them a chance to do so; sadly only his navigator, Flying Officer King, survived as a prisoner of war. A moment later, flames engulfed the Dakota which plunged to earth. Lord received a posthumous Victoria Cross, the only one awarded to a pilot of Transport Command.

German attacks were steadily increasing, for Hitler in an unwelcome tribute to Montgomery's strategic foresight was greatly alarmed by MARKET GARDEN and sent against it reserves from as far away as Denmark. The British units trying to reach Frost were driven back, another posthumous VC being awarded to Captain Lionel Queripel who, though wounded in both arms and twice in his face, covered his men's retirement, firing and throwing grenades until hit again and killed.

Further south, heavy attacks also fell on 82nd US Airborne, but luckily XXX Corps now reached the Americans and helped to drive the enemy back. Attempts on the Nijmegen bridges, however, were again delayed and this had an adverse effect on the general situation because, though no one realized it, the battle had in fact become a race between Allied troops striving to capture the bridges at Nijmegen and German troops striving to regain the one at Arnhem.

During the morning of the 20th, Gavin's paratroopers, the infantry of 1st Battalion, Grenadier Guards and the tanks of its 2nd Battalion fought their way into Nijmegen. At 1500, assault boats carried part of 3rd Battalion, 504th US Parachute Infantry Regiment over the 400-yards-wide River Waal, covered by an artillery barrage and strikes from rocket-firing Typhoons. Enemy fire caused many casualties but 200 men, led by Major Julian Cook, reached the far bank. Aided by later arrivals, they steadily expanded their bridgehead and by 1830 had broken out of it. Half an hour later, they seized the northern end of Nijmegen's railway bridge, the defenders of which fled over it only to be mown down by the Allied troops on the south bank.

Encouraged by the sight of an American flag on the railway bridge, the Grenadiers' Shermans fought their way over the more important road bridge and moved along the Waal's north bank to link up with Cook's men. Behind them, a young sapper officer, Lieutenant Anthony Jones, cut the wires leading to the bridge's demolition charges and threw these into the river, earning a Military Cross in the process.

Sadly, though, the Germans had already secured the bridge that was their crucial target. Frost's 2nd Parachute Battalion had been suffering heavy casualties, among them Lieutenant John Grayburn who had mounted continual counter-attacks despite wounds in the head, arm and back and was awarded another posthumous VC. That afternoon, with its CO wounded and disabled and reduced to a strength of only 140 men, the battalion was at last driven off the bridge and the Germans quickly rushed forces, including tanks, over it to oppose any British advance from Nijmegen.

Other German formations continued to harry the rest of 1st Airborne Division. By 21 September, this had been driven into a narrow salient in the outlying suburb of Oosterbeek. Here it was engaged all day by forces three times its own number, including a unit of forty-five King Tiger tanks, a Mark II version with the usual 88mm gun and much heavier protective armour. Urquhart's men threw back every attack and earned two more Victoria Crosses. Major Robert Cain was wounded but survived; Lance Sergeant John Baskeyfield's was another awarded posthumously.

Nonetheless, 1st Airborne's supplies, especially of ammunition, were running desperately low and it was clear that it had to be relieved very soon. Unfortunately XXX Corps was meeting increasingly strong opposition and on 22 September, a German assault on its right flank cut its supply line for twenty-four hours and compelled Horrocks to send back a brigade to clear the road.

As at the Battle of the Mareth Line, Montgomery recognized an unpleasant truth before anyone else. On 23 September, he warned Dempsey that 1st Airborne should be withdrawn. Horrocks and Browning, however, still hoped that the Polish Parachute Brigade which had been dropped at the village of Driel, opposite Oosterbeek, and 43rd

(Wessex) Division which had been sent to support it might cross the Neder Rijn, join Urquhart and at least retain a bridgehead on the far bank.

It was not to be. Only a handful of men got over the river on the night of 23/24 September and on the afternoon of the 24th, the Germans again cut XXX Corps' supply line, this time for forty-eight hours. Horrocks and Browning were convinced and on the night of 25/26 September, Urquhart and some 2,200 men crossed the Neder Rijn to safety under cover of a heavy rainstorm and a barrage from XXX Corps' guns. Several hundred more, hidden and protected by the Dutch, escaped later but 1st Airborne left behind 1,130 dead and more than 6,000, including Frost, prisoners of war, at least half of them wounded. The Germans had not been unscathed either: at Arnhem and Oosterbeek alone they had had about 3,300 casualties, 1,300 of them fatal.

Since even Montgomery could not say that MARKET GARDEN had gone exactly according to plan, he was content to claim it was 'ninety per cent successful'. This, as Chester Wilmot unkindly but not unfairly points out, was correct 'merely in terms of the number of bridges captured'. There had in fact been several useful gains which will be examined later, but they were tactical ones. The great strategical objectives – to cross the Rhine, threaten the Ruhr, cut off the German forces in Holland, capture the V2 bases and end the war in 1944 – were not attained. General Fuller is right therefore when he calls the operation a failure, though he also comments that: 'None of his [Montgomery's] great battles, not even El Alamein, is likely to lend greater lustre to his generalship' since 'in audacity of conception and execution it stands in a class of its own.'

Equally worthy of admiration is the generous attitude Montgomery, as after GOODWOOD, showed to the men under his command. Browning's biographer tells us that when Urquhart returned after his ordeal, he 'found Montgomery, unlike Boy, totally understanding'. Montgomery publicly thanked and praised 'every officer and man' in 1st Airborne Division. He wrote to the War Office commending both Browning and Urquhart. He was caustic about the broken promises to keep him properly supplied, but in his *Memoirs* the only man in all Twenty-First Army Group blamed by Montgomery is Montgomery himself.

Thus Montgomery rightly declares: 'The airborne forces at Arnhem were dropped too far away from the vital objective – the bridge. It was some hours before they reached it.' Then he states simply and honestly:

I take the blame for this mistake. I should have ordered Second Army and I Airborne Corps to arrange that at least one complete Parachute Brigade was dropped quite close to the bridge, so that it could have been captured in a matter of minutes. I did not do so.

There is much to admire in MARKET GARDEN: the brilliant capture of the Nijmegen bridges by the Grenadier Guards, who Major General Gavin calls 'the best soldiers I saw on either side during the war', and Gavin's own 82nd Airborne which Dempsey hailed as 'the greatest division in the world today'; the gallantry of 1st Airborne with its four Victoria Crosses, three of them posthumous and of its supporting airmen epitomized by Flight Lieutenant Lord. Perhaps at this distance of time can be added the resilience of the German defenders, recovering with remarkable speed from their catastrophic defeat in Normandy.

What a pity then, that some seem determined to remember MARKET GARDEN for and by a clever catchphrase that was certainly not uttered at the time and in the circumstances reported by legend was probably not uttered at all, and would be doubly inaccurate and misleading if it ever had been.

Notes

1. Roberts tells us that the only available maps were of a very small scale, on which Antwerp was 'a little red circle' with 'a blue line going through the middle of it' to indicate the canal.
2. North Beveland was an island off the coast of the peninsula.
3. Horrocks doubts whether the clearance of the Scheldt Estuary at this time would have 'shortened the war by even one day'.
4. It seems that Browning's views were communicated to Montgomery, who made another of his impulsive misjudgements of character and concluded that the Poles had 'no keenness to fight'.
5. Montgomery's later critics have said that his apology was 'mumbled' reluctantly. However, his Head of Administration, Major General Graham, and Tedder – not his friend or admirer – who were present both say it was made openly and honestly. Montgomery may well have been ashamed of his own bad manners.

Chapter Eleven

The Fight for the German Frontier

Another stupid slogan now reappeared to bedevil the Western Allies: 'Unconditional Surrender'. The Nazis had always insisted that this meant Germany's destruction and on 24 September 1944, their warnings appeared to be justified by the publication of a plan for the country's post-war future prepared by Henry Morgenthau, the US Secretary of the Treasury.

By this, Germany would lose East Prussia and Silesia – as indeed she did – and also the Saar and a large area west of the Rhine. The mines and industries in the Ruhr and elsewhere would be destroyed and she would become 'primarily agricultural and pastoral'. This would compel much of her labour force to find work in other countries. She would be policed by her 'continental neighbours', which in defiance of geography were held to include Russia. Despite numerous protests, Roosevelt refused to scrap 'unconditional surrender' or give any indication of what it would mean in practice.

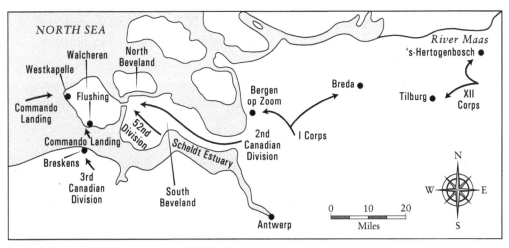

Map 19: The clearance of the Scheldt Estuary.

The result was made abundantly clear by neutral journalists in Germany and intercepted letters home from German soldiers. The majority of the population had no illusions as to the vengeance likely to be inflicted by the Russians, but hoped other enemies would prove more merciful. As defeat appeared more and more certain therefore, support steadily grew for 'letting in' the Western Allies. After the Morgenthau Plan, however, the whole country felt that the only course was to fight on and trust that new weapons or quarrels between the Allies would somehow produce a miracle, and Eisenhower's forces had to face a whole series of grim actions against desperate resistance in increasingly vile weather.

On 22 September, Montgomery had avoided a conference called by Eisenhower. This was not a 'calculated insult' to the Supreme Commander as some have asserted, it was because Montgomery was still bitter about Eisenhower's unfulfilled promises of support and feared he might lose his temper and make matters worse. His decision proved justified: the charming and popular de Guingand got the promises repeated and this time honoured by the cancellation of Patton's wasteful assaults on Metz. As a result, both VIII and XII Corps were able to move up to the line of the Maas on XXX Corps' flanks and the corridor leading to Nijmegen was widened and strengthened, enabling it to be held against repeated attacks.

This alone was a considerable achievement, as was acknowledged by General Student. He declares MARKET GARDEN 'a great success' and points out that 'The conquest of the Nijmegen area meant the creation of a good jumping-board for the offensive which contributed to the end of the war.'

That offensive would be into the Rhineland and then over the Rhine, but the corridor would also provide a splendid start-line for an advance westward to clear the Scheldt Estuary:

'And here,' Montgomery reports in his *Memoirs*, 'I must admit to a bad mistake on my part – I underestimated the difficulties of opening up the approaches to Antwerp so that we could get the free use of that port. I reckoned that the Canadian Army could do it *while* we were going for the Ruhr; I was wrong.'

Since Montgomery then immediately states that 'I remain MARKET GARDEN's unrepentant advocate', he clearly did not feel he should have concentrated on Antwerp instead of launching MARKET GARDEN as has been suggested. His mistake was not turning his whole Twenty-First Army Group against the Scheldt Estuary immediately after Arnhem was lost.

In fact the Canadians had already made useful gains on both banks of the estuary and on 3 October, brilliant precision attacks by Bomber Command smashed the sea defences protecting Walcheren Island, causing flooding that left its garrison holding only the tops of the dykes.[1] At another conference on 5 October, Montgomery did attend and was told by both Brooke and Admiral Sir Bertram Ramsay that he should not leave the opening of Antwerp to the Canadians. He listened and after discussions next day with Dempsey and Simonds – now commanding the Canadians in the absence of Crerar due to illness – changed his mind. On the 7th, he postponed proposed attacks eastward by Second Army and on the 9th expressly ordered that operations by Twenty-First Army Group to open Antwerp for shipping must 'take priority over all other offensive operations'.

Montgomery's plans for clearing the Scheldt Estuary were completed by 16 October. He also urged Eisenhower to appoint one land forces commander – in fairness he did suggest Bradley as well as himself – and expressed criticism of Eisenhower's leadership to Marshall and Bedell Smith. This of course was disgraceful and Eisenhower warned him that if their disagreements continued they would have to be referred 'to higher authority'. Montgomery hastily apologized.

Fortunately, Montgomery's plans for the Scheldt Estuary showed him at his best: clear, simple and realistic. On the Scheldt's south bank, 3rd Canadian Division would attack Breskens. On the north bank, 2nd Canadian Division, reinforced by 52nd Lowland Division and DD tank units, would attack South Beveland. Crocker's I Corps, containing 49th (British), 1st Polish Armoured, 4th Canadian Armoured and 104th US Infantry divisions, would strike north and north-east to Breda and Bergen op Zoom. Ritchie's XII (British) Corps would move westward from the MARKET GARDEN corridor, capture Tilburg and 's-Hertogenbosch, join I Corps and with it secure the south bank of the Maas all the way to the North Sea.

In order to confuse the enemy, these attacks were launched separately in quick succession: the I Corps' attack on 20 October, that on Breskens the next day, that of XII Corps the day after and that on South Beveland on the 24th. All were made over difficult waterlogged country. All were opposed by determined foes who had the advantage of fixed defences. All resulted in bloody fighting, usually at close quarters.[2] Yet all proved successful.

On 26 October, Bergen op Zoom fell, followed by Tilburg and 's-Hertogenbosch on the 27th and Breda on the 29th. By 8 November, Crocker and Ritchie had driven the Germans back over the Maas. South Beveland had been overrun by 31 October; the Breskens area by 3 November. On 1 November, Walcheren was invaded by army Commandos landing at Flushing and Royal Marine Commandos at Westkapelle on its north-west coast. Joined by 52nd Lowland Division at Flushing and 2nd Canadian Division from South Beveland on 3 November, the attackers steadily gained the upper hand and enemy resistance ended on 8 November.

Already work had begun to clear the mines laid in the Scheldt. It is reported that 267 had to be removed before 28 November when the first supply ship, the appropriately Canadian-registered *Fort Cataraque*, reached Antwerp. Even then, the Germans bombarded Antwerp with V1s and V2s, roads had to be improved and railways built to get the supplies to the front line and for several weeks the city was the scene of immense 'traffic jams'. The time taken to clear the Scheldt Estuary despite the preliminary work done by the Canadians shows how right Montgomery was not to have waited for this to be done before delivering his attempt to jump the Rhine.

Nor did the opening of Antwerp to shipping – and that of Ostend, Le Havre, Calais and Boulogne as well – result in any dramatic improvement to Allied progress in North-West Europe. By early December, First US, Third US and the new Ninth US Armies had all ground to a halt. Seventh US Army had liberated Strasbourg, but then been diverted to help Patton. Montgomery's own troops, with VIII Corps striking south-east from Grave and XII Corps north-east from Eindhoven in a pincer movement, had cleared the west bank of the Maas opposite to Venlo, but he was still giving warnings about the dangers of the broad front policy. They would soon receive dramatic confirmation.

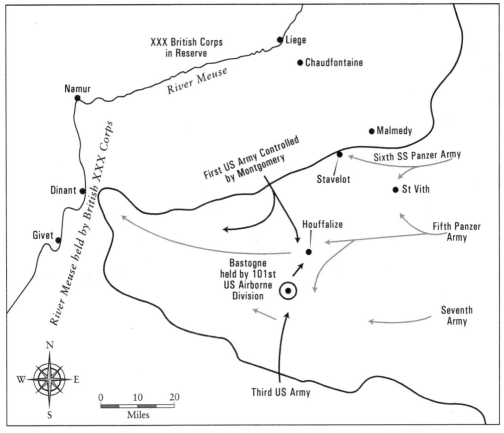

Map 20: The Battle of the Ardennes.

Spurred on by desperation, the Germans had replaced the losses in their panzer units and created new infantry formations called *Volksgrenadier* divisions, with less manpower than usual but very strong in automatic weapons. Hitler was determined to use these reserves to attack through the Ardennes where his Intelligence had told him the Allies were weak, cross the Meuse/Maas and capture Antwerp and Brussels, cutting off the British and Canadian armies. Von Rundstedt declared it would be a miracle if the Germans got as far as the Meuse and when his protests were rejected, 'washed his hands' of the whole business, leaving its implementation to Hitler and Model's Army Group 'B'.[3]

Model commanded three armies and so powerful was Hitler's personality that their young soldiers went into action with morale and confidence high. On the northern flank of the assault was Sixth SS Panzer Army under SS General Josef 'Sepp' Dietrich, a member of the

National Socialist Party from its earliest days and of the SS since it had been merely Hitler's personal guard. His force contained 1st SS, 2nd SS, 9th SS and 12th SS Panzer divisions with a total of about 500 tanks including some 90 Tigers, 3rd Parachute Division and 4 *Volksgrenadier* divisions. Its ultimate objective was Antwerp.

On Dietrich's left came von Manteuffel controlling Fifth Panzer Army: 2nd and 116th Panzer, Panzer Lehr and four *Volksgrenadier* divisions. His objective was Brussels and his own left flank was protected by General Erich Brandenberger's Seventh Army: 5th Parachute and three *Volksgrenadier* divisions.

At 0530 on 16 December, under an artillery bombardment by some 2,000 guns, this formidable force fell upon First US Army which was not well placed to meet it. In the north of the Ardennes it had experienced infantry divisions in prepared defensive positions with strong artillery support, but its remaining 90-mile-wide front was guarded only by one armoured and three infantry divisions, all low in strength and experience.

Since Allied Intelligence had given no warning and bad weather had curtailed air reconnaissance, the assault achieved complete surprise, made worse by many Allied senior officers being distant from the battle-zone. Eisenhower and Bradley, for instance, were at Versailles celebrating the former's promotion to 'five star' general, the equivalent of a British or German field marshal, and it was some time before they sent reserve formations to First US Army's aid.

Nonetheless the soldiers of that army, often without orders, held their ground and fought back. The progress of the German Seventh Army was minimal. The Sixth SS Panzer Army never seriously threatened the vital road junction at Malmedy and though a battle-group of 2,000 men from 1st SS Panzer under Colonel Joachim Peiper did reach the town of Stavelot, this was still 42 miles from the Meuse. Peiper's troops murdered 86 disarmed prisoners, thereby increasing the resolve of American reinforcements that included 82nd US Airborne Division, and were eventually forced back to their start-line with the loss of 1,200 men and all their tanks and other vehicles.

Von Manteuffel's men proved much more dangerous. They trapped 106th US Infantry Division, never previously in action, and on 20 December its 7,000 survivors surrendered: the largest American capitulation in Europe. On the previous day, Fifth Panzer Army captured a vital road junction at Houffalize, but those at St Vith and Bastogne were defended by Brigadier General Robert Hasbrouck's 7th US Armoured Division and Brigadier General Anthony McAuliffe's 101st Airborne Division respectively. Neither would yield and their mood was summed up by McAuliffe, who rejected a demand to surrender in one word: 'Nuts!'[14]

Montgomery, like everyone else, had not expected the assault and first learned of it while relaxing with a game of golf at Eindhoven. He at once flew back to his Tac HQ, where he ordered his liaison officers onto the battlefield to report the situation. As a result, by the evening of 18 December, he was in possession of much more information than any American commander and promptly began to take the action he considered necessary.

Montgomery's first step was to ensure that if the Germans did reach the Meuse, they would be unable to cross it. Learning from Intelligence reports that the Germans were making for bridges south of Liège, he ordered Horrocks and his XXX Corps to take up station between Liège and Namur on the Meuse's west bank. This, incidentally, is much higher than the east bank and so would provide an easily defended obstacle. Montgomery also sent 2nd Battalion, Household Cavalry Regiment, 8th Battalion, the Rifle Brigade and later 29th Armoured Brigade to guard the bridges at Namur, Dinant and Givet and ordered Hodges to block those from Liège to Namur.

Of course Montgomery had no right to give Hodges orders, but he was confident that he would have to take control of not only First US Army but also Ninth US Army stationed north of this and commanded by Lieutenant General William Simpson. Since Bradley's HQ in Luxembourg was out of touch with his troops north of the German breakthrough, this was a sensible if scarcely modest belief, and Montgomery badgered Eisenhower's British Intelligence Officer Major General Strong and his Acting Chief of Operations Major General Whitely to bring it about. After some heated exchanges, Bedell Smith accepted their arguments and took it upon himself to persuade Eisenhower.

At 1030 on 20 December, the Supreme Commander notified a delighted Montgomery and a highly displeased Bradley that the former would take control of First and Ninth US Armies forthwith. Montgomery in turn instructed the ever-helpful Broadhurst to provide full air support for Hodges and Simpson, especially that of the much-feared rocket-firing Typhoons.

Montgomery's control would soon become absolute. Otto Skorzeny, Mussolini's rescuer, had sent small groups of raiders in captured American jeeps and captured American uniforms to spread confusion behind the Allied lines. Wild rumours spread that these were assassination squads. Bradley was forced to travel in an unmarked jeep with tape over the general's stars on his helmet. Eisenhower was made a virtual prisoner in his headquarters, surrounded by guards and forbidden even to take a walk. Neither could give Montgomery any advice or instructions.

It may well be that Montgomery was not displeased by this. Ignoring warnings, on 20 December he set out in a Rolls-Royce, its bonnet decorated with the largest possible Union Jack, to visit Hodges at his headquarters in Chaudfontaine near Liège, having requested Simpson and de Guingand to join them there. From the reports of his liaison officers, he was able to give Hodges and Simpson a detailed summary of the situation; the first that either had ever received.

In addition Montgomery, according to de Guingand, was 'supremely cheerful and confident' and his attitude quickly proved infectious. Montgomery had considered Hodges 'a bit shaken, very tired and in need of moral support.' However, with Montgomery's confidence providing that moral support, he quickly recovered his resolution and his aggressive spirit.

Montgomery then turned his attention to dealing with the German offensive. His detractors would later claim that the Americans had already mastered this. They had certainly disrupted it but von Manteuffel, the ablest enemy commander, was about to renew the assault with his original three armoured divisions reinforced by 2nd SS and 9th SS Panzer transferred to him by Dietrich. He would confirm that it was Montgomery who 'turned a series of isolated actions into a coherent battle fought according to a clear and definite plan'.

Montgomery's plan was to build up a new XIX US Corps behind the battle-lines ready to deliver an effective counter-attack. It would consist of four fresh divisions – 3rd US Armoured from the northern Ardennes, 2nd US Armoured and 84th US Infantry from Ninth Army and 75th Infantry from Normandy – commanded by Lieutenant General 'Lightning Joe' Collins, the captor of Cherbourg. In the meantime

Montgomery proposed to establish a unified front and save many gallant American lives by falling back from endangered forward positions.

Montgomery was particularly concerned about Hasbrouck's 7th US Armored Division, especially its most advanced units under Brigadier General Bruce Clarke east of St Vith. Hasbrouck, though, had been placed under XVIII Airborne Corps and its leader Major General Ridgway believed that retreats were 'un-American'. Throughout 21 December, the defenders of St Vith threw back attack after attack by superior numbers, but late that evening the enemy finally entered St Vith and the next morning Hasbrouck warned Ridgway that unless his men were withdrawn 'we will not have a 7th Armoured Division left.' Ridgway promptly relieved him of his command.

Fortunately, when Montgomery was advised of the situation he reinstated Hasbrouck and confirmed that 7th US Armored's soldiers could retire 'with all honour'. Next morning, Gavin's 82nd Airborne Division was in danger of being overrun. In its previous admittedly short career 82nd Airborne had never retreated and Ridgway had no intention of letting it do so now. Again, however, Montgomery insisted that the Americans fall back to more secure positions, which with some difficulty they reluctantly did.

Montgomery's moral courage can scarcely be praised too highly. He must have known the comments that would be made about a British general who ordered unwilling American units to retreat, but it made no difference to him. Ridgway was much displeased, but Hodges and Gavin accepted the need for Montgomery's actions and Hasbrouck and Clarke gave enthusiastic approval.

Von Manteuffel also admired Montgomery, particularly his 'refusal to engage in premature piecemeal counter-attacks'. Montgomery's detractors of course label him over-cautious and contrast him adversely with the dashing Patton, who with amazing speed organized a counter-attack with 4th US Armored and two US infantry divisions on 22 December, declaring he would reach Bastogne in thirty-six hours and sweep on to Houffalize and St Vith.

Sadly, though, this move did prove to be premature. Though opposed only by the German Seventh Army which had no tanks and had been badly battered in actions against First US Army, Patton only reached Bastogne on 26 December, was unable to move beyond it and suffered such heavy casualties that a fortnight after his offensive began he recorded in his diary: 'We can still lose this war.' It was fortunate that next day the Germans had to direct their attention away from him and onto Montgomery.

Montgomery's first counter-attack had been made on 25 December. On the previous day, von Manteuffel's spearhead, 2nd Panzer Division, had come within 5 miles of the Meuse at Dinant. Here it was halted by 3rd Battalion, Royal Tank Regiment, a unit of the British 29th Armoured Brigade, which destroyed four of its tanks. Then 'Lightning Joe' Collins descended on it from behind with almost 400 tanks and after two days of savage fighting the Germans fled, leaving behind them the wrecks of another 40 tanks and numerous other vehicles.

Since there was a considerable delay before Montgomery followed up this success, he might reasonably have been accused of caution had there not been a motive for this that he was not allowed to reveal. For many years after the war, the Ultra intercepts were a closely guarded secret and, as after Alamein and before the Mareth Line, Ultra now served Montgomery badly. It reported that the Germans planned a new advance on Liège, but was silent when this was cancelled. Montgomery wished to fight on the defensive against it and only when certain it would never take place did he begin his own offensive.

Then on New Year's Day 1945 the Allies suffered a further setback. The bad weather had at last relented on 23 December, enabling the Allied air forces to resume their attacks on enemy troops but also giving the Luftwaffe its opportunity. On 1 January more than 800 German fighters and fighter-bombers struck at Allied airfields in the Low Countries, especially those at Brussels and Eindhoven. They achieved complete surprise and, despite losses, wrecked almost 300 Allied machines on the ground.

Among the formations hardest hit was Broadhurst's 83 Group, but by combining aircraft from different units and bringing forward reserves from England he was able to support Montgomery's offensive which began on 3 January. It was aimed at Houffalize which was good strategy, since on 26 December a raid by almost 300 Lancasters and Halifaxes had reduced St Vith to rubble and so blocked its road system that Houffalize was the only good route left for a German withdrawal. Montgomery's main striking force was 2nd and 3rd US Armored divisions under Collins, but he supported these with British troops: 53rd Welsh Division, 29th Armoured Brigade and two battalions of 6th Airborne Division fighting as infantry.

The offensive soon brought results. On 5 January, the Germans relaxed their pressure on Bastogne, allowing Patton to move forward. On the 8th, Model received Hitler's permission for a general retirement. This was well conducted with continued determined resistance, but the Allies steadily advanced. On 15 January, the ruins of St Vith were occupied, appropriately by 7th US Armored Division, and next day Montgomery's and Patton's forces met at Houffalize and the Battle of the Ardennes was over. It had cost the Germans 80,000 dead, wounded and prisoners as well as vast numbers of tanks and other vehicles, and neither men nor machines could be replaced. The price paid by the Allies was 75,500 American casualties, some 8,400 of them fatal, and 1,400 British casualties, 200 fatal. About 3,000 civilians had also died.

Since Montgomery's actions during the battle had earned the admiration even of his opponents, his conduct in its closing stages appears the more regrettable. Most criticized has been a press conference that he gave on 7 January. He was egotistical and he exaggerated the contribution made by the British, but he made it clear that the battle had been won by 'the good fighting qualities of the American soldiers' and gave their courage the high praise it deserved. His attitude, however, was deplorable. He 'came over' as triumphantly and pityingly superior and naturally this was resented by American officers to whom his behaviour had already been ill-advised and ill-mannered.

On 30 December, Montgomery's persistence, despite previous promises, in making demands, thinly disguised as suggestions, that Eisenhower abandon his broad front policy and appoint a single land forces commander had finally worn away the Supreme Commander's exemplary patience. He made it clear that if his difficult subordinate continued to complain, then the whole matter would be referred to the Combined Chiefs of Staff, which could only have resulted in Montgomery's replacement. Fortunately, de Guingand persuaded Eisenhower to 'hold fire' and then made the danger clear to Montgomery. Genuinely shaken and distressed, Montgomery offered an unqualified acceptance of Eisenhower's authority. Eisenhower graciously accepted the apology and even allowed

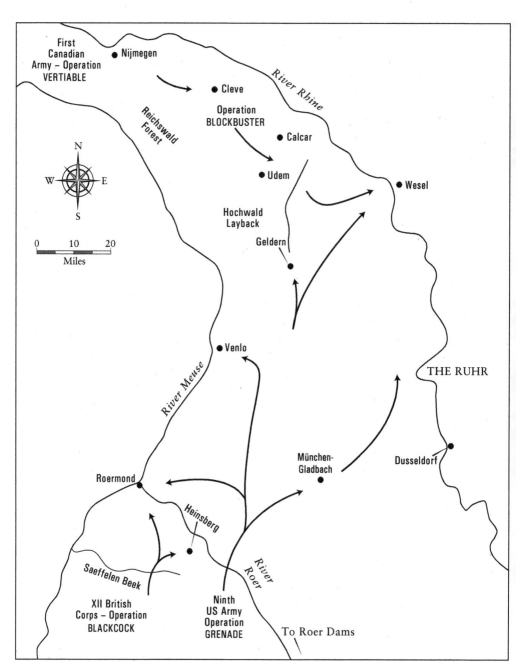

Map 21: The Battle of the Rhineland.

Montgomery to continue to control Ninth US Army, but he would never again be influenced by Montgomery's views.

Worse still, on 25 December of all days, Montgomery had subjected Bradley to savage condemnation, apparently in revenge for Bradley having refused to support his arguments. Bradley would eventually forgive and forget, but for the rest of the war he would be found in the ranks of Montgomery's critics and few will blame him.

It is a relief to turn from Montgomery the petulant complainer to Montgomery the skilled commander. While fighting the Ardennes battle he had, as usual, been planning the battle to follow, or in this case two battles. The first was the Battle of the Rhineland, the objective of which was the occupation of the west bank of the Rhine north of Dusseldorf; the second was the Battle of the Rhine Crossing, the objective of which is self-explanatory.

For the assault on the Rhineland, Montgomery had decided on a pincer movement. He would strike south-eastwards into this from the Nijmegen area captured by MARKET GARDEN. This was Operation VERITABLE which Montgomery, reserving Dempsey's Second Army for the Rhine crossing, made the responsibility of First Canadian Army, strengthened by British troops including Horrocks and his XXX Corps. At the same time, Simpson's Ninth US Army would strike north-eastwards over the River Roer, a tributary of the Meuse/Maas running roughly parallel to the Rhine. This was Operation GRENADE.

There were two major obstacles in Simpson's path. One was the existence of seven dams upriver on the Roer. They were still in German possession and from them a flood could be released onto Ninth US Army's advance. The other was a triangle of land, the sides of which, approximately 20 miles long, were formed by the Meuse/Maas, the Roer and a smaller tributary of the former the Saeffelen Beek, and the apex of which was the fortress town of Roermond where the two main rivers met. It also was still in German hands and from it flanking attacks could be delivered on Ninth US Army. The capture of the dams was left to First US Army, but that of the Roermond Triangle to Ritchie's XII Corps. This was Operation BLACKCOCK.

As usual, Montgomery made every effort to surprise the enemy. The 35,000 lorries carrying food, petrol, ammunition, medical supplies, signals cables and bridging equipment moved to the front line only at night. The petrol and ammunition dumps were stacked so as to resemble natural features like hedges. Tanks and other vehicles were painted white so as to merge with snow-covered ground; if there were thaws, they were hastily covered with mud. These moves were completely successful and the Germans left in ignorance of the timing and direction of all the coming assaults.

First of these was Operation BLACKCOCK, which began on 15 January with a series of attacks on the base of the triangle, supported by 'Funnies' from 79th Armoured Division and a new 1st Canadian Rocket Battery, the missiles of which were the equivalents of 5.5in shells. On the 18th, a posthumous Victoria Cross was awarded to Fusilier Dennis Donnini of 52nd Lowland Division's 4th/5th Royal Scots Fusiliers. Though twice wounded, he constantly rescued fellow soldiers under almost continuous fire until hit again and killed; at just 19 years old he was the youngest VC of the Second World War. Heinsberg on the east of and the key to the triangle's defences fell on 24 January, and three days later the whole area, apart from Roermond itself which was not attacked, had been secured.

Next, Operation VERITABLE began at 0500 on 8 February with a shattering bombardment from well over 1,000 artillery pieces: the usual prelude to an attack but with a new twist. The barrage ceased at 0730 and the Germans, thinking an infantry attack would follow, opened fire. The position of their own guns was thus revealed and when the bombardment resumed ten minutes later, it was directed mainly against them. At 1020, XXX Corps advanced and the defenders, the German 84th Infantry Division, caught by surprise and stunned by the weight of the Allied gunfire, offered comparatively little resistance. By early next day, XXX Corps had broken through the advanced enemy positions.

There would be no quick follow-up, however. The gap between the Rhine and the Maas was a narrow one at the best of times, with much of its southern half blocked by the sinister Reichswald forest. The Germans had reduced it still more by flooding most of the northern half, and heavy rain had turned what remained into a sea of mud in which even tanks became bogged down.

Moreover the whole area was protected by fortified towns, trenches, anti-tank ditches, barbed wire and mines, with a final complex of these called the Hochwald Layback guarding the key town of Wesel. To make matters worse, Horrocks had requested an attack by Bomber Command on the little town of Cleve lying across XXX Corps' main line of advance. Sadly, the airmen had delivered too heavy a raid and that with high-explosive bombs, not incendiaries as Horrocks had wished, leaving Cleve a mass of rubble that provided its defenders with excellent cover. It was not reached until 11 February or cleared until the 12th; meanwhile XXX Corps' supply line became a 'traffic jam' of monstrous proportions.[5]

Of course XXX Corps' difficulties would have been eased had Operation GRENADE commenced on 10 February as originally intended. Unfortunately, Bradley seems to have had little concern with taking the Roer dams. He only directed First US Army against them on 1 February after receiving specific orders from Eisenhower, and by the time all had been gained on the 10th, it was too late. Their floodgates had been jammed open, letting great masses of water pour through and the Roer had burst its banks along the whole length of Ninth US Army's start-line. Until the river had subsided, GRENADE was impossible.

Though Eisenhower was apparently furious, Montgomery remained surprisingly untroubled. It seems certain that his flexible mind appreciated that the situation might turn out to his advantage: that the First Canadian Army, by holding down the bulk of the enemy forces in the Rhineland, might bring about great achievements elsewhere, just as Dempsey's Second (British) Army had done in Normandy. He said as much in a signal to Brooke as early as 10 February and as more and more German formations were moved north to oppose VERITABLE, he became increasingly optimistic. By the 20th, he was proclaiming triumphantly: 'All this is good and is sowing the seeds for a successful GRENADE', and not only for GRENADE as it transpired.

This northern section of the Rhineland as a whole was securely held by First Parachute Army, the last first-class German formation on the Western Front. It was commanded by Lieutenant General Alfred Schlemm who had conducted several successful defensive operations in Italy and its dismounted paratroopers were fully prepared to fight for Fatherland and Führer regardless of losses as Hitler had ordered.

Since the flooding of the Roer protected Schlemm's southern flank, he could and did send strong reinforcements of infantry, armour and artillery to join his battered 84th Infantry Division in the fight against First Canadian Army. On 9 February, 7th Parachute Division reached the front line. On the 11th, so did 6th Parachute Division. On the 12th, so did XLVII Panzer Corps which controlled 116th Panzer and 15th Panzer Grenadier divisions. They contained only some fifty tanks, but that was fifty more than 43rd, 51st and 53rd Infantry divisions from XXX Corps on whom they now fell. Nonetheless, these defended themselves so fiercely and their supporting artillery and anti-tank guns caused such losses that by the following morning, the Panzer corps had accepted defeat and fallen back.

Enemy reinforcements continued to arrive: by 20 February, two more parachute divisions, three more infantry divisions and an old antagonist, Panzer Lehr. Horrocks, though, continued to push forward and on the 21st, his infantrymen, supported by Grenadier Guards tanks and 79th Division Crocodiles, took the vital town and crossroads of Goch.

Next, Operation GRENADE delivered Montgomery's pincer movement. Though Simpson had been told the Roer would only be low enough on 24 February, he risked crossing on the 23rd and thereby achieved surprise. At 0245 came a massive bombardment by more than 1,000 guns; at 0330 four of Ninth US Army's infantry divisions crossed the Roer. They were opposed by four German divisions, but all these had had much of their strength sent northward and by the end of the day the Americans had secured a bridgehead at the cost of just over 1,000 casualties, fewer than 100 of them fatal.

Thereafter GRENADE proceeded as Montgomery had anticipated. By the end of 24 February, the Americans had erected eleven bridges over the river, seven of them capable of carrying tanks. On the 25th, all Simpson's three infantry corps had crossed the Roer, being joined by 2nd US Armored Division on the 26th and 5th and 8th US Armored divisions soon afterwards.

Also on the 26th, Lieutenant General Guy Simonds began Operation BLOCKBUSTER. While XXX Corps secured his right flank, his II Canadian Corps – 2nd and 3rd Canadian Infantry divisions, 43rd (Wessex) from XXX Corps and 4th Canadian and 11th British Armoured divisions – advanced on the Hochwald Layback. Sergeant Aubrey Cousins of the Queen's Own Rifles of Canada was awarded a Victoria Cross for repulsing two German counter-attacks, then leading an assault in which he personally killed twenty enemy soldiers and captured another twenty.

Sadly he would never receive it, being shot dead by a sniper as he left the front line.

By 28 February, Simonds had captured the fortress towns of Calcar and Udem and reached the Hochwald Layback. On 1 March, Major Frederick Tiltson of the Essex Scottish Regiment earned a VC for leading his men to the capture of enemy defences and holding these against heavy counter-attacks despite severe wounds in his hand and both legs. Yet for all their gallantry, the Canadians made slow progress for Schlemm had committed almost his entire remaining strength to holding this last defensive line, including Tiger tanks, Panther tanks, almost all his artillery and some fifty of the deadly 88mm anti-tank guns.

By doing so, however, he left the way clear for Ninth US Army which advanced swiftly over the whole width of the Rhineland. On its left front, it forced the garrisons of strongpoints like Roermond and Venlo into hasty evacuations to avoid being cut off. On its right flank, it swept up the west bank of the Rhine, capturing large numbers of German soldiers as bridge after bridge was destroyed behind them. In the centre, on 1 March it took München-Gladbach, the largest German town yet to fall into Allied hands, and on the 3rd entered Geldern on the south of the Hochwald Layback to make contact with XXX Corps' 53rd Division as this entered Geldern as well from the north-west.

So successful had Ninth US Army's advance been that Simpson suggested he make a snap crossing of the Rhine. Montgomery rejected the idea. He wanted Ninth US Army to help inflict as much harm as possible on First Parachute Army west of the Rhine and then aid Second (British) Army in its major crossing of that river. Moreover Simpson's proposed crossing would have taken him into the heart of the Ruhr, involving him in costly street-fighting which Montgomery – and incidentally Eisenhower – wished to avoid by enveloping the Ruhr and isolating it from the rest of Germany.

Though Montgomery's critics call this over-cautious, his ensuring that Ninth US Army was available to help the Canadians secure Wesel quickly proved justified. On 6 March, Schlemm asked for permission to withdraw, which Hitler reluctantly granted the next day. Schlemm then began to retire in good order, but at the cost of abandoning huge quantities of irreplaceable equipment. On 10 March, the German rearguards escaped over the Wesel bridges, which they then blew up.

So ended what has been called 'The last great stand-up fight' between the Germans and the Western Allies. It had cost the latter almost 23,000 casualties, of which more than 10,000 were British, more than 7,000 American and more than 5,000 Canadian. Enemy casualties were about 90,000, of which 53,000 were taken prisoner. Moreover the victory, as Bradley acknowledged, resulted in 'crumbling resistance up and down the Rhineland'.

Thus on 5 March, First US Army reached the Rhine and on the 7th seized the Ludendorff railway bridge at the little town of Remagen when the charges on this detonated but did not cause it to collapse. Hodges at once had supplemental bridges prepared and four American divisions went over the river, easily repelling hasty piecemeal attacks.[6]

Despite what has been stated elsewhere, Montgomery was delighted with this achievement, declaring its importance 'cannot be over-estimated'. It tied down German reserves, leaving none in the extreme south of the Rhineland. The Third and Seventh US Armies took full advantage of this and overran the area in a week, taking perhaps as many as 100,000 prisoners, and the former followed up by breaking over the Rhine at Oppenheim, some 10 miles south of Mainz. When announcing this success, Bradley was delighted to point out it had not enjoyed 'the benefit of aerial bombardment, ground smoke, artillery preparation and airborne assistance', a sarcastic reference to the preparations for a crossing being made by slow, cautious Montgomery.

This comment was both unfair and unworthy, for Montgomery planned to cross at Wesel which was about 175 miles north of Oppenheim as the crow flies and well over 200 as the Rhine twists and turns. During these, it had been swollen by seven major tributaries, principally the Moselle, and innumerable smaller ones. It was 500 yards wide with a huge flood plain on both sides still covered by the winter rains, high banks and a strong current; an impressive obstacle in its own right. Also the crossing at Oppenheim was virtually undefended, costing only eight dead and twenty wounded and, as Hitler discovered, the reserves in the area consisted of just five mobile anti-tank guns. Montgomery was less fortunate at Wesel.

Montgomery in fact was opposed by the battered but still resolute First Parachute Army. This contained 116th Panzer and 15th Panzer Grenadier divisions with more than fifty tanks, three parachute and two infantry divisions and three admittedly low-class divisions formed from training or maintenance units. It was protected by fixed defences and supported by artillery and sixty of the renowned 88mm anti-tank guns. Since Schlemm had been badly wounded in an Allied air-raid, it was commanded by General Günther Blumentritt.

Von Rundstedt had been held responsible for the misfortunes in the Rhineland and replaced by Field Marshal Kesselring from Italy. An invincible optimist who cheerfully told his staff 'I am the new V3!', he believed his defences and his defenders would confront Montgomery with 'a formidable obstacle'. In contrast to American sneers, he also considered that his opponent's preparations to overcome this were 'exemplary'. Montgomery's soldiers whose lives were saved thereby would undoubtedly have agreed.

Of the items mocked by Bradley, two were preliminary. The 'aerial bombardments' were directed against the German transport system and the Ruhr to prevent reinforcements of men or equipment from reaching the Rhine's defenders. They were carried out by Bomber Command and directed by Tedder who, it is pleasant to report, was in this instance fully co-operative. The 'ground smoke' was an artificial smokescreen that for ten days concealed the details of the Allied forces. It was loathed by the troops because it clung to their clothing and tainted their food, but like the air-raids it succeeded in its aim.

The 'artillery preparation' was part of the plans of Montgomery and his staff for Operation PLUNDER, as the Rhine crossing was somewhat ominously known. It was intended that Second (British) Army would attack north of Wesel with XXX Corps on the left and XII Corps on the right, while Ninth US Army's XVI US Corps would strike south of Wesel. The attackers would be supported by almost 700 tanks including DD amphibious ones and of course by artillery, of which there were more than 5,500 pieces ranging from 240mm guns firing shells of more than half a ton to rocket projectiles.

At 1800 on 23 March, this host of Allied guns opened fire on German positions and gun-sites, achieving a measure of surprise since they had been so well hidden. At 2100, four of 51st Highland Division's battalions set off over the river in amphibious craft, landing successfully four minutes later. At 2200, 1st Commando Brigade also crossed, making for Wesel; it burst into that unhappy town on the heels of a ferocious fifteen-minute raid by Bomber Command that stunned its defenders. Other formations from Second (British) and Ninth US Armies followed on the night of 23/24 March and by the next morning were already pushing forward with the aid of DD tanks.

Then at 1000 on the 24th, the 'airborne assistance' to which Bradley had referred arrived. This was Operation VARSITY, carried out by XVIII US Airborne Corps. The gliders and parachutists of 6th British Airborne Division from airfields in England and those of 17th US Airborne from airfields in France had made a rendezvous over Belgium and now came in supported by almost 900 fighters and closely followed by 240 Liberators to drop supplies to them. Their orders were to capture positions that might obstruct the ground forces and particularly bridges over the next river obstacle, the Issel that ran northward east of and roughly parallel to the Rhine, initially to prevent these being used for German counter-attacks and ultimately to provide easy access from the bridgehead.

Since previous airborne landings had always preceded or at least accompanied the major land assault, VARSITY also achieved surprise but, as has been mentioned earlier, the Wesel area was liberally supplied with AA guns and these shot down many of the swarms of targets provided. When the remaining glider-borne troops or parachutists landed, they were often engaged immediately. An example from each airborne division, however, will show how they mastered all difficulties.

After 2nd Battalion, 513th US Parachute Infantry Regiment had suffered heavy casualties, a private soldier, Stuart Stryker, led the attack on an enemy position. It and 200 prisoners were taken, but Stryker was killed in the fight; he was awarded a posthumous Medal of Honor. Corporal Frederick Topham, a medical orderly in '1 Canadian Para', part of the British 3rd Parachute Brigade, though shot through the nose and in great pain, repeatedly treated wounded men and then carried them to safety under almost continuous fire; he was awarded a Victoria Cross.

This time the planning of the airborne operation was not left to the Airborne Corps but was decided by Montgomery and his staff. VARSITY may have lacked the boldness of MARKET GARDEN, but avoided its mistakes. Thus both 6th British and 17th US Airborne divisions secured their designated bridges over the Issel by landing gliders virtually on top of them. The Germans made repeated efforts to regain them but, aided by the inevitable Typhoons, the Americans retained all their bridges and the British all but one, and that was blown up to avoid capture by the enemy.

Throughout 24 March, both XII British and XVI US Corps made steady progress and by next morning had linked up with their airborne divisions. On their left, XXX Corps was opposed by 15th Panzer Grenedier and three parachute divisions. Major General Thomas Rennie, who had done so much to restore the morale of 51st Highland Division, was killed by a mortar bomb on the morning of the 24th, but by the end of the 26th the northern flank of the bridgehead was secure. By then also, the tireless sappers had erected twelve bridges over the Rhine capable of carrying heavy vehicles and eight divisions from Second (British) Army and six from Ninth US were on its eastern bank. By the end of the 28th, the bridgehead was 35 miles wide and men from 17th US Airborne mounted on tanks of the Guards Armoured Division's 6th Armoured Brigade had advanced 35 miles from the Rhine.

The Battle of the Rhine crossing was over. It had cost the British almost 4,000 casualties and the Americans just over 2,800, but German prisoners alone came to more than 16,000 and the last great natural obstacle in the path of the Western Allies had been overcome. For Montgomery's own contribution to victory, we may turn to *The Battle for Germany* by Major General Hubert Essame, then a brigadier in 43rd (Wessex) Division, who declared:

Judged purely as a military operation, it is impossible to fault Montgomery's plan and its execution – the linking together of the land and air operations, the achievement of concentrated firepower both from the ground and the air, the foresight devoted to tactical and administrative planning and the exploitation to the full of the characteristics of the many components of the land and air forces. It was Montgomery's final masterpiece, executed in a manner soon to be outmoded, but nonetheless, like a [painting by] Constable, a work of art.

Notes

1. The German coastal batteries remained intact, however, and repeated requests that they be bombed were thwarted by Tedder who felt that the RAF was being diverted too frequently from its task of wrecking Germany's industrial capacity.
2. A vivid example of the type of action that took place can be found in the capture of 's-Hertogenbosch as described by Major General Essame in *The Battle for Germany*.
3. Ironically, the newspapers always called this operation 'the Rundstedt offensive'. Von Rundstedt was most displeased.
4. McAuliffe thereby earned a place in *The Oxford Dictionary of Quotations*, where his pithy retort is the shortest entry in that delightful compilation.
5. By contrast, requests by Montgomery for attacks on the bridges at Wesel, the destruction of which would have prevented the escape of the enemy threatened by his pincer movement, were rejected in view of the heavy AA defences.
6. On 17 March, without warning, the Ludendorff bridge did collapse, killing twenty-eight Americans who were working on it. Since it had been closed for repairs some days earlier, however, this had no effect on the bridgehead.

Chapter Twelve

To the Baltic – and Beyond

One of the reasons why Montgomery's preparations for the Rhine crossing had been so thorough was that as usual he was thinking ahead of the current operation. He wanted to ensure his men had enough supplies to enable them to burst through the heart of Germany in the same way they had burst through northern France and Belgium after the Battle of Normandy.

Contrary to what has often been stated, they would face plenty of enemy soldiers. On the northern flank, First Canadian Army's II Corps was reinforced by its I Corps transferred from Italy, but when these advanced into Holland and north-western Germany they were met by superior numbers. About 40 per cent of them were renegade Dutchmen who, having allied themselves to the Germans, could expect little mercy from their countrymen and fought with the courage of desperation.

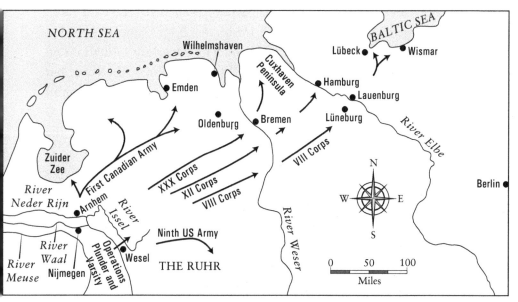

Map 22: The advance from the River Rhine to the Baltic Sea.

Nothing, though, could stop the attackers. On 12 April, 49th (British) Division stationed in the Nijmegen area and serving under I Canadian Corps broke over the Neder Rijn with the aid of 79th Division 'Funnies' and the ever-present Typhoons. Next day, 5th Canadian Armoured Division also crossed the Neder Rijn. Arnhem fell on 15 April and on the 18th, I Canadian Corps reached the southern shore of the Zuider Zee. The German Twenty-Fifth Army and the V2 launching-sites were thus cut off from Germany and the aims of MARKET GARDEN at last achieved. Meanwhile II Canadian Corps raced through north-eastern Holland to the North Sea, securing the whole area by 20 April and moving on to capture Oldenburg and isolate the ports of Emden and Wilhelmshaven.

On 22 April, however, Montgomery ordered I Canadian Corps to halt on the ground it had gained. This was a sensible and humane move, for an assault on the remaining German-occupied part of Holland would have prompted the enemy to flood it, inflicting ruin on the Dutch population who were already coming close to starvation. On 28 April, a formal cease-fire was arranged that lasted for the rest of the war. Next day, British and American bombers dropped 510 tons of supplies and thereafter thousands of tons of food, clothing, medicine and other necessities were regularly delivered by road.

It was First Canadian Army's principal duty, though, to secure the flank of Montgomery's main striking force, made up of both Dempsey's Second (British) and Simpson's Ninth US Armies. The American formations on Simpson's right flank would be detached to help encircle the Ruhr but then rejoin and both armies would advance together, making for Berlin as fast as possible. To ensure this, Montgomery ordered his armour to bypass strongpoints, leaving infantry to 'mop up'. He also stressed the need to capture airfields so as to provide close aerial support.

Montgomery was convinced that his force could reach Berlin – a conviction most senior enemy commanders would later confirm they shared – but only if it contained Ninth US Army. It seemed, however, that he need have no anxiety on this score, for Eisenhower had promised he could control Simpson's army for the rest of the war.

Unfortunately, Bradley was equally anxious that Ninth US Army be returned to his command. He felt its continued absence was an implied criticism of his ability and was not pleased by Montgomery declaring that it had 'done very well in Twenty-First Army Group' and still less pleased by Simpson reporting he was 'far better commanded' under Montgomery than he had ever been previously. Bradley, however, had Eisenhower's ear and on 28 March he achieved his desire.

On that date Simpson was sweeping north and then east of the Ruhr, while Hodges made a similar move south and then east of it, thereby cutting off the Ruhr from the rest of Germany and trapping Model's Army Group 'B' within it. Eisenhower now decreed that as soon as this had been achieved, Ninth US Army would be returned to Bradley. On 1 April, Simpson and Hodges met and Montgomery lost Ninth US Army and any chance of reaching Berlin.

Bradley then turned six of Ninth US Army's divisions together with eight from First US Army and four from a newly-arrived Fifteenth US Army against the Ruhr. This had been so devastated by relentless Allied bombing that it could not possibly provide the fuel and ammunition Model needed. As early as 7 April his subordinates urged him to surrender and as supplies began to disappear, organized resistance withered. On the 17th, it ended completely. At a cost of 10,000 casualties, the Americans had compelled an Axis surrender far exceeding those at Stalingrad or in Tunisia. Field Marshal Model shot himself to avoid capture, but 30 generals and at least 317,000 men became prisoners of war.

Bradley still had the use of thirty other divisions; however, these made not for Berlin but through central Germany towards Leipzig and Dresden. On 13 April, Ninth US Army broke across the River Elbe against minimal resistance and was only 60 miles from the German capital which Simpson believed he could easily have taken, an opinion shared by the German officers who would have had to oppose him. Eisenhower, though, refused to let him advance further, insisting that Berlin was 'nothing but a geographical location'.

It is said that this attitude arose because during March Allied Intelligence had given grave warnings that Hitler and his more fanatical followers would retire to the southern Bavarian and western Austrian Alps. In this area, known as the National Redoubt or Southern Redoubt, aided by various horrific secret weapons, they would fight on perhaps for an entire year. Where this fantasy arose is not known, but Montgomery for one declared that the ruin of the German transport system and the Allied command of the air had in practice made more than token resistance in this area quite impossible. Interrogations of captured enemy officers confirmed that no such plans existed and that Hitler was and intended to remain in Berlin. General Marshall, however, held different views and the myth was only exploded when on 22 April two entire American armies closed in on the supposed site of the redoubt and found nothing!

Even had the redoubt existed, American strength was so great they could have assaulted this and still have taken Berlin and in any case its existence would not explain why Simpson was deliberately prevented from taking the German capital. There must therefore have been other reasons for Eisenhower's attitude.

One was that in the Yalta Conference of February 1945, it had been agreed that Germany should be divided into four zones, one of each to be occupied by the British, the Americans, the Russians and the French. Berlin came in the area of Russian control and, as Bradley who shared Eisenhower's opinions later commented, if the Americans took Berlin they would have to 'pull back and let the other fellow' – the Russians – 'take it' anyhow, so it was pointless to do so.

By the same token, though, it was equally pointless to send huge American forces through central and southern Germany since they would have to be withdrawn, some for as much as 120 miles, to let the Russians take over. It was perhaps the more pointless because the Western Allied troops who took Berlin would only have to withdraw from the Russian one of the four zones into which Berlin, like Germany, had been divided.

Eisenhower, it seems, never considered this. Nor, apparently, that it had been agreed at Yalta that all countries liberated from Nazi rule should hold free elections, yet the Russians had already imposed Communist governments on all the countries they had occupied, even on Poland. For him, Russia could do no wrong and he was willing to oblige her in every way. Thus when asked by the Russians, he would prevent an outraged Patton from capturing Prague but saw no reason to prevent the Russians taking Berlin. Czechoslovakia would become another Soviet satellite; as did Russian-occupied Germany under the name of the German (one-party) Democratic Republic.

It may well be that what finally decided Eisenhower not to attempt to take Berlin was a fear of the casualties this might entail. Bradley had estimated these in the region of 100,000 and so advised the Supreme Commander, declaring that it 'would be a pretty stiff price to pay for a prestige objective'. Eisenhower naturally agreed, but both he and Bradley had missed the point. Quite apart from any prestige value that Berlin might have, it was a vital strategic objective. It was the administrative centre from which Germany's civil and military affairs were controlled and it contained the heart and personification of Germany's will to resist.

A series of defeats, coupled with his determination to conduct every aspect of the war, had reduced Adolf Hitler to a state of physical collapse and mental exhaustion. Yet his amazing willpower was unabated and his tremendous personality still compelled the obedience of his subordinates. This was clearly realized by Montgomery, who on 29 April flatly declared that as long as Hitler was alive, the Germans 'must keep on fighting. Once it is known that he is dead or has cleared out, there will be a big-scale collapse.'

Montgomery also felt that an attack on Berlin by the Americans or the British or both might well not incur anything like the casualties anticipated. Clearly Hitler and his fanatical followers would oppose this, but perhaps the defenders as a whole would not. They did desperately resist the Russians, but then they feared a Russian victory would be followed by an orgy of murder, rape and looting, which indeed it was. They would trust the Western Allies not to do the same and might even welcome them if only to prevent such an ordeal. Certainly when British and American soldiers did enter Berlin after the war, its inhabitants waved and cheered almost as though they were liberators.

Sadly, the days when Montgomery could influence Eisenhower were gone. He was sure that the Supreme Commander was making a strategic mistake and was understandably upset when, despite Eisenhower's previous promises, Ninth US Army was removed from his control and Second (British) Army reduced to a subsidiary role, ordered to take the ports of Bremen and Hamburg but chiefly 'to protect Bradley's northern flank'. Difficult though he often was, however, he was never disloyal and on 9 April, he assured Eisenhower he would do everything possible to discharge this duty.

Subsidiary or not, Second Army's role was not an easy one. The numerous rivers and canals in its path caused less obstruction than might have been supposed, since Montgomery had ensured that enough bridging material would be available even before the Rhine was crossed. The resistance of the German defenders was more serious.

Chief among these was an old opponent, the brave and capable First Parachute Army, and it was reinforced by units either from Denmark or hastily created. Among these was the Training Battalion of 12th SS Panzer Division, the members of which were boys from the Hitler Youth aged only 16 or 17 but thoroughly indoctrinated in the principles of National Socialism and eager to fight and die for their Führer. There was also a force of naval personnel, mainly ex-submarine crews who, although inexperienced in land warfare, fought extremely well. The defenders were provided with large numbers of anti-tank guns and during April, Second Army lost 150 tanks destroyed and 500 more temporarily out of action.

Montgomery's men were not fanatics, but they continued to do their duty and perform acts of amazing heroism. On 2 April, for instance, Corporal Chapman of the Monmouthshire Regiment captured an important enemy position single-handed; then he and his company successfully held it against repeated counter-attacks. On the 3rd, Captain Liddell of the Coldstream Guards cut the wires of demolition charges on a bridge while under continuous fire; then led his men in an attack that took the bridge and forty-two prisoners. Both were awarded Victoria Crosses, but Liddell never received his for on 21 April he died of his wounds.

This 21 April was in fact a sad day for Second Army. Irish Guardsman Edward Charlton won a VC but posthumously. When his Sherman tank was disabled, he removed the turret machine gun and, although twice wounded, resisted units of 15th Panzer Grenadier Division single-handed until receiving a third and fatal wound.

On the same day, Montgomery suffered a personal loss when Major John Poston, the unofficial head of his liaison officers, was ambushed and killed. He had been with Montgomery since becoming his aide-de-camp in the desert in August 1942, and Montgomery, who had always treated him like a favourite son, was quite unable to conceal his grief.

Montgomery used his liaison officers to enable him to keep a close eye on the progress of the fighting, and on the previous day he had given a demonstration of this. By then, XXX Corps had reached Bremen which presented a considerable obstacle, being situated on both banks of the River Weser and garrisoned by paratroopers, SS detachments and ex-submariners. Horrocks had been undecided as to what action to take, but then Montgomery had arrived at his headquarters, briskly remarking he was 'not happy about Bremen'. After learning the full position, he took 'four decisions' which, says Horrocks, 'cleared up the situation'.

Maddeningly, Horrocks does not tell us what the four decisions were, but it seems they brought about the desired result. On 22 April, a raid by 750 Lancasters and Halifaxes devastated the city and on the 23rd, under cover of artillery bombardments, the infantry attacks went in with 3rd Division on the nearer western bank of the Weser and 43rd (Wessex) and 52nd Lowland divisions on the eastern bank. At the same time, the Guards Armoured Division moved north-eastwards to block any relief force coming from Hamburg. The Germans resisted fiercely, but on 27 April Horrocks took Bremen, together with 2 generals and more than 6,000 other prisoners.

Horrocks and his XXX Corps next moved north into the Cuxhaven Peninsula, while the rest of Second Army with XII Corps on the left and VIII Corps on the right advanced to the Elbe; both corps had reached the river by 23 April. It had now been determined that they should cross this and capture ports on the Baltic. Eisenhower was still firmly opposed to the Western Allies taking Berlin – which in any case became impossible by 25 April when the Russians completely encircled this – but he had decided it would be best to avoid complications being caused by the Russians entering north Germany as they had planned to do.

Montgomery had first suggested this move as early as 6 April as part of his desired assault on Berlin, so he was not pleased to hear Eisenhower explaining the 'urgent need' to reach Lübeck, the main port in the area, before the Russians. With scarcely disguised impatience, he retorted that he would have done this long ago had he not been deprived of Ninth US Army. Eisenhower tactfully promised reinforcements, and although the only ones to appear were the 'dismounted' paratroopers of Gavin's 82nd Airborne Division, Montgomery could hardly have asked for anyone better.

Montgomery's major crossing of the Elbe was made near the little town of Lauenburg on the night of 28/29 April. A heavy artillery bombardment began at midnight, and two hours later VIII Corps' 15th Scottish Division and 1st Commando Brigade went over the river in assault boats accompanied by DD tanks. Gavin's men followed them at 0100 on 30 April, upriver from Lauenburg where the Elbe was less wide and less deep. Both crossings successfully gained a bridgehead.

Meanwhile during the 29th, VIII Corps' sappers had been erecting a bridge near Lauenburg. They were harried by artillery fire, mines floated down the river and attacks by Messerschmitt Me 262s carrying anti-personnel bombs. These twin-engine jet aircraft did inflict some casualties but lost thirteen of their number to AA fire, and this was the last contribution the Luftwaffe made to the fighting. None of these efforts halted the completion of the bridge and on 30 May, Montgomery's men poured over this to make their final advances of the Second World War.

First onto the far bank of the Elbe were the remaining divisions of VIII Corps. Roberts and his 11th Armoured Division crossed at midday and headed for Lübeck with the infantry of 5th (British) Division, newly arrived from Italy, riding on the Comet tanks. Close behind came the men of 6th (British) Airborne Division who had raced up from the Rhine in a variety of vehicles including jeeps, civilian vans and trucks and even, it is reported, a steamroller. They joined 82nd US Airborne and both divisions under Gavin's leadership made for Wismar, another Baltic port east of Lübeck. Finally came XII Corps which swung north-westward towards Hamburg.

These advances soon became more like triumphal marches. In the afternoon of 30 April, Hitler and his devoted mistress Eva Braun, who he had married on the previous day, committed suicide. He had appointed as his successor the head of the Kriegsmarine, Grand Admiral Karl Dönitz. That officer had previously seemed willing to fight to the death, but with Hitler's dominance removed, he was anxious only to end the war as soon as possible.

Dönitz only learned of Hitler's death on the afternoon of 1 May. He gave the news to the German people that evening and on 2 May, the 'big-scale collapse' that Montgomery had foretold duly occurred. Roberts and Gavin were hindered mainly by swarms of German soldiers eager to surrender to them, having good cause to believe that if they went into Russian captivity they would never be freed from it. Lübeck and Wismar were both secured a few hours before Russian tanks appeared. That evening the civilian and military authorities in Hamburg agreed to allow XII Corps to take over their city unopposed, which 7th Armoured and 53rd Welsh divisions did the next day. The inhabitants had been ordered off the streets, but the police force lined the road, standing stiffly at the salute.

Far greater surrenders lay just ahead. On 3 May, a delegation from Dönitz arrived at Montgomery's Tac HQ on Lüneburg Heath. It was headed by Dönitz's successor as chief of the German navy, Hans von Friedeburg, who, because naval personnel had been fighting on land, bore the rank of general admiral, much to Montgomery's delighted amusement. The events that followed have often been described and many accounts insist on revealing that Montgomery bullied and belittled the delegation and was harsh, unyielding, dictatorial and generally unpleasant. It is a fair description of his attitude, but there was a reason for this.

Montgomery was almost certain that with Hitler dead, Dönitz would be willing to surrender; almost but not absolutely. Dönitz and the German high command had retired to Flensburg near the Danish frontier and if they fought on the Allies would have to conquer northern Germany, Denmark and perhaps Holland and Norway as well. This might prove lengthy and costly and Montgomery was determined not to risk it, but to push the Germans into a complete capitulation with the minimum of delay.

He did so by producing a map showing the whole military situation, which the Germans apparently had not fully appreciated, declared he was ready and willing to go on fighting and promised dire consequences if this happened. He then demanded the surrender of all German forces in the areas detailed above apart from Norway of which no mention was made. A shaken von Friedeburg miserably replied that he had no power to accept these terms, but would recommend that his superiors do so. Confirmation was received, and at 1830 on Friday, 4 May 1945, the instrument of surrender was signed at Montgomery's Tac Headquarters.

It is rarely mentioned that on 3 May, without waiting for that confirmation, Montgomery had ordered all air-raids to cease, thereby saving many lives. Dönitz was so grateful that he felt honour-bound to respond. He had earlier been determined that all German warships, surface or submarine, should be scuttled rather than handed over to the victors. He now reversed this decision. In fact 221 U-boat commanders ignored these new orders, believing they were false or had been given only under compulsion – Dönitz to his credit would always declare this was not the case – but 156 submarines and Germany's few remaining surface warships did surrender. A request that Dönitz order the capitulation of Dunkirk, not previously mentioned, was also promptly granted.

Hostilities between Germany and Britain officially ceased at 0800 on 5 May, although fighting on other fronts would continue until the 7th. There was naturally much rejoicing, and not only in Britain. As a result of Montgomery's actions, Denmark had been released from Nazi tyranny, spared from being mauled, like France and Italy, as a battleground between Axis and Allied armies and escaped her greatest fear, that of being occupied by the Russians. On 12 May, Montgomery formally entered Copenhagen. He received 'a tumultuous welcome'.

Less joyful were the countries of the Balkans and Eastern Europe which found they had merely exchanged one tyranny for another. Among their number was Poland, which Britain had gone to war to protect in the first place and it was not only the Poles who longed for its deliverance. In ultimately attaining this, Montgomery was destined to play a crucial part.

In July 1945, Montgomery was notified that he would become Chief of the Imperial General Staff when Brooke retired, although this was only officially announced in January 1946 and Montgomery only took over on 26 June. On first learning the news Montgomery, who wanted de Guingand as his vice chief, arranged with Brooke that de Guingand become Director of Military Intelligence at the War Office in September 1945 to give him experience. Unfortunately, de Guingand was far from well and Brooke – Viscount Alanbrooke as he became on 1 January 1946 – told Montgomery bluntly that de Guingand was unbalanced, not to be trusted and not fit to become Vice CIGS.

Since Montgomery had immense respect for Brooke, he felt he must so inform de Guingand. This he did in a most curt and callous manner and then, says de Guingand bitterly, 'rushed off'. Probably this was because he was embarrassed at having to disappoint a loyal subordinate and he later tried to make amends by promising de Guingand that if there was another war 'I would pull you straight in as Chief of Staff.' However, his action has rightly been condemned and would prove an evil omen for his own term as CIGS.

In fact Montgomery was not a good choice for this post. He was never a politician, prepared for compromise and conciliation. As a result, his relationships with his fellow chiefs of staff and with the government of Clement Attlee which had replaced that of Churchill were very unhappy. Nor did it help that he frequently went on trips abroad, during which he took a perverse delight in causing controversy, often on matters on which he clearly knew very little. In one respect, however, his actions were of vital importance.

Only a week after the final German surrender, Churchill was writing to Roosevelt's successor, President Harry Truman, warning him of the threat posed by Russia and, incidentally, particularly condemning her 'attitude towards Poland'. His concern was not at first shared in the United States or indeed in Britain, but it was always held by Montgomery who, as Russia's unwillingness to co-operate and intention of dominating Europe became increasingly obvious, decided he must try to provide an effective defence for Western Europe. His almost obsessive belief in this would lead to his next appointment.

On 1 November 1948, Montgomery left England for Paris to become chairman of the Commanders-in-Chief Committee of the Western Union, this being a military alliance formed earlier that year by Britain, France, Holland, Belgium and Luxembourg. His delight in his appointment was, however, blighted by anxiety over what might happen in Britain after his departure.

Earlier that year, Attlee had argued that Britain should not send an army to the Continent in the event of another European war. Montgomery had persuaded him to abandon this view, but was by no means certain he would not revert to it. Montgomery therefore wanted Crocker, then C-in-C, Middle East, to succeed him as CIGS, being confident Crocker would reassure the other members of the Western Union, particularly the French, that Britain would not desert them. Attlee, however, appointed Slim who had recently become deputy chairman on the board of one of the government's most sacred of cows, British Rail. This would suggest he was a much better politician than Montgomery and indeed he proved a more suitable and much more popular CIGS.

Montgomery's detractors have claimed that he was jealous of Slim. If anything, their writings suggest that the opposite was true. Slim never misses a chance to snigger at commanders who wore more than one cap-badge, studied photographs of opponents to help assess their character, kept devoted staff officers with them or thought their battles went according to plan. His attitude becomes most clear when he describes the staff of General Leese who was appointed Allied Land Forces C-in-C, South-East Asia in late 1944. This, Slim says, had 'a good deal of desert sand in its shoes'. It also had plenty of Sicilian and Italian mud, but what aroused Slim's envy was the desert victories that had made Eighth Army a household name while he and his Fourteenth Army had been 'forgotten'.

By contrast, Montgomery declares Slim 'fit for the highest commands in peace and war', praises his victories on the India/Burma front and ignores the harm Slim caused him after becoming CIGS. This restraint is especially commendable because the real reason why Montgomery did not want Slim to be CIGS was his fear that an Indian army officer who had spent the last three years of the Second World War in the Far East would not favour a 'Continental strategy'. He was quite right: Attlee disavowed former undertakings that Britain would help defend France's frontiers and Slim promptly supported Attlee. Not surprisingly, the French concluded that 'Perfidious Albion' could not be trusted and Montgomery's position as the Western Union's military chief became almost impossible.

Fortunately, Montgomery once more proved adaptable. Shortly after becoming CIGS, he had visited Canada and the United States and urged that co-operation in defensive measures would prevent another war. His efforts received little support in Britain but were welcomed by the two North American countries, which in July 1948 began talks with the Western Union states about a possible anti-aggression pact. Joined by Italy, Portugal, Norway, Denmark and Iceland, on 4 April 1949 they signed a treaty stating that an attack on any one of the signatories would be an attack on all.

Thus was formed the North Atlantic Treaty Organization (NATO), but though an obvious deterrent to aggression, it did not entirely calm French fears. To be able to resist an invasion successfully, they wanted American forces in Europe and Montgomery, recalling his own reception when CIGS, was sure he could persuade the Americans to oblige. Slim and the other chiefs of staff issued objections and warnings but Montgomery ignored them. In November 1949, he went to America and gained the backing he needed. On 2 April 1951, Eisenhower set up the NATO headquarters near Paris as its Supreme Commander, took over the Western Union and appointed Montgomery as his deputy.

In October 1951 Churchill was again elected prime minister, but Slim remained as CIGS. On 30 May 1952, Eisenhower left Europe, shortly to become president of the United States, and although everyone in NATO wanted his Chief of Staff General Alfred Gruenther to succeed him as Supreme Commander, Slim and the other chiefs of staff objected that Gruenther lacked battlefield experience. The Americans therefore appointed Ridgway instead. Montgomery accepted that Ridgway was 'a fine battlefield commander' but considered his temperament unsuited to a long-term project like NATO. Also Ridgway proved unable to maintain the level of international co-operation achieved by Eisenhower. That he rarely bothered to consult Montgomery who he had not forgiven for overruling him in the Ardennes Battle probably did not help.

Luckily, on 1 November 1952 Montgomery's former pupil and subordinate Harding became CIGS. Unlike Slim, he thought that Gruenther, whom he had known in Italy, would be an excellent head of NATO and Gruenther duly became Supreme Commander on 11 July 1953. Montgomery had an ideal relationship with him, as he did with General Lewis Norstad, the American Army Air Force officer who succeeded Gruenther in 1956. In the previous year, Montgomery had gained another of his major objectives when the German Federal Republic (West Germany) became a member of NATO, an event that Montgomery, never vindictive towards Germany, had desired since NATO had first come into being.

Montgomery left NATO on 18 September 1958 and finally retired two days later, but he had passed on to its personnel his conviction that NATO was a long-term commitment. With admirable tenacity and determination they remained ready to fight a war they all prayed would never happen. They were harried by peace movements that were highly approved by the Soviet war machine, but sustained by the obvious desire for freedom of most of Eastern Europe. Poland in particular was the scene of popular unrest and in 1981, for example, martial law was imposed there.

Finally in 1989, NATO proved more durable than its opponents. On 9 November, inhabitants of both West and East Berlin climbed onto its infamous wall that since 1961 had been the visible symbol of the defects of Communist rule, smashing it with sledgehammers and embracing each other while its border guards watched helplessly. This was only the most dramatic of a series of events that saw Russia's Communist puppets in Eastern Europe and the Balkans rejected by their subjects. It did not end history as was stupidly said, or even end wars in Europe; it did not prevent the Continent being threatened by new foes and old foes in new guises; but what was particularly gratifying to Britain was that it brought about the liberation of Poland.

Montgomery did not live to witness these events, some of which would have surprised him; for example, he had never believed that Russia would permit a reunification of Germany. Had he seen them, however, he would have been delighted by their justification of NATO. Since he had played such an important part in the creation of NATO and been for so long a permanent, unifying presence in its senior ranks, it seems fair to consider this the culmination of the battles in North-West Europe fought by Field Marshal Bernard Law Montgomery.

Chapter Thirteen

Master of the Battlefield

That was the title given by Nigel Hamilton to the second part of his three-volume biography of Montgomery, but was this justified?

According to the Roman historian Tacitus, it was better to criticize than praise, for praise can appear servile whereas 'malignancy wears the false disguise of independence'. He certainly followed his own advice, attributing to past rulers and statesmen every possible if usually improbable crime and vice.

So as not to be considered servile therefore, let us be reminded that Montgomery had many very human faults. He was extremely vain and it is really no excuse – though it is true – to point out that he was no more so than say Wellington and Patton, and considerably less so than say Nelson and Mountbatten. He could be arrogant, dogmatic, dictatorial, intolerant, ill-mannered and generally unpleasant. He was always tactless and seemed positively to enjoy causing trouble. No wonder he aroused resentment and hostility.

What was particularly unfortunate was that Montgomery created hostility not just towards himself but also to his ideas. The opposition of Tedder and Admiral Cunningham to his plan for Sicily or that of Eisenhower to his plan for a quick crossing of the Rhine which disappeared after they had got over his bad manners and considered his ideas on their merits provide obvious examples of this.

It also meant that Montgomery was often criticized for actions that were not even noticed if committed by others; for instance, his taking command of Eighth Army two days early in August 1942. Since Rommel's attack was anticipated in only a fortnight's time, this might seem to deserve praise rather than blame, but more significantly, General Alexander who in a similarly difficult situation took over command in French North Africa two days early in February 1943, has never received any criticism. Of course Alexander acted quietly, whereas Montgomery both at the time and later, took gleeful pleasure in his open insubordination.

Montgomery was also accused of being anti-American. He certainly blamed American decisions for failure to end the war in 1944, but Nigel Hamilton has confirmed that he ended his War Diary with the blunt acknowledgement that without the Americans 'we would not have won the war at all.' He praised American courage, quickness to learn and dashing determination. When American commanders or American troops served under him, he treated them with concern, consideration, patience and restraint, as Bradley, Hodges, Simpson, Collins, Gavin, Hasbrouck and others could attest.

Yet as Brooke observed, the Americans could never like Montgomery. His unfortunate mannerisms made even his praise, encouragement or expressions of sympathy come over as patronising or condescending.[1] This impression was reinforced by his attitude towards Eisenhower who was very much liked by everyone.

Montgomery, though often arrogant and difficult, was never disloyal or dishonest but he did subject Eisenhower to constant criticism that reached its culmination with the publication of his *Memoirs*. In retrospect the fuss caused by these seems exaggerated, for while Montgomery was very disparaging of Eisenhower's generalship, he praised his patience and good nature, sincerity and common sense, ability to inspire trust and confidence and concludes by declaring him 'a truly great man'.

Unfortunately, although Americans would tolerate criticism from fellow countrymen,[2] any by a British officer caused outrage. Montgomery's tendency towards hasty and ill-considered judgements also engendered hostility. He could be unfair in refusing to retain subordinates who he considered 'useless', a favourite word. On the other hand, he never tried to find scapegoats, as his treatment of Dempsey after GOODWOOD and Browning after MARKET GARDEN shows. He was also willing to give second chances to those he considered unfairly treated by others: for instance Ritchie, who had been made a scapegoat by Auchinleck.

Curiously enough, Montgomery's most regrettable fault, his egotistical vanity, proved beneficial to his generalship and hence to his country. His arrival in the Middle East to take command of Eighth Army is thus described by Major General Fuller in *The Decisive Battles of the Western World*: 'Montgomery was a man of dynamic personality and supreme self-confidence...[that] electrified his men. He was the right man in the right place at the right moment; for after its severe defeat the Eighth Army needed a new dynamo and Montgomery supplied it.'

Montgomery's effect on Eighth Army was confirmed by the victory of Alam Halfa which everyone could see had been won by Montgomery's decisions and the alterations he had made to previous plans. Montgomery was well aware of the lift this had given to morale and therefore increased it by maintaining that everything had gone exactly according to plan. It was an attitude he would adopt in all subsequent battles and was justified since it made his men's confidence in him absolute.

In reality, in every battle matters did not go according to plan, at least in regard to its details. Montgomery was well aware of this and we have seen instances of his expressly or implicitly accepting it. These admissions, however, were made privately and were not allowed to be noticed by his soldiers. Unfortunately, Montgomery's vanity prompted him to continue this fiction long after the close of hostilities. It was extraordinarily stupid for a whole number of reasons.

For a start, it concealed one of the best features of Montgomery's generalship. It will have been noticed how often he proved variable of thought and adaptable in changing circumstances. This was of far more service to his troops than if he had stuck rigidly to a previous plan. His insistence that he had always done so, as Liddell Hart points out, has 'deprived him of the credit due to him' in respect of his most unusual 'combination of flexibility with determination'.

Then again, this insistence robs Montgomery of the sympathy to which he was surely entitled for his constant bad luck with the weather. This was exceptionally unpleasant in the winters of 1943–44 and 1944–45 and in the latter it came unusually early, thereby having a considerable adverse effect on MARKET GARDEN as General Student generously accepted. There was also the 'torrential' rain in the desert, the violent storm that wrecked Benghazi and handicapped Montgomery's advance on Tripoli, the unusually bad summer weather that upset his plans for the D-Day landings and the worst summer storm for forty years that crippled his build-up in Normandy. It has been said Montgomery was a lucky general, but that seems somewhat unlikely.

Most of all, though, Montgomery's insistence that everything always went exactly according to plan left him wide open to the attacks of his critics. They had no difficulty in finding incidents in his battles that he had not intended and perhaps not anticipated. These could be triumphantly revealed and, however unimportant, be exaggerated to such an extent that it sometimes appears as if Montgomery never gained a victory at all.

As General Fraser relates in *And We Shall Shock Them*, the British Army finished the Second World War triumphant 'under Slim in Burma, under Alexander in Italy, under Montgomery in North-West Europe.' In order to assess Montgomery's generalship therefore, it may be helpful to compare him not with commanders who failed but with these other two very successful ones.

The most attractive feature of all three generals was their empathy with their soldiers. All were very able, hard-working, determined and undaunted by the most adverse circumstances. In this respect, it can be argued that most credit must go to Slim, whose experiences were very unpleasant.

In November 1940 Brigadier Slim, as he then was, was instructed to capture the Sudanese frontier fort of Gallabat that had been taken by the Italians and Metemma, the corresponding Italian fort in Abyssinia. He did recapture Gallabat, but his advance on Metemma was repulsed amid some panic; the Italians then drove him out of Gallabat as well. In March 1942, Lieutenant General Slim commanded Burma Corps – two infantry divisions and an armoured brigade – opposed by a single Japanese division, but he suffered a series of defeats ending only in May with the flight of his remaining troops into India.

Throughout his misfortunes, Slim's resolution never faltered and his fighting spirit, evidenced by his bulldog features, jutting chin and perpetual scowl, inspired respect from the men of Burma Corps and later of his Fourteenth Army. This was increased by the knowledge that 'Uncle Bill' had been with them in bad times as well as good. Nevertheless, his actual achievements in the lean years hardly deserve mention alongside those of Alexander and Montgomery in their great time of trouble, the retreat to and evacuation from Dunkirk.

Brooke would pay tribute to both Alexander and Montgomery, but he believed that while Montgomery realized their perilous circumstances and was stimulated by them, Alexander did not. In fact, Alexander fully appreciated the situation but, more quiet and restrained than Montgomery, believed it his duty to radiate a calm serenity. This inspired all who served with or under him and played a very great part in the success of the evacuation.

Montgomery, by contrast, showed his greatness during the retreat. His achievements have already been described; suffice to recall that his 3rd Division had fewer casualties than any other and Brooke 'thanked heaven to have a commander of his calibre'. Less dramatic but equally commendable was his provision of 'rations on the hoof' for his men. The need to secure supplies was something that the staffs of all commanders had to consider, but Montgomery would make it his personal concern.

In two books, *El Alamein to the River Sangro* and *Normandy to the Baltic* that appeared under his name – really they were written by Belchem under his supervision – Montgomery constantly refers to this necessity under the heading of 'administration'. In the former one when the supply lines were more perilous, there are chapters dealing solely and separately with administration in North Africa, Sicily and Italy. This was typical of Montgomery's wide interest in all aspects of generalship in several of which he excelled even men of the calibre of Slim and Alexander.

For example, there was Intelligence. In his *Defeat into Victory*, Slim complains: 'I had not at my disposal the sources of information of the enemy's intentions that some more fortunate commanders in other theatres were to invoke. We depended almost entirely on the Intelligence gathered by our fighting patrols.' This ignores the considerable information gained by air reconnaissance as well as that from Ultra intercepts which Michael Smith, a former Intelligence officer, declares in *The Emperor's Codes* was especially important during the crucial actions at Kohima and Imphal and included 'a complete order of battle of the Japanese forces' both army and army air force. Since Slim admitted this in private, his statement just quoted was either deliberately untrue or, one would prefer to believe, a reflection of a personal disinterest in Intelligence.[3]

Alexander, by contrast, took a great interest in Intelligence and was particularly impressed by Ultra. He was not always well served by this in his Italian campaigns, but it seems that he or at least his Intelligence officers felt that as long as they had Ultra, there was little need to bother about other sources.

Montgomery was also greatly interested in Intelligence, but in a more calculated fashion. He gratefully listened to Ultra intercepts – although as we have seen, he too was misled by them on several occasions – but he also tried to obtain confirmation from all other possible sources. These included air reconnaissance – it will be remembered how he specifically requested a pair of Mosquitos to assist in this – specialized ground reconnaissance, for instance by the Long Range Desert Group, and day-to-day knowledge from his liaison officers. Moreover Williams confirms that Montgomery as 'the complete professional' well understood his German opponents and often helped his Intelligence staff interpret confusing or seemingly contradictory items of information.

Montgomery also excelled in the use of new weapons, from the Scorpion flail tanks at Alamein, through the anti-tank 'Pheasants' at Medenine to the 'Funnies' at D-Day and thereafter. It can be argued that Alexander and Slim did not have the same opportunities to use new weapons, but Montgomery alone had a hand in the creation of one: his conversion of Shermans into Fireflies. It is also worth considering the use made by all these officers of a weapon all did possess: their supporting air forces.

Slim in particular suffered from Axis air supremacy. His defeat by the Italians resulted from the battering his troops received from the *Regia Aeronautica*. A couple of months later he was shot in the buttocks by a strafing Italian fighter. Yet in the first Burma campaign, he ignored the danger from a dominant Japanese Army Air Force and suffered accordingly. It would appear that he only learned the lesson as late as February 1943.

On the 14th of that month, 3,200 men under Brigadier (later Major General) Orde Wingate crossed the Chindwin River to operate in Japanese-held territory. That British and Indian troops could outfight and outwit the Japanese in the jungle caused a dramatic rise in morale and the transfer of Wingate's supply lines and supporting fire to the air showed how to counter superior Japanese manoeuvrability on the ground. Slim at first was delighted. After Wingate's death in an air crash, Slim declared him to have more than one 'attribute of genius' and be 'irreplaceable'. Sadly, it seems that Slim later became jealously resentful of the praise bestowed on Wingate, dismissing his raid as 'an expensive failure' magnified by 'somewhat phoney propaganda'. At least he now accepted the need for co-operation of ground and air forces.[4]

Neither Montgomery nor Alexander had ever doubted the importance of aerial support, but it was the former who achieved this from the moment he arrived in the Middle East and moved his headquarters from the Ruweisat Ridge to the coast next to that of the Desert Air Force. Aerial action proved crucial at the Battles of Alam Halfa and El Alamein and with Broadhurst's co-operation produced a magnificent culmination at the Battle of the Mareth Line with the storming of the Tebaga Gap.

During these operations many of the subsequent refinements of close support aerial missions were introduced: the consultation of army and air force planning staffs; the presence of air force officers in the front line to direct strikes; and the standing patrols of ground-attack warplanes, ready for action if needed. These developments would later be directed with skill and success by Alexander in Italy and by Slim on the India/Burma front, but most credit belongs to Montgomery because he was the first to employ them. He also expanded on them in his own later operations. His use of heavy bombers has been criticized, though, as we have seen, often in connection with matters beyond his control, but his use, again with Broadhurst's essential aid, of the rocket-firing Typhoons in Normandy was admitted, even by his enemies, to have been decisive.

From specific aspects of generalship, we turn to the basics: strategy and tactics. In the most simple terms, strategy determines objectives and the routes of advance or retreat should this prove necessary and so dictates where battles are fought. Tactics decide how they are fought: the general's plans, the combination of the different branches of an army and its co-operation with its supporting air force.

According to General Fraser, Slim was more imaginative than Montgomery. If so, this was clearly not in the field of strategy. In the first Burma campaign, the Japanese, having taken Rangoon, had two lines of advance into Upper Burma: the valleys of the Irrawaddy and Sittang Rivers. The former was blocked by Slim's Burma Corps and the latter by two Chinese formations called 'armies', but each only equal to a British corps in manpower and vastly weaker in equipment, transport and supporting units. In addition, Slim faced only one Japanese division while the Chinese were confronted with three.

Since the Chinese understandably proved unable to hold their ground, Slim's left flank was continually open to attack. Yet Major General James Lunt in *A Hell of a Licking* reports that Slim declared his 'intention to recapture Rangoon before the monsoon broke in mid-May'. Slim's memoirs discreetly omit this, but do confirm his constant desire to counter-attack. He never seems to have realized that the further south his counter-attacks progressed, the more chance there was of his men being cut off when his left flank gave way, and the more men who took part, the more were endangered.

Slim showed little more strategic imagination at later times. By the end of 1944, shattering Japanese defeats at Kohima and Imphal had been followed by still greater ones elsewhere, notably in October 1944 the titanic Battle of Leyte Gulf. In this the Japanese fleet was eliminated, ensuring their loss of the Philippines and the natural resources for which they had gone to war in the first place. After this, their army in Burma could not be strengthened but lost troops who were sent to the Pacific.

In these circumstances, the strategy of Slim and the theatre's Supreme Commander, Mountbatten, was very limited: that of 'reaching Mandalay before the monsoon'. It was Leese, after his arrival as Commander-in-Chief, Land Forces in November 1944, who urged the much more daring and successful strategy of taking Rangoon as well. As he would write to his wife, 'When I first came out here it was never even thought of.'

Slim never acknowledged Leese's action and was still more ungenerous about the part played by Alexander in the first Burma campaign. In his writings and in interviews he complained that Alexander had been 'out-generalled', denied Alexander's immense contribution to the maintenance of morale, sneered at Alexander's legendary personal courage which he preferred to call 'foolhardy' and concluded that Alexander had not had 'the faintest idea of what was going on'.

This was unfair and untrue. In reality Alexander, unlike Slim, had the strategic vision to see that the defence of Upper Burma was unrealistic: the Japanese could be reinforced which he could not and they had complete command of the air. Had it not been for the arrival of the Chinese, Alexander would have carried out an orderly evacuation of Burma as swiftly as was consistent with destroying strategic prizes like the Yenangyaung oilfields to prevent their falling into enemy hands. For political reasons, though, he had to co-ordinate his movements with those of the Chinese, which crippled his freedom of movement.

Slim's reluctance to retreat and bold but futile counter-attacks made Alexander's position still more difficult. In late April it became impossible. The Chinese collapsed completely and, apart from one division that made for India, fled to their homeland. Alexander then ordered a retirement to Imphal, but a covering force was prematurely withdrawn – by Slim of all people – and although most of Burma Corps' soldiers escaped, it was at the cost of most of its equipment. It was not Alexander who had not had 'the faintest idea of what was going on'.

Alexander's clarity of strategic vision was displayed on many subsequent occasions: his appreciation of the value of Malta as a base from which the enemy's supply lines could be disrupted; the consequent need to recapture the Martuba airfields; the importance of Naples and Foggia; and the need to keep up pressure in Italy and so compel the Germans to retain forces there that might have proved decisive on other fronts.

Above all, Alexander realized that his strategy must take account of political as well as military matters, in particular the needs and wishes of Britain's allies. He was sometimes too gracious when failing to curb the mistakes of a subordinate, like those of Slim in Burma. He sometimes allowed political considerations to dictate unwise actions, as when he permitted Patton to head for Palermo rather than Messina. These faults, though, were far outweighed by his natural charm and ability to unite men from different countries in a common purpose as he did so well in French North Africa and Italy.

Montgomery, as he would readily admit, lacked Alexander's noble qualities and hated political interference in military matters. It seems fair therefore to agree with Eisenhower and acknowledge Alexander as 'Britain's outstanding soldier in the field of strategy'.

Not that Montgomery was a poor strategist; Rommel in fact would declare that 'it would be difficult to accuse Montgomery of ever having made a serious strategic mistake.'[5] On his arrival in the Middle East, Montgomery at once realized, as Auchinleck had not, that if the Alamein positions fell, Egypt would be impossible to defend. He shared Alexander's appreciation of the importance of Malta, Martuba, Naples and Foggia. Later he saw the need for a concentrated thrust through North-West Europe as against a 'broad front' policy; for taking the Ruhr quickly; and for reaching the Baltic ports ahead of the Russians. Later still, he would realize that the defence of Europe required the presence of the Americans and would set about obtaining it despite the lack of support from Attlee and Slim.

In one respect indeed, Montgomery was a finer strategist than Alexander. Alexander was sometimes too far-sighted and found strategic prospects such as the landing at Anzio or a proposed advance from north

Italy to Vienna so attractive in principle that he overlooked their short-term tactical problems. Montgomery's strategic vision was not so far-reaching but it was more down-to-earth and realistic and as a superb tactician he would never have been misguided in this way.

That Montgomery was a superb tactician becomes clear if only from the sheer variety of his battles. Slim never carried out an amphibious landing; those in Burma were executed by Lieutenant General Christison, including the one in May 1945 that led to the capture of Rangoon before the Fourteenth Army could reach it. Alexander did carry out several amphibious missions in the Mediterranean, gaining special credit for his coolness when that at Salerno threatened to become a disaster. None, however, in difficulty or importance can be ranked equal to Montgomery's achievement as 'NEPTUNE's general'.

Both Alexander and Slim carried out river crossings, one by Slim over the Irrawaddy being the widest of any by British and Commonwealth troops. This, however, was opposed only by members of the 'Indian National Army' formed by Subhas Chandra Bose, once president of the Congress Party, from soldiers who had changed sides after being taken prisoner by the Japanese.[6] They sought only an opportunity to desert and were despised by British and Japanese alike. None of these river crossings, therefore, in difficulty or importance, can be ranked equal to Montgomery's crossing of the Rhine.

As regards victories in defensive battles, Alexander's in French North Africa were won mainly because the Germans were more concerned with the threat from Montgomery's Eighth Army in their rear. That won by Slim at Sinzweya in February 1944 – the Battle of the Admin Box – was won by overwhelming superiority on land and in the air and in *Battle for Burma*, Brigadier 'Birdie' Smith, with delicious irony remembering Slim's own belittlement of Wingate, remarks that it was 'not nearly as great a victory as was claimed in the glowingly phrased communiqués issued.'

Slim's twin victories of Kohima and Imphal really were great ones. While Fourteenth Army had fewer than 17,000 casualties, the Japanese had 53,000 that could never be replaced and so ensured a subsequent British reconquest of Burma. The Japanese, however, were very inferior in numbers of men, artillery, armour – only fifteen Japanese tanks appeared and these of inferior quality – and in the air. They were also desperately short of ammunition, medical supplies and even food. Yet the battles were won only after savage struggles of attrition lasting from early March to early July 1944 and compared by participants on both sides to the brutal conflicts of the First World War. That emphasizes the courage and tenacity displayed by British, Indians and Japanese alike – Bose's double-deserters dishonourably excepted – but would not normally be regarded as a tribute to the generalship on either side.

Compare the generalship shown in Montgomery's defensive battles. At Alam Halfa with the two sides nearer to an even balance than at any other time and the enemy possessing superior tanks and anti-tank guns, Montgomery won by a combination of determination and flexibility plus an admirable use of his supporting air power. The same qualities won the Ardennes Battle. Medenine, on the other hand, was a deliberate attempt to trap and destroy German armour: a new concept that a desert veteran like Kippenberger could call a 'masterpiece'.

Turning to battles fought on the offensive, we find all three generals winning brilliant victories, but Montgomery again taking the greatest personal interest in every aspect of generalship. Deception measures had always been a part of any offensive, but those of Montgomery before Alamein, given their own code-name of Operation BERTRAM, established the importance of deception for all time and influenced all subsequent operations.

Similarly, Montgomery's ability to plan not only for the present but for future battles and his adaptability in those battles, many examples of both of which have been observed previously, were very much his own and were unequalled even by officers of the calibre of Alexander and Slim. This is also the case with his use of different divisions on different tasks for which they were best suited.

In *The Battle for Berlin*, Major General Sir John Strawson rather slightingly states that: 'Montgomery never really advanced in his tactical ideas beyond the First World War "push". The difference of *his* "pushes" was that they succeeded.' Well, that was perhaps a not unimportant difference but in any case, Montgomery not only varied the direction of his 'pushes' in the course of the battle, but adopted a variety of different tactics as the basis for them.

An examination of Montgomery's different forms of attack can be aided by reference to Major General Fuller's *The Second World War 1939–1945*. In this Fuller details four basic types. One is the penetration attack that breaks through the enemy's front and then turns on one or both of the unattacked parts. This Fuller calls an Arbela manoeuvre after a victory of Alexander the Great, though in fact the main cause of victory was the premature flight of the Persian King Darius III that caused the disintegration of his multi-racial army.

The other basic tactics detailed by Fuller are the attack on one enemy flank which he calls 'single envelopment', the attack on both flanks or 'double envelopment' and the attack on the enemy's rear by a force operating separately from its main body. These he names respectively Leuthen, Cannae and Chancellorsville tactics after victories by Frederick the Great of Prussia, Hannibal Barca of Carthage and Robert Edward Lee, a general of the Confederate States of America in that country's tragic civil war.

Of the victories of the modern Alexander, Tunis, from which he gained his title, was a Leuthen attack. His final advance to the River Po was a Cannae attack. His most brilliant victory was the Battle for Rome: Operation DIADEM. This was planned as a Cannae attack, trapping the Germans between Fifth US and Eighth (British) Armies moving north-west from the area of Cassino and VI US Corps moving north-east from the Anzio bridgehead. Unfortunately, Clark's obsession with the Italian capital turned the attack into a reinforced Leuthen manoeuvre that captured Rome but not most of the enemy troops.

Slim's most brilliant victory, the Battle of the Irrawaddy Shore, was always intended to be a Leuthen operation. It bore a considerable although it seems unnoticed similarity to Montgomery's previous Leuthen attack in Normandy; so much so that one wonders if it was consciously or unconsciously influenced by this. The basic idea was that the British XXXIII Corps should tie down the enemy on the Allied left front by threatening not Caen but Mandalay, while the British IV Corps on the Allied right would capture the enemy supply base, not Alençon but Meiktila some 70 miles south of Mandalay and trap the Japanese in the equivalent of the Falaise pocket.

As it happened, the Japanese, though losing Mandalay, Meiktila and most of their equipment and being driven eastward in disorderly retreat, were not trapped. The reason was that at Meiktila the Japanese administrative troops and even patients summoned out of hospital showed the same ferocious determination as their front-line soldiers. Slim called the Japanese 'the most formidable fighting insects in the world' and it is often assumed that they were the most dangerous of all opponents. Ronald Lewin, however, in *Ultra Goes to War: The Secret Story*, specifically compares them with the SS formations in Normandy and rates these 'even more formidable'. They certainly had better equipment. The soldiers advancing on Mandalay encountered just thirteen obsolescent light tanks – promptly wiped out by anti-tank Hurricanes – but those advancing on Caen faced from 520 to 725 tanks that were far from obsolescent.

Indeed, before examining Montgomery's offensive battles it is worth considering the difficulties he faced. He did have a superiority in numbers, though nothing like as great as that enjoyed by Slim or, for that matter, by Auchinleck in the battles of July 1942. On the other hand, he fought very capable enemies: the SS troops and parachutists in North-West Europe and *Panzerarmee Afrika* in the desert. He often had to overcome strong, skilfully prepared fixed defences and always had to cope with weapons of superior quality; principally tanks, anti-tank guns and mortars.

In addition, Montgomery was opposed by enemy commanders of a very high standard. Slim did not have the same problem, for the best Japanese generals were not wasted on a sideshow like Burma but were in the Philippines, Iwo Jima or Okinawa. Alexander was opposed by Rommel in Tunisia only briefly, but his chief rival there and in Sicily and Italy was Kesselring, the brilliance of whose defensive operations was acknowledged by friend and foe alike. Montgomery, though, was still more sorely tried. He was up against Rommel in North Africa from Alam Halfa to Medenine and the list of his opponents in North-West Europe is an impressive one: Rommel, von Rundstedt, Model, Kesselring, Student, von Manteuffel and several others of only slightly lesser ability.

Of the various offensive tactics, Montgomery apparently favoured the Leuthen one most. In addition to Normandy which proved more successful than even the finest efforts of Slim and Alexander, he used this at El Agheila and in Sicily and in his move beyond the Sangro. He employed the penetration tactic on three occasions, to all of which he added his own distinctive touch. His attack on the Gabes Gap on a moonless night contrary to his usual practice was unremarkable, but the same cannot be said for the other two. At Alamein he did not complete his penetration but halted on vital ground that the enemy was desperate to regain; he thus obtained the advantages of fighting on the defensive in an offensive action, and won this uniquely on the counter-counter-attack. At MARKET GARDEN he supported and speeded up his assault by the airborne seizure of crucial bridges.

In his Cannae operations, Montgomery again introduced personal variations. The continually mobile activities of both his flanking movements towards Tripoli helped to confuse his foes, and he was quick to see that the enforced 'stagger' of his flanking attacks in the Rhineland would draw the bulk of his enemies onto the first one, leaving them wide open to the assault of the second one. Although he was assisted by airborne missions in Sicily, the D-Day landings and the Rhine crossing, he made only one 'rear attack proper' as Fuller calls it. This was on the Tebaga Gap during the Battle of the Mareth Line. It is summed up by Fuller in *The Decisive Battles of the Western World* as 'a superb manoeuvre – reminiscent of that of Lee at Chancellorsville.'

Of course, not all aspects of Montgomery's tactics have earned praise. Rommel, for instance, declares that he was 'excessively cautious'. Montgomery's detractors have eagerly seized on this description, but it referred to Montgomery's advance from El Alamein to El Agheila and we have already noted that it is expressly contradicted by German historian Paul Carell who got his information from Rommel's chief subordinates. Indeed, Rommel personally admits that Montgomery frequently moved faster than expected, preventing the Axis troops from rallying or reorganizing.

Nor was this the only time that Montgomery's forward moves – unexciting but well-planned and enforced with ruthless persistence – progressed faster than had been thought possible. In Tunisia, Montgomery's thrust through the Mareth Line and the Gabes Gap amazed Eisenhower and Bedell Smith. In Italy, despite having to move his supply lines from the west to the east of the peninsula, Montgomery continually advanced faster than the aggressive Clark. In Normandy, Montgomery reached the Seine sooner than anticipated by anyone, including Montgomery himself.

Rommel was more accurate when saying of Montgomery, 'command of a force in mobile battle was not his strong point.' This, though, was true only of Montgomery's early battles in the desert when he deliberately avoided mobile battles in which Rommel's men were at their best. This he was surely wise to do; Rommel confirms that had he not done so at

Alam Halfa, he would probably have lost that vital encounter. In later battles he was much more mobile.

The Americans usually contrast Montgomery's deliberate moves unfavourably with the eye-catching dash of General Patton. This again is unfair. Patton made spectacular advances in Sicily and Normandy when his enemy had already been broken by others, but it was a different story when he was faced with determined resistance. Witness his inability to defeat very inferior numbers of Germans and Italians in Tunisia, his mindless battering against Metz and the Saar, regardless of casualties, and his counter-attack at Bastogne, unkindly described by Major General Strawson in *The Battle for the Ardennes* as 'a masterpiece of bad planning, inadequate preparation [and] poor tactics.'

Montgomery proved very capable of dealing with determined resistance, but he also moved rapidly enough when circumstances were favourable. Ironically, when Patton made his dramatic sweep through France to the Seine, he was under Montgomery's command and his action had been laid down long before as part of Montgomery's plan. Observe also how Montgomery turned the Buerat defences, took the Tarhuna-Homs escarpment 'on the run' and captured Tripoli in one continuous series of moves, or his dash from the Seine to the Scheldt, followed by his dramatic if unsuccessful attempt to seize the Rhine bridges.

This last – Operation MARKET GARDEN – is often quoted as showing that Montgomery was quite prepared to take risks, and he took greater ones. Whatever MARKET GARDEN did or did not achieve it could not endanger the basic security of Montgomery's Twenty-First Army Group, as was confirmed by this never being seriously threatened during the Ardennes offensive. On other occasions failure could have brought serious consequences. There was Montgomery's assault on Tripoli with only ten days' supplies in hand. There was Montgomery's advance into Tunisia to help First (British) Army, dangerously over-extending his forces and causing him to have 'sweated a bit at times'. Most of all there was his call for D-Day to be launched on 6 or even 5 June in clearly adverse conditions.

Ultimately the main credit for the decision to 'go at once' must be given to Eisenhower. Yet Eisenhower must have been heartened and encouraged by the obvious confidence of the Land Forces Commander and a disaster might well have ended Montgomery's career. Eisenhower was too honest and too honourable to have avoided responsibility – indeed he prepared a message to be issued in case of failure personally accepting all blame – but Tedder and Patton probably and Morgan and Kay Summersby certainly would have made sure most of it was 'passed down'.

Montgomery's 'caution', incidentally, did not extend to his own personal safety. De Guingand notes resignedly that Montgomery 'was always to be seen in the danger area of the battlefield, being quite unmoved by any unpleasant incident.' De Guingand, Horrocks, Williams and others refer to a number of such 'incidents' from artillery fire, bombing raids, strafing attacks and so on, and there were even occasions when Montgomery seems have been wilfully reckless.

During the advance from Alamein, for example, Montgomery's Tac HQ was further forward than that of any corps or divisional commander and he was in genuine danger of being captured, as were Mainwaring and Richard Carver. In Normandy, his Tac HQ was only 3 miles from the front line. In the Ardennes Battle, when the threat of assassination drove Bradley to abandon his badges of rank and kept Eisenhower inoperative, surrounded by guards, Montgomery drove about openly in his Rolls-Royce with its huge Union Jack on the bonnet. His attitude won the admiration of his men and increased their confidence in victory.

> 'But what good came of it at last?'
> Quoth little Peterkin.
> 'Why that I cannot tell,' said he,
> 'But 'twas a famous victory.'

The poet Robert Southey was clearly a confirmed cynic. All the same, it may be of interest to examine the contributions made by our three very able generals to winning the Second World War and the benefits that resulted.

In the case of Slim, through no fault of his own, it was practically none. In *Defeat into Victory*, Slim makes great play with the Japanese advance on Imphal, assuring us they hoped to take the 'glittering prize' of India and 'change the whole course of the world war'. In fact, as Slim knew very well from intercepted signals, all the Japanese planned was a seizure of the Imphal plain to provide a better defensive position than the Chindwin River, the weakness of which had been exposed by Wingate's raid.

So far were the Japanese from intending the conquest of India that they threw away their best chance of attaining their limited objective. They made no attempt to capture the main Allied supply centre at Dimapur as they could easily have done. It would have given them the food and equipment they desperately needed and deprived Fourteenth Army of the base for its counter-offensive, but it would have taken them too deeply into India.

Slim's subsequent conquest of Burma, though splendidly conducted, did not shorten the Second World War by a day or by an hour. Nor did it restore the prestige lost by the British in the disasters of 1942. Within three years of the war's end, the magnificent Indian army was broken up by the partition of the sub-continent, Bose's followers were hailed as patriotic heroes by the Congress Party, and Burma not only ceased to be a British colony but left the Commonwealth entirely.

Alexander's efforts gained better rewards. The evacuation from Dunkirk ensured that Britain would fight on. As the Army Group Commander he must be given the chief credit for the liberation of Tunisia and the consequent Allied control of the Mediterranean. Finally he freed first Sicily, then the Italian mainland from its own dictator, its German Army of Occupation and any threat of its control by Russia.

Once again, however, Montgomery earned the greatest gratitude of posterity. Major General Fuller in *The Decisive Battles of the Western World* includes three victories by the Western Allies in the struggle with Germany: El Alamein in 1942, Tunis in 1943 and Normandy in 1944. Of these, Alamein or perhaps more accurately Alam Halfa and Alamein together ensured the Allied retention of the Middle East and North Africa; both were planned and won by Montgomery. For Tunis we have already given chief credit to Alexander, but his strategy was secured by Montgomery's victories, especially that at the Mareth Line. Normandy was also planned and won by Montgomery and resulted in the liberation of Western Europe from both Nazi Germany and Soviet Russia. To this Montgomery's part in the formation of NATO added the subsequent liberation of Eastern Europe and in particular that of Poland.

Taking all the above points into account, surely as a general Montgomery must be ranked even above the other two who led British armies to victory. This was the opinion of General Fraser who praises all three but concludes with a tribute to Montgomery, saying: 'He mastered events. He made battle and enemy conform to his will and his will was of steel.' Ronald Lewin makes the same comparison and also comes down in favour of Montgomery. 'Greatly as I admired Alexander and Slim,' reports Field Marshal Harding, 'if I had to go to war again, I would sooner go under a plan prepared and conducted by Monty than by anybody else who lived through either war.'

Nigel Hamilton's assessment of Montgomery as 'Master of the Battlefield' does not seem exaggerated then. It is in fact echoed by his subordinates and staff officers. Richardson calls Montgomery 'without a doubt a supreme master of the battlefield'. Roberts declares bluntly that no one except Montgomery could have won either Alamein or Normandy. Leese, who incidentally saw at close quarters how both Alexander and Slim won battles, considers Montgomery 'the greatest soldier of our age', often 'most difficult and even exasperating' to his equals and superiors, yet 'as a commander to serve under on the battlefield, it's Monty for my money any day.'

Perhaps, though, the greatest tribute to Montgomery comes from Major General Sir Francis 'Freddie' de Guingand. As Montgomery's invaluable chief of staff, he was well aware of how 'difficult' and 'exasperating' Montgomery could be and saw him in rare moments of concern and worry. He was worked terribly, almost cruelly hard by Montgomery but was curtly rejected from selection as Vice CIGS, a blow that hurt him so bitterly that he resigned from the War Office and then from the army altogether.

Yet Montgomery's faults of character could never conceal his military ability from de Guingand. When de Guingand produced his wartime reminiscences – in 1947 soon after his disappointment – far from joining Montgomery's critics, he actively condemned adverse comments on his old chief as 'ill-informed and unfair'. He called his book *Operation Victory* and Montgomery's battles 'these golden pages of the history of British arms'.

It is significant that of those who saw at first hand Montgomery's skill at overcoming all difficulties, few indeed are willing to join his critics. See for instance Robert Merriam, head of the section in the US Army Historical Division dealing with the Battle of the Ardennes. In this, Montgomery's egotistical manner had aroused much American resentment. Merriam, though, had personally fought in that conflict and, like de Guingand, insists that 'brutal criticism of Montgomery's tactics does not square up with the facts' and can only 'indicate ignorance of the situation'.

Also significant is the praise of Montgomery's generalship by his ablest opponents: Kesselring, Student and von Manteuffel among others, not to mention von Rundstedt who declares simply: 'Montgomery is the ablest of the British generals.' 'There were some at the time,' recalls Harding, 'and there are more now who write books and so on' – he was speaking in 1977 – 'who think they could have done better [than Montgomery]. For my part I am thankful they weren't given the chance to try.'

It must of course always be remembered that neither Montgomery nor any other successful general could have achieved anything but for the skill, discipline, determination, resilience and sheer raw courage of the men who served under him. The service his men gave to Montgomery was overwhelming. By the time Tripoli was reached, the sick rate in Eighth Army had fallen to just one man in every thousand. By the time the central Tunisian plain was reached it was a fraction over one in every 2,000. Horrocks tells us that men who had been wounded and evacuated to Egypt, on recovering 'thumbed lifts for over a thousand miles to rejoin their units at the front'.

Some Eighth Army divisions did not react well to the bocage conditions in Normandy, but after getting new commanders, they were soon 'back in their old form'. By the end of hostilities, the officers and men of Montgomery's Twenty-First Army Group were high in morale, determination and total confidence in final victory.

Montgomery, to his credit, was always conscious of, grateful for and ready to acknowledge the debt he owed to his men, of whom he was rightly proud. 'The soldiery gave of their best,' he proclaims. The supporting airmen did 'brilliant and brave work'. 'Few commanders,' he assured his Twenty-First Army Group, 'can have had such loyal service as you have given me. I thank you from the bottom of my heart.' 'They gave me their complete confidence,' he says of Eighth Army, 'what more can any commander want? My only fear was that I myself might fail these magnificent men.'

In return, Montgomery lavished every possible care on those who fought for him. He showed them that they mattered. He never ceased to encourage and hearten, to appreciate and praise. He instinctively understood their wishes and concerns and did his best to meet these. He tried to further the careers of his chosen officers. Those who had been wounded, Harding and Horrocks for instance, would always remember his kindness and compassion.

When caring for his men, even Montgomery's personal flaws became benefits, sweeping aside anything that might stand in his way. In the desert, he cancelled orders preventing nursing sisters being brought up to the forward areas, declaring – he was no doubt dogmatic – that the wounded 'then knew they would be properly nursed. No nursing orderly can nurse like a woman, though many think they can.' On the Normandy beaches, he defied Churchill – he was no doubt dictatorial – by arranging for dentists' chairs to be landed so his men's teeth could be checked regularly. In the vicious winter of 1944–45, he required every soldier to have at least one hot meal a day and urged – he was no doubt tactless – that his American allies must follow his example.

Nor was Montgomery's concern inspired only by the knowledge that his troops would fight better if they were well looked after, as is the impression given by some successful commanders. Alan Moorehead in his *Eclipse* reports that Montgomery 'treated his army as a kind of family and he drove among them for hours every day'.

When thinking of Montgomery, one's mental picture is often that of the commander: studying with fierce concentration maps of the area where he intended to fight a battle; informing a roomful of senior officers how he planned to fight it; and eagerly watching its progress through his binoculars. It would be more suitable, though, to picture him where he was most happy: in the middle of his fellow fighting men, waving delightedly to the cheering troops, meticulously acknowledging the salutes of the officers; first, last and always, the soldiers' soldier.

Notes

1. When Richardson was Deputy Chief of Staff (British) in Clark's Fifth US Army, he and Clark's own Chief of Staff, a certain Major General Alfred Gruenther, used to pass on only a summary of messages from Montgomery, knowing that Montgomery's unfortunate wording must often be resented.
2. General Douglas MacArthur, for instance, derided Eisenhower as 'the best clerk I ever had'.

3. In 1956 when *Defeat into Victory* appeared, 'Ultra' was still a closely guarded secret, so Slim could not have referred to it directly. However, he could and should have praised Intelligence generally, as did Alexander and Montgomery.

4. Full details of Slim's changing attitudes may be found in *Wingate and the Chindits: Redressing the Balance* by David Rooney, a former senior lecturer at Sandhurst.

5. This and his other statements quoted come from *The Rommel Papers* edited by Captain Liddell Hart.

6. The Gurkhas, as might have been guaranteed, remained loyal to a man.

Bibliography

Primary Sources:

Alexander, Field Marshal the Earl, *The African Campaign from El Alamein to Tunis* (*The London Gazette* Supplement, 1948)

Alexander, Field Marshal the Earl, *The Alexander Memoirs* (Cassell, 1962)

Alexander, Field Marshal the Earl, *The Allied Armies in Italy* (*The London Gazette* Supplement, 1950)

Alexander, Field Marshal the Earl, *The Conquest of Sicily* (*The London Gazette* Supplement, 1948)

Arnold-Forster, Mark, *The World at War* (Collins, 1973)

Beevor, Anthony, *Ardennes 1944: Hitler's Last Gamble* (Viking, 2015)

Beevor, Anthony, *Arnhem: The Battle for the Bridges 1944* (Viking, 2018)

Beevor, Anthony, *D-Day: The Battle for Normandy* (Viking, 2009)

Behrendt, Hans-Otto, *Rommel's Intelligence in the Desert Campaign* (Kimber, 1985)

Belfield, Eversley and Essame, Major General H., *The Battle for Normandy* (Batsford, 1965)

Bradley, General Omar N., *A Soldier's Story: The Allied Campaigns from Tunis to the Elbe* (Eyre & Spottiswoode, 1951)

Bryant, Sir Arthur, *The Turn of the Tide 1939–1945* (Collins, 1959)

Bryant, Sir Arthur, *Triumph in the West 1943–1946* (Collins, 1959)

Carell, Paul, *The Foxes of the Desert: The Story of the Afrika Korps* (Macdonald, 1960)

Carver, Field Marshal Lord, *Dilemmas of the Desert War: A New Look at the Libyan Campaign 1940–1942* (Batsford, 1986)

Carver, Field Marshal Lord, *El Alamein* (Batsford, 1962)

Carver, Field Marshal Lord, *Harding of Petherton* (Weidenfeld & Nicolson, 1978)

Carver, Field Marshal Lord, *The Imperial War Museum Book of the War in Italy 1943–1945* (Sidgwick & Jackson, 2001)

Carver, Field Marshal Lord, *Out of Step* [Memoirs] (Hutchinson, 1989)

Carver, Field Marshal Lord, *Tobruk* (Batsford, 1964)

Churchill, Sir Winston, *The Second World War*: Vol. IV, *The Hinge of Fate* (Cassell, 1951), Vol. V, *Closing the Ring* (Cassell, 1952), Vol. VI, *Triumph and Tragedy* (Cassell, 1954)

Clark, Lloyd, *Arnhem: Jumping the Rhine 1944 and 1945* [Both MARKET GARDEN & PLUNDER/VARSITY] (Headline Publishing Group, 2008)

Clark, General Mark, *Calculated Risk* (Harrap, 1951)

Clarke, Sir Rupert, *With Alex at War: From the Irrawaddy to the Po 1941–1945* (Leo Cooper, 2000)

Collier, Richard, *The Sands of Dunkirk* (Collins, 1961)

Connell, John, *Auchinleck* (Cassell, 1959)

De Guingand, Major General Sir Francis, *Generals at War* (Hodder & Stoughton, 1964)

De Guingand, Major General Sir Francis, *Operation Victory* (Hodder & Stoughton, 1947)

Eisenhower, General Dwight D., *Crusade in Europe* (Heinemann, 1948)

Ellis, Major L.F. with Allen, Captain G.R.G. RN, Robb, Air Chief Marshal Sir James M. and Warhurst, Lieutenant Colonel A.E., *Victory in the West*, Vol. I, *The Battle of Normandy* (HMSO, 1962), Vol. II, *The Defeat of Germany* (HMSO, 1968)

Elstob, Peter, *Hitler's Last Offensive* (Secker & Warburg, 1971)

Essame, Major General H., *The Battle for Germany* (Batsford, 1969)

Florentin, Eddy, *Battle of the Falaise Gap* (Elek Books, 1965)

Follain, John, *Mussolini's Island* (Hodder & Stoughton, 1965)

Fraser, General Sir David, *Alanbrooke* (Collins, 1982)

Fraser, General Sir David, *And We Shall Shock Them: The British Army in the Second World War* (Hodder & Stoughton, 1983)

Fraser, General Sir David, *Knight's Cross: A Life of Field Marshal Erwin Rommel* (HarperCollins, 1993)

Fuller, Major General J.F.C., *The Decisive Battles of the Western World*, Vol. III (Eyre & Spottiswoode, 1957)

Fuller, Major General J.F.C., *The Second World War 1939–1945* (Eyre & Spottiswoode, 1948, revised edition, 1954)

Hamilton, Nigel, *Monty*, Vol. I, *The Making of a General 1887–1942* (Hamish Hamilton, 1981), Vol. II, *Master of the Battlefield 1942–1944* (Hamish Hamilton, 1983), Vol. III, *The Field Marshal 1944–1976* (Hamish Hamilton, 1986)

Hamilton, Nigel, *Monty: The Battles of Field Marshal Bernard Law Montgomery* (Hodder & Stoughton, 1994)

Hamilton, Nigel, *Monty: The Man Behind the Legend* (Lennard Publishing, 1987)

Hastings, Max, *Overlord: D-Day and the Battle for Normandy 1944* (Michael Joseph, 1984)

Haswell, Jock, *The Intelligence and Deception of the D-Day Landings* (Batsford, 1979)

Hibbert, Christopher, *The Battle of Arnhem* (Batsford, 1962)

Hinsley, F.H. with Thomas, E.E., Ransom, C.F.G. and Knight, R.C., *British Intelligence in the Second World War: Its Influence on Strategy and Operations*, Vol. II (HMSO, 1981)

Holland, James, *Together We Stand* (HarperCollins, 2006)

Horne, Alistair with Montgomery, David, *The Lonely Leader: Monty 1944–1945* (Macmillan, 1995)

Horrocks, Lieutenant General Sir Brian, *A Full Life* (Collins, 1960)

Howarth, T.E.B. (edited), *Monty at Close Quarters: Recollections of the Man*. Articles by Dawnay, Lieutenant Colonel C.P., 'Inside Monty's Headquarters'; Harding, Field Marshal Lord, 'In Memoriam'; Williams, Brigadier Sir Edgar, 'Gee One Eye, Sir' (Leo Cooper, 1985)

Jackson, Robert, *Dunkirk* (Arthur Barker, 1976)

Jackson, General Sir William, *The Battle for Italy* (Batsford, 1967)

Jackson, General Sir William, *The Battle for Rome* (Batsford, 1969)

Jackson, General Sir William, *The North African Campaign 1940–43* (Batsford, 1975)

Kesselring, Field Marshal Albert, *Memoirs* (Kimber, 1963)

Kippenberger, Major General Sir Howard, *Infantry Brigadier* (Oxford University Press, 1949)

Lewin, Ronald, *Montgomery as Military Commander* (Batsford, 1971)

Lewin, Ronald, *Rommel as Military Commander* (Batsford, 1968)

Lewin, Ronald, *The Life and Death of the Afrika Korps* (Batsford, 1977)

Lewin, Ronald, *The Other Ultra* (Hutchinson, 1982)

Lewin, Ronald, *Ultra Goes to War: The Secret Story* (Hutchinson, 1978)

Liddell Hart, Captain B.H., *History of the Second World War* (Cassell, 1970)

Liddell Hart, Captain B.H., *The Tanks: The History of the Royal Tank Regiment and its Predecessors* (Cassell, 1959)

Lucas, James and Barker, James, *The Killing Ground: The Battle of the Falaise Gap August 1944* (Batsford, 1978)

Lucas Phillips, Brigadier C.E., *Alamein* (Heinemann, 1962)

Lucas Phillips, Brigadier C.E., *Springboard to Victory* [Kohima] (Heinemann, 1966)

Lunt, Major General James, *A Hell of a Licking: The Retreat from Burma 1941–2* (Collins, 1986)

Macintyre, Captain Donald, *The Battle for the Mediterranean* (Batsford, 1964)

Macksey, Kenneth, *Kesselring* (Batsford, 1978)

Macmillan, Harold, *The Blast of War* (Macmillan, 1967)

Majdalany, Fred, *The Battle of El Alamein* (Weidenfeld & Nicolson, 1965)

Masters, David, *With Pennants Flying: The Immortal Deeds of the Royal Armoured Corps* (Eyre & Spottiswoode, 1943)

Mead, Richard, *General 'Boy': The Life of Lieutenant General Sir Frederick Browning* (Pen & Sword, 2010)

Mead, Richard, *The Men Behind Monty* (Pen & Sword, 2015)

Mellenthin, Major General F.W. von, *Panzer Battles* (Cassell, 1955)

Merriam, Robert E., *The Battle of the Ardennes* (Souvenir Press, 1958. Reissued as *Battle of the Bulge*, 1965)

Molony, Brigadier C.J.C., *The Mediterranean and Middle East*, Vol. V, *The Campaign in Sicily 1943 and the Campaign in Italy 3rd September 1943 to 31st March 1944* (HMSO, 1973), Vol. VI with Jackson, Sir William and Gleave, Group Captain T.P., *Victory in the Mediterranean* (HMSO, 1973)

Montgomery, Field Marshal the Viscount, *A History of Warfare* (Collins, 1968)

Montgomery, Field Marshal the Viscount, *El Alamein to the River Sangro* (Hutchinson, 1948)

Montgomery, Field Marshal the Viscount, *Memoirs* (Collins, 1958)

Montgomery, Field Marshal the Viscount, *Normandy to the Baltic* (Hutchinson, 1947)

Moorehead, Alan, *Eclipse* (Hamish Hamilton, 1967)

Moorehead, Alan, *Montgomery* (Hamish Hamilton, 1946)

Moorehead, Alan, *The Desert War: The North African Campaign 1940–1943* (Hamish Hamilton, 1965)

Nicolson, Nigel, *Alex: The Life of Field Marshal Earl Alexander of Tunis* (Weidenfeld & Nicolson, 1973)

Owen, Roderic, *The Desert Air Force* (Hutchinson, 1948)

Pack, Captain S.W.C., *Operation Husky: The Allied Invasion of Sicily* (David & Charles, 1977)

Playfair, Major General I.S.O. with Molony, Brigadier C.J.C., Flynn, Captain F.C. and Gleave, Group Captain T.P., *The Mediterranean and Middle East*, Vol. III, *British Fortunes Reach their Lowest Ebb* (HMSO, 1960), Vol. IV, *The Destruction of the Axis Forces in Africa* (HMSO, 1966)

Potter, E.B. and Nimitz, Fleet Admiral Chester W., *The Great Sea War* (Harrap, 1961)

Richards, Denis and Saunders, Hilary St G., *Royal Air Force 1939–1945*, Vol. II, *The Fight Avails* (HMSO, 1954), Vol. III, *The Fight is Won* (HMSO, 1954)

Richardson, General Sir Charles, *Flashback: A Soldier's Story* (Kimber, 1985)

Richardson, General Sir Charles, *From Churchill's Secret Service to the BBC: The Biography of Lieutenant General Sir Ian Jacob* (Brasseys (UK), 1991)

Richardson, General Sir Charles, *Send for Freddie* [De Guingand] (Kimber, 1987)

Roberts, Andrew, *Masters and Commanders* (Allen Lane, 2008)

Roberts, Major General G.P.B., *From the Desert to the Baltic* (Kimber, 1987)

Rommel, Field Marshal Erwin (edited by Liddell Hart, Captain B.H.), *The Rommel Papers* (Collins, 1953)

Rooney, David, *Wingate and the Chindits: Redressing the Balance* (Arms & Armour, 1994)

Roskill, Captain S.W., *The Navy at War 1939–1945* (Collins, 1960)

Rostrom, Peter, *The Military Life & Times of General Sir Miles Dempsey: Monty's Army Commander* (Pen & Sword, 2010)

Ryan, Cornelius, *A Bridge Too Far* (Hodder & Stoughton, 1974)

Ryan, Cornelius, *The Longest Day* (Victor Gollancz, 1970)

Ryder, Rowland, *Oliver Leese* (Hamish Hamilton, 1987)

Sayer, Ian and Botting, Douglas, *Hitler's Last General: The Case against Wilhelm Mohnke* (Transworld Publishers/Bantam Press, 1989)

Seaton, Albert, *The Fall of Fortress Europe* (Batsford, 1981)

Shilleto, Carl, *Pegasus Bridge: Merville Battery* (Leo Cooper, 1999)

Slim, Field Marshal the Viscount, *Defeat into Victory* (Cassell, 1956)

Smith, Brigadier E.D., *Battle for Burma* (Batsford, 1979)

Smith, Michael, *The Emperor's Codes* (Bantam Press, 2000)

Stewart, Adrian, *Eighth Army's Greatest Victories* (Leo Cooper, 1999)

Stewart, Adrian, *Six of Monty's Men* (Pen & Sword, 2011)

Stewart, Adrian, *The Campaigns of Alexander of Tunis 1940–1945* (Pen & Sword, 2008)

Stewart, Adrian, *The Early Battles of Eighth Army* (Leo Cooper, 2002)

Strawson, Major General Sir John, *The Battle for Berlin* (Batsford, 1974)

Strawson, Major General Sir John, *The Battle for North Africa* (Batsford, 1969)

Strawson, Major General Sir John, *The Battle for the Ardennes* (Batsford, 1972)

Tedder, Marshal of the Royal Air Force Lord, *With Prejudice* (Cassell, 1966)

Thompson, R.W., *The Battle for the Rhineland* (Hutchinson, 1958)

Toland, John, *The Last 100 Days* (Arthur Barker, 1965)

Tuker, Major General Sir Francis, *Approach to Battle* (Cassell, 1963)

Turnbull, Patrick, *Dunkirk: Anatomy of Disaster* (Batsford, 1978)

Tute, Warren with Costello, John and Hughes, Terry, *D-Day* (Sidgwick & Jackson, 1974)

Urquhart, Major General R.E. with Greatorex, Wilfred, *Arnhem* (Cassell, 1958)

Whiting, Charles, *The Battle of the Bulge* (Sutton Publishing, 1999)

Whiting, Charles, *The Last Battle: Montgomery's Campaign April–May 1945* (Crowood Press, 1989)

Wilmot, Chester, *The Struggle for Europe* (Collins, 1952)

War Diaries of the various armies, corps, divisions and brigades at The National Archives, Kew.

Index

Note: Except for Montgomery himself, all service personnel are given the rank they held at the time of the incidents described.

INDEX OF MILITARY FORMATIONS AND UNITS

ALLIED
BRITISH & COMMONWEALTH

UNITED STATES

OTHER ALLIED COUNTRIES

AXIS
GERMAN

ITALIAN